Bridging Transcultural Divides

The contributors of this remarkable book explore a wide range of topics relating to the discipline of Asian Studies in Australian higher education. From perspectives ranging from that of senior academics to postgraduate students and area expertise from Indonesia to Japan, they give concrete and often personal accounts of their teaching and/or learning of Asian languages and cultures. However, they all have one aim in common: to bridge the divide at the many interfaces of this endeavour, whether they are cultural, pedagogical or political. All those who are interested in creating a more culturally diverse and sensitive world should read this book.

Professor Kam Louie
Dean, Faculty of Arts, University of Hong Kong

One of the most important recent trends in universities in English-speaking countries has been the massive increase in the number of Asian (mostly but not all Chinese) students coming to study for degrees. The impressive and stimulating essays in *Bridging Transcultural Divides* deal with the cultural and educational issues in the Australian context. They offer insights into the shift of the centre of the world towards Asia, challenge the conventional wisdom on some of Western education's most treasured — but often least defined — concepts, and give sound advice on dealing with issues such as plagiarism, language learning and training in social science research. The book's central message is that education for Asian students in Australia, and more broadly in the West, can no longer been seen as a one-way transfer of knowledge, but must be understood as a process of reciprocal learning in which both teachers and students are changed by the experience. This important book addresses both theoretical and practical issues and will appeal to a broad range of interests — those concerned with the 'rise' of Asia, including China, and its cultural implications for the West; educational theorists and policy makers seeking ways to respond to the influx of foreign students; and higher education classroom teachers keen to deliver the best and most productive experience to incoming students.

Professor Tim Wright
Emeritus Professor of Chinese Studies, University of Sheffield

This volume presents the diverse approaches and achievements of scholars of Asian cultures and languages in today's global academy. Recent vast increases in student numbers and ethnic diversity have created pressing challenges for a higher education which engages with contemporary concerns for Asian societies as well as for Asian students involved in Western education. This collection of scholarly analyses demonstrates the centrality and significance of Asian Studies and languages for these globalising academic communities. Significantly, it demands a rethinking of traditional 'intercultural' education. In so doing, it brings empirical knowledge as well as multicultural interpretation and multilingual expertise to throw new light on the challenges in higher education today, and to open up new understandings of the demands of the future.

With the focus on pedagogy, the chapters here present the original perspectives of multilingual, globally-educated university staff in Australia, as well as the learning experiences of their diverse students. All the contributors are actively engaged with the educational challenges they identify and, as a result, their writings provide sharply relevant theoretical perspectives and cutting edge innovations to practice. Through contextually situated analysis, the studies here interrogate global trends in Asian cultural studies, in addition to curriculum transformations in the teaching of Asian languages, and they represent a rich diversity of rhetorical styles and methodological approaches. Taken together this collection provides a new and ground-breaking perspective on the teaching of Asian students in globalised higher education. Inspired primarily by the understandings of Asian scholars in Australian universities, it offers uniquely authentic theoretical insights and practical initiatives. As such it succeeds admirably in its goal to celebrate difference while overcoming division, and providing practical strategies for achieving educational opportunity and social justice in the living contexts of Western higher education.

Professor John Makeham
Head, Department of Chinese Studies, Australian National University

This book is available as a fully-searchable pdf from
www.adelaide.edu.au/press

Bridging Transcultural Divides:

Asian Languages and Cultures in Global Higher Education

edited by

Xianlin Song
Centre for Asian Studies, The University of Adelaide

and

Kate Cadman
School of Social Sciences, The University of Adelaide

Published in Adelaide by

University of Adelaide Press
The University of Adelaide
Level 1, 230 North Terrace
South Australia
5005
press@adelaide.edu.au
www.adelaide.edu.au/press

The University of Adelaide Press publishes externally refereed scholarly books by staff of the University of Adelaide. It aims to maximise the accessibility to its best research by publishing works through the internet as free downloads and as high quality printed volumes on demand.

Electronic Index: this book is available from the website as a down-loadable PDF with fully searchable text. Please use the electronic version to serve as the index.

© 2012 The Authors

This book is copyright. Apart from any fair dealing for the purposes of private study, research, criticism or review as permitted under the *Copyright Act 1968* (Cth), no part may be reproduced, stored in a retrieval system, or transmitted, in any form or by any means, electronic, mechanical, photocopying, recording or otherwise without prior written permission. Address all inquiries to the Director at the above address.

For the full Cataloguing-in-Publication data please contact the National Library of Australia: cip@nla.gov.au

1. Oriental languages — Study and teaching (Higher)
2. Asia — Civilization — Study and teaching (Higher)

I. Song, Xianlin.
II. Cadman, Kate.

ISBN (paperback) 978-1-922064-30-1
ISBN (ebook) 978-1-922064-31-8

Project Editor: Patrick Allington
Cover design: Emma Spoehr
Book design: Zoë Stokes

Contents

Acknowledgements — ix

List of Contributors — x

Foreword — xiii

Part I: Another pedagogy is possible

1. Embracing *trans*cultural pedagogy: An epistemological perspective — 3
   Kate Cadman and Xianlin Song

Part II: Re-locating teaching and learning

2. What are the implications for learning in Australian universities if and when the centre of the world shifts towards Asia? — 29
   Mobo Gao

3. (Post) Modern times: Transcultural exchange and the circumstances of postgraduate social science research — 49
   Greg McCarthy

Part III: Transforming curriculum in Asian language teaching

4. Teaching Asian languages from an intercultural perspective: Building bridges for and with students of Indonesian — 73
   Anthony J Liddicoat and Michelle Kohler

5. A Study Skills Action Plan: Integrating self-regulated learning in a diverse higher education context — 101
   Kayoko Enomoto

6	The challenge of motivation: Teaching Japanese *kanji* characters to students from diverse language backgrounds *Naomi Aoki*	131
7	Personal growth through intercultural communication: Engaging native speakers and reflective learning in Japanese language curriculum *Akiko Tomita*	155

Part IV: Capitalising on Asian social and cultural studies in contexts of diversity

8	Increasing cultural flexibility: A psychological perspective on the purpose of intercultural education *Delia Lin*	191
9	Reflections of a 'Korean' teaching about Japan in globalising Australia *Sejin Pak*	209
10	Critiquing critical thinking: Asia's contribution towards sociological conceptualisation *Shoko Yoneyama*	231

Part V: Bridging learning gaps

11	Chinese culture and plagiarism: A convenient cause for an inconvenient issue in the academy *Ming Hwa Ting*	253
12	Education with(out) distinction: Beyond graduate attributes for Chinese international students *Xianlin Song and Kate Cadman*	269

Acknowledgements

For the joy and fulfilment that have been generated by this project we owe a special debt of gratitude to the many people who have shared their vision, as well as their time and energy, with us along the way. Our on-going dialogues with all those involved have led us to new places, and to new ideas.

First and foremost, we would like to thank our fellow authors in this collection, and to take this opportunity to recognize their expertise and the ground-breaking work that routinely informs their contributions to Asian Studies.

Our appreciation is extended to all our collegiate readers and mentors, including the anonymous reviewers, and particularly to Professor Chihiro Thomson (UNSW), Dr Laura Dales (UWA), Dr Julia Miller (UA) and Dr Simon Smith (UA) for their insightful evaluations and feedback on our drafts.

This volume would not have been possible without the financial assistance of the following organisations, and we thank them sincerely for giving us the freedom to explore our educational interest in Asia and its students at this critical moment in the globalisation of Higher Education:
- Centre for Asian Studies, University of Adelaide, South Australia
- School of Social Sciences, University of Adelaide, South Australia
- Confucius Institute, University of Adelaide, South Australia.

We would also like to express our thanks to Professor Kent Anderson for his personal interest and generous support for this work.

We are grateful to the University of Adelaide Press, especially to Dr John Emerson and Dr Patrick Allington, without whose belief in the project and rigorous professional commitment this collection would not have come into being.

And last, but by no means of least significance, we would like to acknowledge the unique and invaluable contribution of students of Asian cultures and languages to Australian Higher Education today, and to express our sincere appreciation for all they have taught us on our mutual 'transcultural' journeys.

Xianlin Song and Kate Cadman
July 2012

List of Contributors

Ms Naomi Aoki is a Lecturer in Japanese in Asian Studies at The University of Adelaide. She specialises in Teaching Japanese as a Second/Foreign Language and develops various teaching resources including textbooks and e-learning materials. Her research interests include curriculum design by focusing on learners' motivation and information literacy.

Dr Kate Cadman is Adjunct Senior lecturer in the School of Social Sciences at The University of Adelaide, where for over 10 years she was Coordinator of research education and bridging programs for students with English as an Additional Language. She is on the Editorial Board of the international *Journal of English for Academic Purposes*, and an Editor of *TESOL in Context*. She conducts invited research education consultancies in USA, South Africa, China, Singapore and SE Asia, as well as Australia. Her research focuses on critical strategies for developing an inclusive global academy.

Ms Kayoko Enomoto is a lecturer in Japanese at The University of Adelaide. Kayoko's research focuses on adult second language acquisition and its implications for classroom teaching. Her recent research examines several educational initiatives which explore approaches to engage and motivate students from a wide variety of linguistic, cultural and disciplinary backgrounds and to meet the diverse learning needs of such a cohort. Kayoko has won various excellence in teaching awards, including a national ALTC (Australian Learning and Teaching Council) Citation for Outstanding Contributions to Student Learning (2011).

Professor Mobo C F Gao is Professor of Chinese Studies at the Centre for Asian Studies and Director of the Confucius Institute at The University of Adelaide. Professor Gao's publications include four monographs and numerous journal articles and book chapters as well as popular media essays. He is the author of the critically acclaimed book *Gao Village* and of *Introduction to Mandarin Chinese*, which are widely used at tertiary institutions. Professor Gao's most recent publication is *The Battle for China's Past: Mao and the Cultural Revolution*.

Dr Michelle Kohler is a Research Fellow at the Research Centre for Languages and Cultures, University of South Australia, and Lecturer in Languages Education at Flinders University. Michelle has contributed to a number of national projects including the Report on Intercultural Language Teaching and Learning, Intercultural Language Teaching Learning in Practice, Standards for Languages Teaching, The Current State of Indonesian Language Education in Australia Schools and the recent Student Achievement in Asian Languages Education. Michelle's research interests include intercultural language teaching and learning, languages curriculum and assessment, and Indonesian language education.

Professor Anthony J Liddicoat is Professor in Applied Linguistics at the Research Centre for Languages and Cultures at the University of South Australia. His research interests include language and intercultural issues in education, conversation analysis, and language policy and planning. His research has focussed on ways on issues relating to the teaching and learning of culture through language study. His publications include *Languages in Australian Education: Problems, Prospects and Future Directions* (2010, with Angela Scarino), *Language Planning in Local Contexts* (2008, with Richard Baldauf), *Discourse Genre and Rhetoric* (2008), *Introduction to Conversation Analysis* (2006), *Language Planning and Literacy* (2006), *Australian Perspectives on Internationalisation* (2003, with Susana Eisenchlas and Susan Trevaskes), *Perspectives on Europe* (2002, with Karis Muller), *Striving for the Third Place* (1999, with Joseph Lo Bianco and Chantal Crozet) and *Teaching Languages, Teaching Cultures* (2000, with Chantal Crozet).

Dr Delia Lin is a Lecturer with the Centre for Asian Studies at The University of Adelaide. She holds a B.A. in Linguistics and M.A. in Applied Linguistics from China and a PhD in the Humanities (Chinese political culture) from Griffith University. Delia Lin has won awards in translation and teaching and has over a decade of teaching experience in the Chinese language, English/Chinese translation, interpreting and Chinese culture at both Chinese and Australian universities.

Professor Greg McCarthy wrote his PhD dissertation on societies in transition from capitalism and pre-capitalism to socialism in the 1980s. He is now supervising PhD students analysing societies in transition from socialism to capitalism. His publications include *Telling Tales: the State Bank of South Australia* (Australian Scholarly Publishing 2001).

Dr Sejin Pak is a lecturer in Japanese studies in Asian Studies at The University of Adelaide. His teaching areas are in Japanese society and culture and East Asian Political Economy. His research interests are in the comparative study of Japan and Korea, currently in the area of the politics of identity and spirituality.

Dr Xianlin Song is Senior Lecturer and Head of Discipline at the Centre for Asian Studies, The University of Adelaide. She has been teaching Chinese language, cultural and society and Asian Studies courses for the past 15 years. She has done extensive work in translation and interpretation. Her research focuses on the current cultural transition, gender issues and government discourse in contemporary China, and higher education learning in Australia. Her most recent publications include a co-authored book on contemporary Chinese feminist writing with Professor Kay Schaffer, *Women Writers in Post-Socialist China* (Routledge 2012)

Dr Ming Hwa Ting has a PhD from the the Centre for Asian Studies, The University of Adelaide, and is a member of the Pacific Forum-CSIS 'Young Leaders' program. He was also the inaugural Bill Cowan Barr Smith Library Fellow. His previous works have been published by Academia Sinica, Taipei, Taiwan, Australasian Political Studies Association, New Zealand Asian Studies Society, Society for South-East Asian Studies, Vienna, Austria, and the European Institute for Asian Studies, Brussels, Belgium.

Ms Akiko Tomita is an Associate Lecturer in the Centre for Asian Studies and a doctoral candidate at the Discipline of Linguistics at The University of Adelaide. She has many years of teaching experience in the Japanese language at Australian universities and her research interests include teaching/learning Japanese Language, Japanese politeness, and bilingual and bicultural identities.

Dr Shoko Yoneyama is a Senior Lecturer in Asian Studies at The University of Adelaide. Her fields of research are the sociology of education and Japanese studies. She is the author of *The Japanese High School: Silence and Resistance* (Routledge 1999 & 2007) and the social science editor of *Japanese Studies*.

Foreword

Since the turn of the 21st Century a radical change has occurred in Australian higher education: the student body has internationalised. While euphemistically we refer to this by the neutral and politically correct term of 'international students', in fact the change has been the 'Asianisation' of the student body so that roughly a quarter of the students on our campuses are from Asia.[1] The Asian Century has arrived in higher education, and Australian universities are the better for it now and going forward.

How we think about the new demographics of the Australian campus has evolved over time. International students have been chiefly understood for the financial benefit their participation has brought. International students were merely seen as a utilitarian response to a constricted funding model in Australia. With the capping of domestic fees (and until recently the capping of domestic student numbers) international students were one area where universities could charge the market rate for students and thereby diversify and increase their revenue.

The fact that international students were paying more understandably led to the charge and criticism of 'cross-subsidising' by international students of the domestic student educational experience and universities' research. The fact that the new students could pay more contributed to the image and stereotype of a rich, spoiled Asian student driving a flash car and living in an expensive apartment. This of course hid the reality of parents making serious sacrifices and drawing on long-term savings to provide the students mobility and the marginal living and employment conditions many international students were enduring. Within this context, international students from Asia were understood merely for the economic benefit they brought universities.

Shortly after the beginning of the increase in Asian students across the sector, a second image of international students emerged. Wizened professors at first welcoming began to complain about the language and contextual fluency of the new students. The charge of every generation about the diminishing of standards was thrown about at faculty meetings across the country and anecdotes of the poor oral exam and questionable grammar on essays was shopped among like-minded colleagues.[2] The fact that most of these criticisms echoed of the previous generation of academics' handwringing with the middle-classification of university education in the baby boomer era passed most by. More recently universities have responded to the criticisms by improving their selection process for those coming from systems outside of Australia, by increasing the amount of tutorial assistance available on campus, and by collecting the data that disproves the anecdotal claims.[3] The result is today the quality of international students' experience on campuses is better than it was and education support for all students has also improved.

Over a decade into the new century and a more exciting third trend is emerging. Rather than seeing international students as a financial crutch or educational liability, some lecturers, some schools and some universities are understanding the improved pedagogy and research environment that a greater number of non-Australian students (and more Australian students from non-traditional cultural backgrounds) can bring to the university classroom. Simply put: Internationally diversified classrooms can deliver better education and research for all students and academics. This is the dynamic area where this book treads.

The crux of the new pedagogy is that intercultural transformations are not restricted to a Western civilizing notion of education but embrace transcultural learning that moves multidirectionally, that is in both the geographical sense (eg South to North) but also in the power sense (eg student to instructor). The book canvases a number of real life examples of how this is working in the classroom. The book's focus on Asian Studies is an interesting one as this newer discipline is less wedded to the classical disciplines' doctrines and embraces non-Western voices.

Let me add my narrative to the excellent examples included. I recently taught a Law and Film course that explored what is meant by 'justice'.[4] The traditional venue for this conversation is in a Jurisprudence or Legal Theory course where English positivist scholars such as Hart and Dworkin (on the shoulders of Aristotle and Hobbes) are set against the American realists such as Holmes and Cardozo (and followed by the Critical Legal Scholars like Duncan Kennedy and Catharine MacKinnon).[5] Eschewing this Western lexical discourse, my course seeks to use the non-traditional legal text of film, particularly those made by non-Western directors such as Akira Kurosawa.[6] My purpose in this approach is not to be cosmopolitanly clever, but rather to turn the tables so that the students are the holders of expertise and knowledge as they are more fluent in film and Asian contexts than I am. By empowering students and particularly those familiar with Asia, it is hoped that a different notion of justice might emerge. My role as teacher correspondingly shifts from imparting knowledge of the Western tradition and testing that it has been sufficiently absorbed, to setting materials that evoke interesting questions and shepherding debate so that it covers the core points of established doctrine but allows for venturing into areas I would not know or feel confident to guide on my own.

I provide this example because it suggests this 'Asian Studies approach' can be deployed in traditional disciplines — such as Law — and even in one of the areas most fundamental to 'Western thought'. The chapters here point out that one of the challenges in pursuing these different pedagogies is rewarding front line lecturers for investing in development of non-traditional methods, but I would add a second challenge is ensuring the support of academic colleagues for such unconventional approaches.

This book presents a cogent argument with real world examples for a challenging new approach to teaching university students in the 21st Century — the Asian Century. Universities in Australia have changed over the last decade and that trend is now spreading to other Anglo-institutions as well as throughout Asian higher education itself. As Australia has led the internationalisation of universities, this book will lead the third wave of thinking on how an internationalised classroom can be, and should be, adapted to a new and more progressive environment. The Asianised classroom can be a better classroom and this book will lead others to how to make this a reality.

Kent Anderson
Pro Vice Chancellor (International)
University of Adelaide

Notes

[1] Australian Bureau of Statistics, 'Australian Social Trends, 4102.0: International Students in Australia', 16 December 2011 available at <http://www.abs.gov.au/AUSSTATS/abs@.nsf/Lookup/4102.0Main+Features20Dec+2011>.

[2] See Anita Devos, 'Academic Standards, Internationalisation, and the Discursive Construction of "The International Student"', 22 *Higher Education Research and Development* 155 (2003).

[3] See, eg, Alan Olsen, Zena Burgess and Raj Sharma, 'The Comparative Performance of International Students in Australia', 42 *International Higher Education* (2006) (noting that based on the results of 338,000 full-time student studying at 22 Australian universities there was no discernable difference between domestic and international students); Brian C Lovell, 'Academic Performance of International Students in Electrical Engineering at the University of Queensland' (2003) at <http://espace.library.uq.edu.au/eserv/UQ:10710/ACEE.pdf> (providing a useful example of the faculty common room discussions, and showing international students outperformed domestic students in this one school's discipline).

[4] For a full discussion of this course and its objectives, see Kent Anderson, 'Reflections on I Just Didn't Do It, the Lay Judge System, and Legal Education in and out of Japan', 6 *Asian Journal of Comparative Law* — (forthcoming 2012). On the law and film pedagogy more generally see, Alan A. Stone, 'Teaching Film at Harvard Law School', 24 *Legal Studies Forum* 573 (2000).

[5] See generally Surya Prakash Sinha, *Jurisprudence: Legal Philosophy in a Nutshell* (1993).

6   For an interesting discussion on using Kurosawa films in law school teaching, see David S Sokolow, 'From Kurosawa to (Duncan) Kennedy: The Lessons of Rashomon for Current Legal Education', 1991 *Wisconsin Law Review* 969; Ann Althouse, 'Invoking Rashomon', 2000 *Wisconsin Law Review* 503; Orit Kamir, 'Judgment by Film: Socio-Legal Functions of Rashomon', 12 *Yale Journal of Law and the Humanities* 39 (2000).

Part I

Another pedagogy is possible

Embracing *trans*cultural pedagogy: An epistemological perspective

Kate Cadman and Xianlin Song

> Father and Mother, and Me,
> ...
> And all good people say,
> That all nice people like us are We,
> And everyone else is They:
> But if you cross over the sea,
> Instead of just over the way,
> You may end by (think of it!) looking on We
> As only a sort of They!
>
> — Rudyard Kipling, *We and they*, 1926.

Introduction

'We' are the good people who research and teach in a typical research-intensive Australian university; 'they' are the diverse, multi-ethnic students we are now, literally, in the business of educating. And in our specifically Asian Studies context, we are particularly interested to know how these students interpret their educational achievement, so, at the end of their courses, we ask them to describe what they have learned. One Chinese-background student who was at the end of his undergraduate degree program, wrote curtly in a shaky hand: 'Multiculturalism is a big fat lie'. In such a comment it seemed to us this student was expressing what they, and many of their colleagues, had personally experienced as the failure of the Australian education process to provide them with learning experience that was equitable, relevant and satisfying for them. In so many cases, the internationalising of higher education in Anglo-Celtic countries such as Australia has quite simply not been able to produce the kinds of teaching that are demanded when international, largely Asian, students enter existing degree programs in large numbers. In these teaching contexts, institutional respect, status and professional security are still conferred almost exclusively on traditional research outcomes and incomes. Consequently, the pedagogic innovations that would be needed to ensure appropriate and fulfilling educational experiences for all student groups are, more often than not, conspicuous for their absence.

The title of this introductory section speaks our position: *Another pedagogy is possible*. As the editors of this volume, our goal here is to interrogate, and to substantiate, this conviction. Together with all the contributors, most of whom are themselves of Asian background, we are committed academic educators of the diverse and complex student cohorts enrolled in the disciplines known as 'Asian Studies'. We are thus located where the forces of globalisation on academic teaching have been most directly and strongly felt, and where theoretical and practical innovation has been an immediate imperative. This collection investigates and showcases these recent innovations, to engage proactively and publically with some of the less visible ways in which Anglo-Celtic higher education programs today are being reviewed and transformed as a result of the international encounters they engage. To this end, we begin here by examining the implications of a 'postmodernist archaeological perspective' (Scheurich 1997), in order to argue for 'another' pedagogy in global higher education, one which embraces the *trans*cultural. In disciplines of Asian Studies we are, significantly and not before time, beginning to look upon 'They' as only a sort of 'We' (see the Kipling epigraph above), and grappling with the implications of this for teaching and learning.

As may already be apparent, in this endeavour we are following the inspiring lead of Boaventura de Sousa Santos (2007), whose declaration that *Another knowledge is possible* advanced the powerful contribution of his internationally collaborative project series, *Reinventing Social Emancipation*. Santos and his colleagues open one of their substantial analyses by stating their intellectual position unequivocally:

> The main argument of this book is that there is no global social justice without global cognitive justice ... a new critical theory and new emancipatory practices must start from the premise that the epistemological diversity of the world is immense, as immense as its cultural diversity ... [T]his book is intent to show that the reinvention of social emancipation is premised on replacing the 'monoculture of knowledge' by an 'ecology of knowledges' [which constitutes] an invitation to the promotion of non-relativistic dialogues among knowledges ... aimed at both maximising their respective contributions and at decolonizing knowledge and power. (Santos, Nunes & Meneses 2007, pp. xix–xx)

Santos's (2007) rigorous exploration of the real-world epistemological diversity of so-called 'southern'[1] communities provides the groundwork for a worldview that seriously questions the exclusive dominance of Anglo-Celtic scientific and social-scientific ways of knowing. Erik Wright (n.d.), acclaiming this book series in an admiring review, reinforces the point:

> In the 1980s Margaret Thatcher declared, 'There is no alternative.' At the beginning of the 21st century the World Social Forum replied, 'Another world is possible.' The [Santos] project ... is a passionate and wide-ranging effort at enriching our vision of that other world.

That 'other world' is characterised by its epistemological diversity and its dialogic possibility. And central to this possibility is the role of those educators whose work is at the spearhead of the 'knowledge ecology' that comes to life in the global multicultural space that is Northern, metropolitan higher education today. Thus, our goal here is to extend Santos' theme of possibility to the locus of teaching — another pedagogy is possible, and if we are serious about education, whether it is designed to be freely given to our own familiars or sold as a product to strangers from overseas, it is our responsibility to engage fruitfully with that possibility.

Asianising Asian Studies

The contexts for the discussions we present here are fairly typical in terms of their settings in Asian Studies disciplines, which bring together the researching and teaching of Asian cultures and languages in contemporary globalised higher education. Over the past decade, Australian and other metropolitan universities have witnessed vast increases in international student numbers; as early as 2003 it was estimated that there were about two million students actively participating in the transnational flow of higher education (Davis 2003). This movement has produced a competitive marketing of degree programs, and posed daunting challenges for university policy makers and the academic staff who implement them. That these challenges have not been effectively met at the institutional level has been rigorously and vehemently demonstrated by Simon Marginson and others (Birrell 2006; Marginson 2009a; Marginson & Eijkman 2007). The impact of misguided national government policy approaches to international education upon educational outcomes, and even upon the nature of university education itself, has been cogently argued. In a 2009 article in *Campus Review*, Marginson stressed the gravity of neglecting educational goals in favour of commercial ones:

> Australia is the only country in the world that uses its top 200 research universities to shore up the balance of trade. We are the only nation where these universities enrol 10,000 fee-paying international students purely to balance

their books… Australia has become a byword for quantity not quality, and hustling not scholarship, in the international education market. (Marginson 2009b, p. 9)

Individual institutions have clearly become dependent for their level of operations, if not their survival, upon international student fees. Management structures have been 'corporatised', with courses of study increasingly commodified and packaged for commercial sale (Starfield 2004). In Australia, as in the UK, it has been widely acknowledged that 'the public face of internationalisation is the face of the international student' (Wells 2003, p. 9), and all teaching contexts are affected by their changing student profiles to a greater or lesser degree.

Because the majority of these large numbers of international students are Asian, the significant increase in their numbers creates some of its most strategic challenges in Australian universities. Asian students' parents and societies in general place great value on a foreign degree, as they perceive the holder to have better professional skills and employability prospects in the highly competitive Asian human resources markets (Bodycott 2009; Gareth 2005). Northern metropolitan universities are capitalising on these motivations as economic incentive to recruit students to their institutions. Aggressive marketing procedures are now standard practice in Asia, based on a simplistic, pseudo-mathematical formula:

---

high school graduation + IELTS (or equivalent) English score + the ability to pay fees

= the potential for success in an academic degree

Clearly what is missing from this formula is any consideration of the appropriateness of the education that these students are being offered, for their own development. The fact that they frequently appear to be unable to master the learning required in the Anglo-Celtic education tradition has been extensively identified in recent scholarship (see, for example, Hayes & Introna 2005; Ho, Peng & Chan 2001; Holmes 2004). However, students' previous educational experience, requisite skills level, and motivation for learning have no necessary bearing on the recruitment strategies that attract them, nor, after they arrive at their destinations, on the educational curricula designed to serve their interests.

Meanwhile, for academics who have until recently seen their task as delivering a Northern metropolitan style of education, and training researchers and educators to carry on that tradition, the challenge of this 'Asianisation' is immediate. What used to be a relatively manageable practice of *knowledge transfer* to English-mother-tongue, Australian-school-educated students (see Cadman 2000) has turned into a demand for transnational growth characterised by the multicultural and multilingual perspectives required for *knowledge exchange*. For teaching staff this routinely creates pressure to engage with students' unfamiliar profiles and needs, as well as exertions over English competency (Birrell 2006) and newly sharpened anxiety about readings, research writing, and plagiarism (McGowan 2009; Stappenbelt, Roles & May 2009). Our first hand experience of this Asianisation is showing us that the stark *difference* in these students' educational histories, aptitude, and skill from the mainstream, is rapidly becoming *division*. Unquestionably, it is cultural divides and their ramifications for learning and teaching that are most immediately confronting for both students and staff in the internationalisation of Australian higher education today.

What has become apparent through this process is that the changing conditions of teaching require a fundamental redefinition of education. Our Northern traditions are no longer the exclusive preserve of an Anglo-Celtic minority; the liberal education philosophies and goals derived from European classical backgrounds are now, thanks to globalisation, a focus of considerable interest for Asian and other international communities, and we in the metropole are in a prime position to generate educational dialogues around them. As Mignolo and Schiwy (1997) have argued, it is up to us *all* now to actively reinscribe the historical legacy of colonial difference: '[T]he question … is no longer one of dualism. We are no longer facing the question of "the West and the Rest" but "the Rest *in* the West" as well as "the West *in* the Rest"' (p. 18, emphasis added). If higher education is to grapple with the implications of these integrations, the most pressing issues become whether, and how, it is possible to bridge the cultural divides that come into focus as these diverse epistemological traditions intersect. In our metropolitan centres, we have to work towards a new imaginary which is prepared to account for our own worldview, in other words to prise open for articulation and scrutiny the dominant Northern assumptions of what constitutes knowledge and knowledge-making in our own contexts. Eminent cultural theorist Gayatri Spivak (1990) insists that the first vital step towards emancipation in the colonial contact is taken by 'working critically through one's beliefs, prejudices and assumptions and understanding how they arose and became naturalised' (p. 121). Thus, if 'We' are not to remain stuck within the restricted parameters of vision humorously evoked by Kipling in the epigraph above, we will need to overcome our fear and shock-horror of the changing interpersonal and knowledge landscapes we now inhabit ('think of it!'). It is our human as well as professional responsibility to develop alternative pedagogies that grapple with the diverse values and practices inherent in internationalisation (Gillespie 2002), and turning our gaze to our own backyard beliefs and practices is the best place to start.

Archaeologies of knowing

For the conceptual framework that informs our own pedagogic theory and practice, we are indebted to the insightful work of James Scheurich (1997; Scheurich & Young 1998) in the USA. In his in-depth analysis of *Research method in the postmodern*, Scheurich (1997) extends Foucault's 'discursive regularities' and 'archaeological' systems[2] (Foucault 1971/1973, 1972) specifically to throw light on research and the academic production of knowledge. In doing this Scheurich first explains the all-encompassing effects of '*social* regularities' (p. 94, emphasis in original), which he defines as 'the rules or assumptions that *constitute* the nature of reality, the way to know reality, the nature of the subjectivity of the knower, etc.' (1997, p. 163, emphasis in original).

As developed by Scheurich, this social construction represents 'powerful "grids" or networks of regularities' (p. 98) that are not only reflective but inherently constitutive of social behaviours. These regularities emerge by common 'rules of formation' through which we come to understand how it is possible for us to *be* in the world, as our cultures establish 'formational sets' in relation to the social regularities that are at any one time historically dominant. Consequently, 'to be a member of [a] culture is to live — think, act, talk, be — literally in the terms of its interlinked categories or nodes of social construction' (p. 163). Scheurich explicitly labels the interactive intersections of these categories as 'an archaeology', and 'viewing a culture in this way' as 'an archaeological perspective' (1997, p. 163). He notes that what he calls the *deepest* 'rules and assumptions of the multi-formational archaeology' operate outside the reflective consciousness of culture members, and thus are most often unconsciously reproduced (p. 167).

Such a theoretical position locates the intellectual activity of individuals in specific 'archaeological' contexts that will quite clearly have enormous bearing on the learning that is possible for them when they relocate to other cultural environments. Scheurich makes the process clear:

> To say that an individual, a single self, thinks is, if you want to speak archaeologically, to say that the archaeology is calling forth or enacting an event that we think of as an 'individual thinking'. When I think, the 'I' that thinks is that which I have learned to have as an 'I' in my particular culture. When I think, the categories I use to think with are the categories of my culture, categories that derive their meaning from the linked web or array of other categories. When I think, what I understand as thinking has been taught to me by my culture, by my archaeology. (1997, p. 165)

While Scheurich also acknowledges the unique and dynamic nature of the interactive intersections that constitute any individual person's growth to subjectivity and knowledge, his goal is to stress the interdependence of cultural context and individual performance: 'it is critically important to understand that the fundamental rules, assumptions etc. of the overall multi-formational archaeology are almost exclusively those of the dominant formation, which is … the key source of its dominance' (p. 167). How this affects the conduct of research, of thinking about research, and of the learning that is involved in an academic education, irrespective of the language in which it is carried out, is thus not a simple matter of grasping new conceptual material or language structures. Rather, it is a deeply embedded and complex interaction of personal, social and ecological dimensions. As Scheurich (1997) says:

> To be a researcher, then, is not to be a free, self-defining entity. It is like being an aspect of an ecology in which no single aspect of the ecology moves freely and independently or can be said to have an independent existence, instead … it is the whole interwoven ecology that lives and moves, not just some individual part. The researcher does not speak the archaeology; the archaeology speaks the researcher. (p. 171)

Such a process inevitably has deep and challenging significance for educators who would aim for the knowledge development, and for the research and thinking skills, of learners who have grown and been schooled in diverse cultural backgrounds.

Implications for international education – embracing the *trans*cultural

In presenting this 'postmodernist archaeological perspective', Scheurich (1997) explains that, because it operates most often beyond the conscious intention of individuals, it acts, archaeologically, at a *civilisational* level. As corollary, in relation to education and knowledge-building, he shows how the assumptions that are invisibly embedded in the currently dominant white, Anglo-Celtic academy act 'civilisationally' on ways of researching, teaching and learning to engage our imaginations within the restricted social regularities that are familiar to us. As a result, in the present contexts defined by globalised higher education, they produce conditions of educational discrimination that it is now vital we recognise and interrupt.[3] As we have noted elsewhere, Scheurich explores in considerable detail how these 'civilizational' understandings that emerge directly from the ontologies, epistemologies and axiologies of the dominant group, 'have become so deeply embedded that they are typically seen as "natural" or appropriate norms rather than as historically evolved social constructions' (p. 139; see Cadman 2005b). In this they are quite distinct from 'individual', self-conscious acts of prejudice or discrimination (p. 133), as well as conceptually different from those 'institutional and social' processes that involve 'standard operating procedures … [norms, concepts, habits, expectations] that hurt members of one or more races in relation to members of the dominant race' (p.135).

Scheurich explores these *individual* and *institutional* 'levels' of discrimination specifically in relation to epistemological and educational processes. In our Australian contexts, while we clearly see the same trends as those detailed by Scheurich, we are also aware that, in both individual and institutional activities, there have been ground-breaking attempts to grapple with the complexities that have resulted from internationalising universities. Of course it will always be the case that certain individual power brokers among both faculty and administration staff act routinely to serve their own interests by marginalising those they perceive as different. Significantly, however, today many individuals working in a leadership capacity for multicultural equity, often against the grain of their own self-interest, are increasingly being seen and heard (Delaney 2002; Teekens 2003; Van der Wende 2003). Further, at the institutional level, enormous advances have been achieved by feminist and post-structural scholarship exploring how human beings see and relate to the world around them in terms of cultural, social diversity and gender related issues. In the higher education sector, multiculturalism and pluralism have clearly gained ground in creating spaces for equity considerations to be conceptualised and respected within the dominant paradigms of learning. Nevertheless, despite these advances, it remains the case that policy goals and directives, often including basic pedagogical procedures and curricula, have been slow to accommodate the educational diversity we now experience.

In making this observation we strongly agree with Scheurich (1997) that such institutional short-sightedness is a logical result of generic failure of vision at the *civilisational* level, that is, the imaginative frame which 'creates or constitutes the possibility for all of the [other] categories' (p. 133). As education providers in the dominant power positions, we have inadequately recognised the fundamental distortion effected by the *epistemological* lens we bring to our task, which colours all in its own hue. Scheurich states: 'The lens constructs the world according to the nature of the lens, and ... archaeology knows this, while realism imperially thinks its lens is a window onto the really real' (pp. 173–4). If we continue to believe that the Enlightenment 'reason' we have historically and geographically inherited provides us with truths of universal application (what Scheurich describes as 'modernism's royal road to Truth about the really real' [p. 171]), we will remain trapped blindly in our own civilisational ways of knowing. Conceptually, we, as the purveyors of Anglo-Celtic education, are in danger of being stuck within the certainty of our Northern epistemological supremacy, thus effectively impoverishing our own as well as others' possibilities for gaining and sharing new knowledge.

The argument we want to advance here, then, is that, if we choose to articulate and engage seriously with the implications of the recent globalising trends in education, there are very positive steps we can now take. First, it is of course necessary that difference and diversity should be named, foregrounded, and analysed, but not then ignored, sidelined or forced to conform to shapes demanded by ill-informed pedagogies that do not respond to up-to-date, global intercultural understanding. In fact, we believe that the huge intercultural divides we observe for both teachers and students in Australia today need to be addressed in ways which extend beyond the individual and institutional innovations that are currently taking place. It *is* possible for us to bridge our educational differences effectively and successfully, if we address pedagogic challenges at the 'civilisational' level. In other words, human beings have the capacity to learn how to interrogate their own assumptions and beliefs through the imaginary of another, to engage with each other's epistemological premises and worldviews, and to grow in understanding of each other's ways of knowing about the world. In human societies, *civilisations* do not clash; it is empires that clash, not the ontological and epistemological concepts that sustain them (Liu 2004). Both educators and learners can bridge the existing divides we are experiencing, but only if we in the power positions are prepared to reconsider new possibilities for pedagogies that problematise our own operational understanding of interculturalism, and thus facilitate a new conceptual step towards the principles of *trans*culturalism that globalised education now demands.

The notion of the 'transcultural' has grown out of an early concept of 'transculturation' coined in 1940 by Cuban historian Fernando Ortiz (1995) to throw light on the contemporary multiracial and multicultural issues then existing in Cuba. According to Mignolo and Schiwy (2003/7, p. 20), Ortiz was seeking to correct the perception that, in the dynamic cultural exchange between migrant and settled communities, change and growth occur as a unidirectional flow, as represented in the historical concept of 'acculturation'. In an introduction to Ortiz's work, the anthropologist Malinowski refers to 'acculturation' as

> an ethnographic word with a moral meaning: the immigrant has to acculturate, just like indigenous peoples, pagans, infidels, barbarians and savages were subjected to Our Great Western Culture … The ignoramus must receive the benefits of 'our culture'; it is he who must change and become one of 'us'. (Malinowski in Ortiz 1995, p. 4)

For these scholars it is imperative to recognise that, in the intercultural encounter, 'cultural transformations do not only go from East to West but also from West to East or North-South and South-North', that, 'following Ortiz, transculturation works bidirectionally in the social life of things' as well as of people (Mignolo & Schiwy 2003/7, p. 21). More recently, Onghena (2003/6) has further explained that, for Ortiz, the transcultural encounter, 'more than being an end result, was a project, a *possibility*' through which 'a new and complex reality emerges; a reality that is no mechanical mixture of characters, nor mosaic, but instead a new, original and independent phenomenon' (pp. 182–3, added emphasis). In the present century of globalisation, as Onghena points out, we are being forced to reinterrogate these ideas so that we can see and come to terms with the conceptual frames that we ourselves are operating within. Onghena (2003/6) argues that we need again to embrace the full implications of Ortiz's concept of *bi*directional, *trans*cultural learning which, as he says,

> better expresses the different phases of the transitive process of shifting from one culture to another, since these do not solely entail the acquisition of a new and distinct culture, as suggested by the English word 'acculturation'; instead… to describe this process, the Latinate word transcultural provides us with a term that does not suggest the idea of one culture having to lean towards another, but of a transition between two cultures, both active and participating parties, both contributing in their own ways, cooperating in the advent of a new civilisational reality. (Ortiz 1995 in Onghena 2003/6, pp. 182–3)

For our own pedagogy we engaged early with the convincing analysis of '[t]he difficulties of interculturalism' presented by Roberto Salvadori (1997), who touches on the idea of transculturalism specifically in the personal intercultural encounter between teacher and student. Salvadori argues that to overcome the difficulties experienced in intercultural teaching, we must accept that '[e]ducation will only be valid when both parties to the relationship — teacher and pupil — are involved in the same way … and they transform each other. Something changes in the culture of both' (p. 187; see Cadman 2000). Salvadori's goal is 'achieving transculturalism and creating a common culture, which … certainly will be different from the original cultures of both teachers and students' (p. 188) and which effectively works towards 'the creation of a critical, comparative and systematic perspective of existing cultures' (p. 189).

Both Salvadori (1997) and Onghena (2003/6), however, want to stress the discomforts and antagonisms involved for all parties who grapple with these transcultural divides. Salvadori speaks of confusion, loss, and weakening of identity (p. 187). Onghena points to the tensions involved in asymmetric power relations as we, mainstream academics, feel the need to 'reinforce this sense of "us" that, according to some, has become vulnerable faced with the invading "other"' (p. 183; see also Kraidy 2009, pp. 13–14). Meanwhile, for our students, 'the combining of practices is not undertaken freely — because not everyone enjoys the same freedom at the moment of combining or interpreting cultural factors' (Onghena 2003/6, p. 183). These divisive potentials are inescapable aspects of intercultural encounters and in the global education enterprise they demand our professional and, above all, our pedagogic expertise. In this we strongly endorse Onghena's (2003/6) call when she says: 'A new social imaginary is needed ... And more than ever it is necessary to reconsider the processes and effects of cultural diversity within a new framework and with a new language' (p. 184). For us this means embracing the *trans*cultural along with the pedagogic risks that are required.

Reframing pedagogy

In clarifying this pedagogic goal we are aware that we are choosing a path that takes us philosophically in the opposite direction from the dominant thinking of Northern, metropolitan universities. The prevalent 'civilisational' and therefore intuitive response to the discords and perceived threats caused by Asianisation is for universities to move towards a more stringent and explicit homogenisation of course curricula and assessment outcomes. In their zeal to protect the traditional 'standards' of Northern, Anglo-Celtic education, institutional policy-makers have shown a marked tendency to deal with escalating student diversity, ironically, by demanding 'standardised' course profiles for all teaching across the disciplinary contexts of the university (for example, University of Adelaide, 2009/2010) and creating mandatory, one-size-fits-all 'graduate attributes' for the students (see Song & Cadman, Chapter 12, this volume). Such policy moves are clearly attempts to effect the acculturation, if not the assimilation, of the diverse 'other' exactly in the manner described and rejected by Ortiz (above). While these are, in Scheurich's (1997) terms, 'institutional' imperatives, they are inherently embedded in 'civilisational' assumptions emanating from a set of shared, unconsciously held academic values which still see native speaker English and a traditional metropolitan education as the keys to superior knowledge of the world as well as to personal career advancement, irrespective of a learner's ethnic, cultural or language background. Such a focus requires students to turn their backs on their own intellectual heritage and subjects them to boundaries for learning that effectively exclude or marginalise other knowledges and learning traditions.

The overt homogenising of policies and practices is not, however, without its critics. It has been clearly shown that such a response to student diversity reflects a regressive 'monolingual framing' that not only fails to capitalise on the lived realities of international education for both students and staff, but also generates a continued discourse of 'intellectual imperialism' which acts to exclude students from mainstream educational processes (Liddicoat & Crichton 2008). Millar (2009) addresses these trends and advocates strongly for 'the art of inclusive teaching', taking his definition from the Centre for Instructional Development and Research at the University of Washington:

> *Inclusive teaching* means teaching in ways that do not exclude students, accidentally or intentionally, from opportunities to learn. (p. 3, emphasis in original)

He then cites the Washington list of teaching behaviours that exclude students:

- Conveying disrespect, unfairness, or lack of confidence in students
- Disregarding student backgrounds, preparation, or life events that affect learning
- Interacting with only a sub-set of students
- Teaching in ways that favour particular backgrounds or approaches to learning. (p. 3)

The point Millar wants to make here is that, while few university teachers would intentionally act in these ways, many might do so unintentionally, '[g]iven the pressure under which they work' (p. 3). In our view it is not just the pressure of work that results in teaching which routinely reproduces the behaviours listed here, but rather the unthinking collusion of academics like ourselves in the 'archaeological' regularities identified by Scheurich (above). These uninterrogated beliefs characterise our understanding of Anglo-Celtic superiority in epistemological and discursive performance, and thus promote our participation in imperialistic practices. Such practices have been described as effecting an 'educational neocolonialism' that is advanced as Northern, metropolitan paradigms act 'to shape and influence educational systems and thinking elsewhere through the processes of globalization' (Nguyen et al. 2009, p. 109).

Increasingly, scholars with progressive vision for globalising education are seriously resisting these neocolonial advances with arguments that demand new pedagogic approaches and 'curriculum contestations', in favour of

> providing students the vital learning to enable them to transgress the monocultural protectionism of White-nation, English-only politics in order to secure their economic well-being via the corporate multiculturalism of the world's multilingual knowledge economies.' (Singh 2005, p. 115)

Leaders in this project like Michael Singh and his colleagues, are uncompromising in their pressing demand for democratising educational procedures towards the delivery of a truly equitable and 'responsive education' in globalising contexts. This, they say,

> requires a consideration of innovative ways of renovating the policies, pedagogies, and politics concerned with educating students *for* life. This means graduating students who can think critically and have deep understanding of ideas, developing students able to produce knowledge by drawing on resources

from different fields and integrating these with their own experiential knowledge so as to speak to their real life contexts. (Singh, Kenway & Apple 2005, p. 10, emphasis in original)

In a very powerful investigation of the place of Chinese knowledge in educational research in Australia, Singh (2009) argues that the most fertile way for us to begin a transformation of pedagogy is by focussing on our own 'cross-cultural ignorance', in other words by integrating, pedagogically, what we *don't* know into our curriculum designs, and 'engaging … students from other cultures in ways that use their intellectual capital, about which the [academic teacher] knows very little' (p. 8). In this discussion, Singh shows in convincing detail the primary educational outcomes achieved by those who, with no matter how much goodwill, focus their teaching on perceived student difference and deficit. He describes the work of these 'conscientious academics' who are civilisationally blind to the discriminating effects of the transmission pedagogies they adopt 'in good faith'. These effects do not, as they would hope, enhance the adaptation of multiethnic students to an unfamiliar academic culture and make them more competitive in their academic performance. Rather, they maintain the remedial positioning of those student groups that do not possess the taken-for-granted knowledge and skills, and continuously renew the authority of the Anglo-Celtic teacher (Singh 2009, p. 8).

And it is through these processes that we see a set of standard attitudes to Asian students being consolidated in our institutions, based on a highlighting of their difficulties rather than their strengths, and a myopic, culturally-biased construction of their 'remedial' needs (Millar 2009). As Liddicoat & Crichton (2008, p. 371) have argued, the prevailing monolingual framing of such international education results in a dominant, taken-for-granted 'discourse of inadequacy' in which the term 'multilingual' signifies a problem which needs to be addressed, rather than a resource to be celebrated, exploited and built upon (Liddicoat & Crichton 2008, pp. 371–2). The extent to which we, as individuals and institutions, want to interrupt this discourse and offer *all* students educational opportunities that build upon their existing skills and advance their future goals, is the extent to which we will succeed in weakening the prevailing force of neoliberal and market-oriented policy objectives in higher education. Only in this way will we succeed in reinvigorating a global discourse that again sees education as a path to equity and social justice rather than primarily to commercial gain.

Thus, we argue that, as scholarly educators, our pressing challenge is to transcend the civilisational framing we inherit and welcome the epistemological possibilities opened up by globalisation. Focussed, transcultural pedagogy is an effective and practical step towards international student emancipation in our own local teaching contexts. However, it inevitably means participating in change to the same degree that we expect from students, as well as recognising and engaging with our own vulnerability in the teaching project. To transform pedagogy touches every aspect of our professional and academic endeavours; it requires that we reconfigure course content, teaching objectives, processes, tasks and activities, materials, assessment and reporting. Significantly, transculturalism demands that we account explicitly for our own taken-for-granted epistemological assumptions about ways of knowing, and approaches to learning, since these are contestable in multicultural contexts. Above all, such a pedagogy engages each teacher in a sincerely reflexive investigation of their own personal investment in these value-laden expectations, as well as in dialogues that both respect and integrate the, possibly quite alien, investments of their students.

In earlier work we have acknowledged the powerful conceptual approaches that have informed our understandings of the kind of pedagogic transformation we are advocating here. These approaches include Simon's (1987, 1992) conception of a 'pedagogy of possibility' as 'one committed to the expansion of the range of human capacities contained within the requirements of securing diversity, compassionate justice, and the renewal of life' (1992 in Cadman 2000, p. 101). They also include the 'pedagogy of engagement', defined by hooks (1994) as the 'connection between ideas learned in university settings and those learned in life practices' and later extended by Pennycook (1999, p. 340), who argues that 'such issues as gender, race, class, sexuality, and postcolonialism [are] so fundamental to identity and language that they need to form the basis of curricular organization and pedagogy' (see Cadman 2005a, p. 355). Finally, we have drawn extensively on the 'pedagogy of connection' we developed in these contexts, which aims consciously 'to privilege opportunities for connecting — people, understandings, knowledges, feelings — in the diverse ways that a [transcultural] teaching context makes possible' (Cadman 2005a; see Lin, Chapter 8, and Song & Cadman, Chapter 12, this volume). All these innovative pedagogic approaches require conditions of possibility for their effectiveness. The most immediate of these is the creation of a learning environment that is designed to be hospitable — a place where students want to be — where both their affective and intellectual energies are engaged and they can connect to the teacher, the other students, and the learning process in relevant and fulfilling relations. Above all, as we have argued above, the teaching/learning relationships must here be horizontalised in key ways so as to articulate what both teachers and students *do* and *don't* have epistemological investment in, what Onghena (2003/6) has called the 'relationship-based exchange' that is at the heart of a transcultural pedagogy.

Multiple perspectives: Bridging *trans*cultural divides in the teaching of Asian languages and cultures

Asian Studies departments in Australia, in many ways, have been at the forefront of these revolutionary movements in the globalisation of higher education. Initially established to teach Asian languages, cultures and societies in the last millennium, increased student diversity has impelled these departments to confront and experiment with a new paradigm of teaching practice that bridges the transcultural divides in the higher education experience. The educators whose work comes together in this volume represent the professional and scholarly diversity of Asian Studies today. With a focus on pedagogy, this collection speaks directly to the centrality and significance for globalising societies of a university education which addresses contemporary concerns both for and about Asia and Asian people. Notably, most of the authors here are multicultural, multilingual and globally educated. Their combined analyses provide a cutting edge perspective on the importance of Asian studies and languages in educating students for immediate transnational futures, as well as for their long-term roles as global citizens.

All the contributors to this collection are teaching and researching at the forefront of the educational challenges they identify. They range from internationally recognised scholars to mid-career academics, early career researchers and PhD candidates, thus embodying the living population of the Australian higher education workforce. The contributions here demonstrate innovative and eclectic approaches to practice; they noticeably represent a wide range of diverse rhetorical arguments, and demonstrate the creative research writing that is taking place today in contemporary social sciences. Overall, the combined insights of these writings articulate a politics of difference not division, inspired by an ethics of connection and social justice informed by recent linguistic, cultural, and educational theories.

The chapters are organised to focus primarily on the missions that typically inspire the work of Northern metropolitan centres for Asian Studies and languages. Part II (chapters 2 and 3) speaks to the conceptual and political ideas which inform 'transcultural' teaching and learning. In Chapter 2, Mobo Gao immediately challenges the focus of an Asian Studies education in his provocative question, 'What are the implications for learning in Australian universities if and when the centre of the world shifts towards Asia?'. In an in-depth analysis of some of the distorting epistemological and social effects resulting from the 'us' and 'them' mentality of traditional scholarly analysis, Gao shows how world narratives now have to be rewritten and decentred from Western interests. In this he furthers the ecological arguments presented above, and argues that the 'West' now needs urgently to interrogate some of its 'currently unthinkable' assumptions, including that the prevailing locus of epistemological superiority and power may be on the move from the Anglo-Celtic academy to a new location such as China.

In Chapter 3, Greg McCarthy again raises the problematic effects of Western scholarly traditions which rest on a set of epistemological and ontological assumptions that take for granted their own universal application. With a focus on the research education of Asian, in this case Chinese, postgraduate students, McCarthy argues that significant distortions may be experienced by both supervisors and novice researchers, and these can profoundly influence students' capacity to undertake the critical theoretical work that is now imperative for any challenge to Western epistemological dominance and neoliberal market forces. He identifies the untapped potential of a transcultural pedagogy to open up much needed cultural spaces in research education for speaking truth to power, and actively engaging international postgraduates in extending the dominant boundaries of reason and critique.

Part III (chapters 4 to 7) explores curriculum transformations in the teaching of Asian languages. New interrogations of pedagogy, of ways of knowing, learning styles, and student motivation are seen here as creative responses to new demands on students and teachers in Asian language classes. In Chapter 4, Anthony Liddicoat and Michelle Kohler draw on notions of language, culture, and the intercultural in language learning to argue that teaching which rests on the one-way transfer of linguistic and cultural knowledge is no longer adequate for the complex roles required of multilingual speakers in globalising contexts. Today, foreign language learners have to be able to mediate actively in intercultural encounters. By analysing Indonesian teaching situations, these authors show how enlightened intercultural language teaching can effectively build bridges between cultures, as students are led to 'gain independence from a single linguistic and conceptual system through which to view the world', and thus to resist the tyranny of monolingual vision cautioned against by Gao.

In Chapter 5, Kayoko Enomoto uses a theoretical model of action planning to design a Study Skills Action Plan (SSAP) for an extremely large cohort of first-year students of Japanese, most of whom have had their previous educational training in Asian contexts. The SSAP learning plan explicitly integrates students' responses to teacher feedback into the learning and assessment program. A key aspect of this procedure is a requirement that students complete a reflective journal, assessing their own performance and motivation. Through detailed analysis of both quantitative and qualitative data, Enomoto shows how the SSAP methodology has led to a demonstrated increase in students' development of 'deep' learning strategies, including taking responsibility for their own learning. As a result she is able to point to the transferability of study skills action planning to other disciplinary contexts.

At the second year level, Naomi Aoki (Chapter 6) again signals the crucial point that today's new levels of student diversity clearly demand a re-evaluation of traditional teaching methods and materials. Here Aoki investigates the effectiveness of a range of different pedagogic strategies for teaching Japanese *kanji* characters to students from four different language groups, English-only, Chinese, Korean, and Malay, who have diverse levels of familiarity with these characters. Here she analyses students' written feedback on a self-reflexive questionnaire focussed on motivation, learning strategies and evaluation of self-study, in addition to students' test scores. The conclusions showed marked and significant differences in preferred study and learning practices among the four language groups. Aoki argues that investigations into the affective factors influencing students' learning are now vital for curriculum design, and that carefully scaffolded, student-centred learning strategies need to be integrated into language teaching programs for today's multilingual, multicultural learners.

Advanced level language students frequently express the need for intercultural exchange that will extend them beyond purely linguistic competence. To meet this demand, Akiko Tomita (Chapter 7) presents a study evaluating her integration of authentic, real-life interactions with Japanese native-speaking exchange students into language curriculum activities and assessment. Drawing on the principles of Cadman's (2005a) 'pedagogy of connection' and Liddicoat's (2008) framework of intercultural language teaching, Tomita conducts quantitative and in-depth qualitative analysis of students' written reflections on this initiative. In this context the language students attributed high levels of warmth and personal value to their growth in understanding of their own and the 'other's' culture, through the interpersonal dialogues that were generated. Tomita argues that not only does strategic interaction with native speakers enhance motivation for advanced-level language learners, but it also significantly enriches their personal growth and well-being by fostering life-long openness to other cultures, ideas and people.

Part IV (chapters 8 to 10) extends the theme of transcultural transformation to explore the richness of Asian social and cultural studies for deepening our insight into how Asian perspectives contribute to global understanding. In Chapter 8, Delia Lin problematises the one-way teacher-to-student process inherent in accepted understandings of 'intercultural competence' as a teaching goal, and advances an alternative, psychological framework which she calls 'cultural flexibility'. Following Salvadori's (1997) call for an authentically '*trans*cultural' pedagogy in which teachers and students 'change together' (see Cadman & Song, this volume, Chapter 1), she explores concepts of flexibility and inflexibility drawn from a psychological theory known as Acceptance and Commitment Therapy (ACT). Lin's resulting model of 'cultural flexibility' challenges the dominant restricted interpretation of intercultural 'competence', and proposes an alternative conceptualisation of the intercultural by making explicit the key elements needed for transcultural and dialogic teaching in multicultural educational contexts.

In a starkly different rhetorical exploration of the roles of teachers and students in progressing transcultural relations, Sejin Pak (Chapter 9) presents an auto-ethnographic analysis of his own experience as a Korean man, teaching cultural studies subjects that focus on contemporary Japan. Pak here situates himself intellectually, emotionally and ethnically in the lived reality of the multi-ethnic situations that his teaching demands. In addition, he also links students' previous educational histories with their attitudes to key topic areas. In this way he shows how core intellectual concepts in his courses are open to contestation and divergent interpretation at the point of learning, with diverse, sometimes noticeably disturbing, effects for students. Through this auto-ethnographic inquiry, Pak offers a reflexive analysis of the impact of his own 'Koreanness' on his students' learning about Japan and, by drawing on what he has learned from students' own reflexive writing, he emphasises the central importance of the exercise of reflection itself, not only as a strategy for learning but also for life.

In Chapter 10, Shoko Yoneyama shows again how central an Asian Studies education is to the contested spaces in higher education opened up by globalisation. Yoneyama here brings a uniquely Asian, sociological perspective to the now almost banal assumptions underpinning 'Western' attitudes to 'critical thinking' and Asian students. She explores discourses from a range of scholarly disciplines in the global academy to identify the Orientalism that sits at the heart of Western understandings of 'critical' analysis, especially in their relationship to education and 'Confucian-heritage cultures' such as Japan. By bringing critical thinking into a specifically Asian frame of interrogation, Yoneyama argues that the relational aspects of conceptual learning which are integral to Asian cultures are currently missing from dominant understandings of the critical. She advances the concept of 'connected knowing', which involves empathetic and dialogic engagement with the position of the other in truly 'critical' interaction, and potentially extends to 'realms of the soul and spirit'. She finally proposes a 'tabula' or sociological model for a new, connecting critical thinking, forged through the synthesis of Western intellectual values and the most positive aspects of Eastern social relations.

The final chapters, in Part V, address a third mission often ascribed to pedagogies for Asian studies and languages; that is:

> Bridging the gap between Asian and Anglo-Celtic education systems by capitalising on students' previous learning and enhancing their academic experiences in Australia. (University of Adelaide 2009)

The first issue highlighted under this mission is plagiarism, which Australian universities have identified as an increasingly serious academic problem for Asian international students, and related largely to the difference in cultural and educational training of students from Asian backgrounds (Devlin 2002). In Chapter 11, with a focus on Chinese-background students, Ming Hwa Ting presents an explicitly Asian perspective. He argues that to assume a direct correlation between a student's culture and their textual practice of plagiarism is an over-simple causal explanation for a complex problem. Ting here shows how analysts, including scholars of Chinese background, express conflicting views: on the one hand, Chinese culture and education are seen to be conducive to both the social and textual practices of plagiarism; on the other, it is argued that Chinese writing does not assume a lack of attribution of erudite sources, and is often required to constitute original, non-derivative prose. Drawing on his experience as an academic teacher and assessor, Ting argues that occurrences of plagiarism relate more directly to economic and social issues than to cultural influences. In his view, English composing skills can be taught, and learned, by motivated students: what is needed is hard-line implementation of regulatory policies, together with sympathetic, active and consistent teaching interventions that are not constrained by the belief that Chinese culture somehow locks its students into the unshakeable habit of plagiarising the words of their masters.

In the final chapter, we, Song and Cadman, present our analysis of a skills-based, *Research Project* course designed to address social studies research and communication skills that Chinese-background students' educational histories may not have covered. The course was inspired firstly by the Confucian belief that all people are educable, and *all* have the right to an appropriate and relevant education. Secondly, we were required to address a mandated set of homogenised 'graduate attributes', which are believed to represent the 'educated' person in Australia. A compulsory co-requisite subject provides content reading and conceptual ideas so that course teaching can be directed exclusively to the skills students need to conduct and communicate research. A significant pedagogic innovation is that the course is taught, and learnt, bilingually. Students are free to use Chinese or English at any time, and assessed writing is required to demonstrate Northern, metropolitan principles of deductive logic in either language. Course evaluations and outcomes demonstrate clearly that in its first semester this course effectively met the mandatory generic institutional attributes, even as it fulfilled our own transcultural, educational and political goals for the Confucian ideals which motivated us.

Conclusion

In all these ways, then, the chapters presented here speak forcefully to the pedagogic possibilities currently being pursued at the local level in the teaching of Asian cultures and languages in Australia. And in relation to the larger goal for this project, we have here bridged transcultural divides in a wide variety of ways. Ideologically, it is largely agreed that the incredulous interjections of the speaking voice heard in our epigraph — that delightful child persona of Kipling's poem 'We and they', who echoes the adult attitudes around him as he exclaims, 'would you believe it?', 'isn't it scandalous?', 'impudent heathen!', 'think of it!' — beautifully characterise the white ruler's horror at even the *idea* that his own cultural and epistemological worldview (that of the dominant 'We') might be considered equivalent to that of any other ('they'). For us, the humorous mimicry of this voice only barely conceals the social and epistemic violence created historically by the gendered and supercilious worldview it conjures. The potential loss to this child of the world he would naturally inherit is so clearly glimpsed here as devastation and degradation that we fully understand his obdurate resistance to the progress that would be needed to bring it about. Today the Northern academy is just so resistant, but if we continue, as we are starting, to engage with pedagogic possibility as it is realised in the examples of Asian studies education shown in this collection, our collaborative endeavours will move us confidently towards that fertile ecology of knowledges that globalisation allows us to imagine.

Notes

[1] In our own writing we have adopted the North/South terminology of the United Nations and so referred to the dominant Anglo-Celtic global academy as 'northern' and 'metropolitan', in line with the work of Connell (2007) and Santos (2007). Other authors in the volume have retained the terms 'West' and 'East' for their own purposes.

[2] Foucault (1972) distinguishes between linguistic analysis which provides from given, defined samples, 'rules that make it possible to construct other statements than these', and discursive analysis which answers the more socially situated question: 'how is it that one particular statement appeared rather than another?' (p. 27). In this framework, Archaeology is the method of investigating the social and historical conditions that allowed such statements to be made.

[3] Scheurich and Young (1997, 1998) construct these conditions as assumptions and acts of epistemological and educational racism. In the present discussion we feel that a discourse of racism is not fruitful for our purposes and so have chosen not to engage in those terms with what for us are still extremely salient issues.

References

Birrell, B 2006, 'Implications of low English standards amongst overseas students at Australian universities', *People and Place*, vol. 14 no. 4, pp. 53–64.

Bodycott, P 2009, 'Choosing a Higher Education study abroad destination: what mainland Chinese parents and students rate as important', *Journal of Research in International Education*, vol. 8 no. 3, pp. 349–372.

Cadman, K 2000, '"Voices in the air": evaluations of the learning experiences of international postgraduates and their supervisors', *Teaching in Higher Education*, vol. 5 no. 4, pp. 475–491.

Cadman, K 2002, '"English for academic possibilities": the research proposal as a contested site in postgraduate genre pedagogy', *Journal of English for Academic Purposes*, vol. 1 no. 2, pp. 85–104.

Cadman, K 2005a, 'Towards a pedagogy of connection in research education: a "REAL" story', *Journal of English for Academic Purposes (Special Edition on Advanced Academic Literacies)*, vol. 4 no. 4, pp. 353–367.

Cadman, K 2005b, '"Divine discourse": plagiarism, hybridity and epistemological racism', in S May, M Franken & R Barnard (eds), *LED: refereed proceedings of the inaugural international conference on language, education and diversity*, University of Waikato Press, Hamilton, NZ [CDRom].

Coley, M 1999, 'The English language entry requirements of Australian Universities for students of non-English-speaking background', *Higher Education Research & Development*, vol. 18 no. 1, pp. 7–17.

Connell, R 2007, *Southern theory: the global dynamics of knowledge in social science*, Allen & Unwyn, Sydney, NSW.

Davis, TM 2003, *Atlas of student mobility*, Institute of International Education (IEE), New York.

Delaney, AM 2002, 'Enhancing support for student diversity through research', *Tertiary Education and Management*, vol. 8, pp. 145–166.

Devlin, M 2002, *Minimising Plagiarism*, Centre for the Study of Higher Education, The University of Melbourne, Melbourne viewed 6 February, <http://www.cshe.unimelb.edu.au/assessinglearning/03/plagMain.html>.

Eisenchlas, S, Trevaskes, S & Liddicoat AJ 2004, 'Internationalisation: the slow move from rhetoric to practice in Australian universities', in AJ Liddicoat, S Eisenchlas & S Trevaskes (eds), *Australian perspective on internationalising education*, Language Australia, Melbourne, pp. 141–149.

Foucault, M 1971/1973, *The order of things: an archaeology of the human sciences*, Vintage, New York.

Foucault, M 1972, *The archaeology of knowledge*, Pantheon, New York.

Gareth, D 2005, 'Chinese students' motivations for studying abroad', *International Journal of Private Higher Education*, vol. 2, pp. 16–21.

Gillespie, SH 2002, 'The practice of international education in the context of globalization: a critique', *Journal of Studies in International Education*, vol. 6 no. 3, pp. 262–267.

Hayes, H, & Introna, LD 2005, 'Cultural values, plagiarism, and fairness: when plagiarism gets in the way of learning', *Ethics and Behavior*, vol. 15 no. 3, pp. 213–231.

Hooks, b 1990, *Yearning: race, gender and cultural practice*, South End Press, Boston.

Kraidy, MM 2009, 'Critical transculturalism', paper presented at the annual meeting of the International Communication Association, New York City, NY, viewed 12 December 2010, <http://www.allacademic.com/meta/p14237_index.html>.

Liddicoat, AJ & Crichton J 2008, 'The monolingual framing of international education in Australia', *Sociolinguistic Studies*, vol. 2. no. 3, pp. 367–384.

Liu, LH 2004, *The clash of empires*, Harvard University Press, London.

Marginson, S 2009a, 'University rankings and the knowledge economy', in MA Peters, S Marginson, & P Murphy (eds), *Creativity and the global knowledge economy*, Peter Lang, New York, pp. 185–216.

Marginson, S. 2009b, 28 April, 'Our gift to the world', *Campus Review*, vol. 19 no. 8, pp. 8–10.

Marginson S, & Eijkman, H 2007, *International education: financial and organisational impacts in Australian universities*, Monash University Centre for Economics of Education and Training, Clayton, Vic.

McGowan, U 2005, 'Does educational integrity mean teaching students NOT to "use their own words"?', *International Journal for Educational Integrity*, vol. 1 no. 1, viewed 20 December 2010, <http://www.ojs.unisa.edu.au/index.php/IJEI/article/view/16/6>.

McGowan, U 2008, 'International students: a conceptual framework for dealing with unintentional plagiarism', in TS Roberts (ed.), *Student plagiarism in an online world: problems and solutions*, Hershey, New York, pp. 92–107.

McGowan, U 2009, Sept 28–30, 'Research apprenticeship: is this the answer to inadvertent plagiarism in undergraduate students' writings?', refereed Proceedings of the 4th Asia Pacific Conference on *Educational Integrity*, University of Wollongong, Wollongong, NSW, viewed 28 March 2010, <ro.uow.edu.au/cgi/viewcontent.cgi?article=1034&context=apcei>.

Mignolo W & Schiwy, F 2007/2003, 'Double translation: transculturation and the colonial difference', in B Streck & T Maranhão (eds), *Translation and ethnography: the anthropological challenge of intercultural understanding*,

University of Arizona Press, Tucson, AZ.

Millar, G 2009, 'Working with international students: Applied linguistics and the art of inclusive teaching. *TESOL in Context*. Special Edition on Pedagogies of Connection, vol. S2, viewed 23 November 2010, <www.tesol.org.au/Publications/Pedagogies-of-Connection>.

Nguyen, PM, Elliott, JG, Terlouw, C & Pilot, A 2009, 'Neocolonialism in education: cooperative learning in an Asian context', *Comparative Education,* vol. 45 no. 1, pp. 109–130.

Onghena, Y 2003/2006, 'Transculturalism and relation identity', in *Intercultural dialogue between Europe and the Mediterranean*, Consortium of the European Institute of the Mediterranean, IEMed, Barcelona, pp. 181–184.

Ortiz, F 1995, *Cuban counterpoint: tobacco and sugar*, trans. H. de Onís, Duke University Press, Durham, NC.

Pennycook, A 1999, 'Introduction: Critical approaches to TESOL', *TESOL Quarterly,* vol. 33 no 3, pp. 329–348.

Salvadori, RG 1997, 'The difficulties of interculturalism', *European Journal of Intercultural Studies,* vol. 8 no. 2, pp. 185–191.

Santos, BS 2007, *Another knowledge is possible: beyond northern epistemologies*, Verso, London.

Santos, BS, Nunes, JA, & Menesis, MP 2007, 'Introduction: opening up the canon of knowledge and recognition of difference', in BS Santos (ed.), *Another knowledge is possible: beyond northern epistemologies,* Verso, London, pp. xix–lxii.

Scheurich, JJ 1997, *Research method in the postmodern*, The Falmer Press, London and Washington.

Scheurich, JJ & Young, MD 1998, 'In the United States of America, in both our souls and our sciences, we are avoiding white racism', *Educational Researcher,* vol. 27 no. 9, pp. 27–32.

Singh, M 2009, 'Using Chinese knowledge in internationalising research education: Jacques Ranciere, an ignorant supervisor and doctoral students from China', *Globalisation, Societies and Education*, vol. 7 no. 2, pp. 185–201.

Singh, M, Kenway, J & Apple, M 2005, *Globalizing education: policies, pedagogies and politics*, Peter Lang, New York.

Spivak, G 1990, 'The intervention interview, with T Threadgold & F Bartowski', in S Harasym (ed.), *G. Spivak: the postcolonial critic: interviews, strategies, dialogues*, Routledge, New York, pp. 113–132.

Stappenbelt, B, Rowles, C & May E 2009, Jan 29–30, 'Cultural influence on attitudes to plagiarism', refereed proceedings of the 18th Annual Teaching Learning Forum *Teaching and learning for global graduates*, Curtin University of Technology, Perth, WA, viewed 28 March 2010, <http://otl.curtin.edu.au/tlf/tlf2009/refereed/stappenbelt.html>.

Starfield, S 2004, 'Why does this feel empowering? Thesis writing, concordancing, and the "corporatizing" university', in B Norton & K Toohey (eds), *Critical pedagogies and language learning*, Cambridge University Press, Cambridge, pp. 138–157.

Teekens, H 2003, 'The requirement to develop specific skills for teaching in an intercultural setting', *Journal of Studies in International Education*, vol. 6 no.1, Spring, pp. 108–119.

Van der Wende, M 2003, 'Globalisation and access to higher education', *Journal of Studies in International Education*, vol. 7 no. 2, Summer, pp. 193–206.

Wells J 2003, Internationalisation and Australian universities', *Frontline: NTEU National Women's Journal*, vol. 11, pp. 9–10 & 24.

Wright, EO n. d., review: Boaventura de Sousa (ed), *Democratizing democracy: beyond the liberal democratic canon*, Verso, New York, viewed 6 December 2010, <www.sirreadalot.org/reviews/0101.htm>.

Part II

Re-locating teaching and learning

What the implications for learning in Australian universities if and when the centre of the world shifts towards Asia?

Mobo Gao

Introduction

In this chapter I aim to argue that the centre of the world has begun to shift away from the West and towards Asia — the 'West' and 'Asia' in terms of geography but more importantly in terms of cultural tradition and political values — and that this centre shifting will have wide-ranging and far-reaching implications for learning at Australian universities. This argument contains three related tasks. The first is to outline briefly that the centre of the world has been the West for a long time, arguably since Columbus's symbolic sail to America. The second task is to demonstrate that there are at least indications and preliminary evidence that the centre has begun to shift, with the rising of China and India in recent years. Note that I do not wish to claim that the centre of the world will be Asia for the foreseeable future. I only argue that the overwhelming dominance of the West is a thing of the past. The final task of this chapter is to postulate some implications for learning at Australian universities as a result of the rise of Asia in general, and China in particular, on this globe where there will be different claims of value supremacies and legitimacies.

Issues, concepts and the change of global forces

When we talk about the learning of Asian languages and studies of Asian culture, it is usually taken for granted that that is what we should do at a university in Australia. But Asian languages and cultures are not courses that must necessarily be taught at an Australian university, in the same way as mathematics, English or physics. There remain the questions of *why* Asian languages and cultures should be subjects to be taught here, as well as *how* they are taught. If we look at these issues from the market point of view, these courses will be taught if there is a demand. We will respond to economic pressure and teach these courses in a way that satisfies the market. Or, from the point of view of national interest, Australia can dictate what Asian languages and cultures will be offered at what university by allocating resources in the name of Australia's national interest. However, neither of these considerations is something that can be taken for granted either. What a market is, is not self-evident — markets can be explored and created. Nor can we take it for granted what the Australian national interest is.

These issues are even more complex if we consider the change of global forces. For a few hundred years in modern history the West has been dominating the world stage in military force, in cultural values and in language. Because of this hegemony, in Australia, as a nation of Western traditions and possessing a Western value system, studies of Asian cultures and languages have been taken as exotic or curiosity subjects by a small percentage of people, and as pragmatic tools by an even smaller number of people for the necessity of dealing with bearers of these cultures and languages in diplomatic and intelligence services. But now there are indications that Western domination is about to come to an end. There is a change occurring in the movement of global forces that is increasingly made clear with the rise of China. Since I locate myself primarily as a China studies specialist, I will explore the issue of learning at Australian universities in relation to the study of Chinese language and culture.

But first, I need to consider some conceptual problems to clear the way for later discussion. Any concept, term or name can be deconstructed so as to question its validity and legitimacy. The same is true of the concepts used in this chapter, concepts like 'Western', 'Asia' and 'modernity'. Let me start with a commonly used concept, 'the West'. What is the West or Western? For instance, Japan has been considered part of the West politically for at least as long as the period from the end of World War II when Japan began to be occupied by the USA. Ever since the Meiji Reform the influential Japanese elite have wanted to lift Japan out of Asia to join Europe (Sun Ge 1999). Japan has to a large extent succeeded in doing that because of its economic success and its seemingly Western style of democratic political system (Gao 1992). Its success is such that even the white apartheid regime in South Africa at some point in its history considered the Japanese to be 'honorary whites' (Time 1962). With similar geographical complexity, Australia is geographically in the Asia Pacific but considers itself part of the West. And of course the US is not strictly located in the western part of the globe. So 'West' or 'Western' seems to be denoting certain kinds of values, and, to many, the colour of skin. For example, the Liberal Party of Australia holds the view that Australia does not have to choose between its geography and its history (presumably both sets of values) to engage with Asia (Abbott 2010).

By the same token, the Japanese case illustrates the problematic of what is 'Asia' or 'Asian'. The Japanese are undoubtedly Asian ethnically (if there is such a thing as ethnicity) and culturally. But by way of articulation, the Japanese think of themselves and are thought of as different from other Asians. What are these differences that people trouble to make? Is it because Japan is a democracy? Whatever one may mean by a 'Western' style of democracy, India, and even Pakistan, are democracies. But India and Pakistan, the latter having a very close but tense relationship with the US, are not considered 'Western' either by themselves or by the West. One might consider that it is the US occupation or military bases that make Japan different. But that consideration cannot be seriously sustained since the US occupies many places, and has military bases all over the world, and many of these nations or areas have not been, and are not, considered 'Western', like Saudi Arabia for instance.

The Japanese case is interesting because it really touches the nerve of all the conceptual problems discussed here. Let us propose that some countries have some similarities with Japan but also differences in such a way that it is legitimate to consider Japan part of the West. India and Japan are supposedly both democratic and in that respect they are similar. But one important difference is that modern India has not been occupied by the leader of the Western world, whereas Japan has. Saudi Arabia is occupied by the US but it is not a democracy and therefore it is different from Japan. What makes Japan stand out? Maybe it is its wealth and modernity. In what respect is it that Japan is seen to be 'modern'? Is it in industry, in manufacturing, in technology, in lifestyle? What if countries like China and India are catching up rapidly with the West's affluence and industrialisation? Furthermore, what if China not only catches up with the West in terms of wealth and modernity but also maintains its political system, which is not a Western-democracy? Here is the crux of the issue: the rise and rise of Japan does not bother us much since we consider it part of the West. However, the rise and rise of China (and India) does set alarm bells ringing because this will challenge the so-called 'Western' values and supremacy that we take for granted.

Western dominance and learning at Australian universities

Before I continue to explicate the change of global forces and its significant implication for learning at Australian universities, it is necessary to establish how learning in Australian higher education is still based on the assumption of Western dominance. It is probably not an exaggeration to say that modernization is largely Westernization. The Western way of doing things is the way to go, and the Western way of making judgement is the way of judgement. Some daily life examples that everyone takes for granted are enough as evidence to support this statement. In societies such as Singapore, Taiwan, Hong Kong, and increasingly China, a person is not considered very educated if they do not have a Western education. Huge numbers of people in China are learning English and very often when you apply for promotion in a government office, you need to pass a test in English even if your work has nothing to do with English (Zhang & Gao 2001, Zhang 2007). The Golden Arches of McDonald's have flattened the globe (Friedman 2005), so to speak, and nowadays many Chinese consider it a privilege to eat a meal in one of the thousands of these places in China. Similarly, in visual entertainment — or brainwashing, depending how you look at it — when you think of blockbusters you think of Hollywood. The Academy Awards are promoted internationally as the standard bearers in the film and entertainment industry. And Chinese film directors like Zhang Yimou have made films such as *Raise the Red Lantern* to satisfy Western audiences and to win awards and prizes.

In the all-important field of the media, Western dominance is even more persuasive. In many countries in Asia and Africa, citizens constantly hear the news about their own country through the Western media, and mostly sourced by the four dominant Western news agencies. And when it comes to international affairs, non-Western countries are even more at the mercy of the Western media, which selects what is news and what is not and sets the agenda for international consumption"

> Twenty-four hours, day and night, for 20 days one billion Chinese viewers sat glued to their television sets as soldiers fought in Iraq. They watched live coverage of government leaders' speeches one after another, government press conferences one after another, official slogans and national flags one after another. They were watching government and military-approved journalists travelling, eating, sleeping, chatting, and laughing with soldiers. These journalists were broadcasting live with 'their' troops. You might have thought it was just the classic propaganda of the communists and the communist-controlled media. In actuality, the Chinese were watching CNN and Rupert Murdoch's channels. Since the first day of the war, the Chinese government handed over the country's five most popular TV channels to CNN and Murdoch. All the images and messages the Chinese audience got from their TV sets were filtered by CNN and Murdoch's people (Li Xiguang 2005).

Last but not least, military dominance by the West goes without saying. The annual military expenditure by the US, according to one estimate, is more than all the annual military expenditures of the other top ten countries put together (SIPRI Yearbook 2011). Western countries, especially the US, have the most sophisticated military technology and weapons in space, land and sea. US spy planes continually keep surveillance missions around China and take it as their natural right to do so (Bamford date; Kan et al. date). Imagine what the Western reaction would be if Beijing sent spy planes to carry out regular surveillance flights to watch over the US.

Western dominance is not just recent, of course. It goes back to European colonialism — ever since the so-called 'discovery' of America by Columbus. Armed with a sense of either religious righteousness or racial superiority, or both, Europeans could simply sail to a place in the Americas or Africa and declare that the land belonged to them. And their sustained power was not just a result of the supremacy of technology. In fact, diseases brought over by Europeans decimated indigenous peoples in the Americas and Australia.

Western dominance has been sustained by its advancement in technology, by its monopoly of knowledge and intellectual property rights, and by a very sophisticated international structure that comprehensively exploits peripheral states for the wealth and well-being of the core Western countries (Cope 2011, p. 9; Wallerstein 1974).[1] The intellectual property rights regime, with the West's advantage of being more advanced in technology, being the centres of finance and receiving great subsidies to agriculture, have combined to condemn non-Western countries to work in impoverished conditions to earn a living while the structure itself creates a virtual 'working class aristocracy' in the West (Cope 2011).

In recent years, economic rationalist policies pursued by politicians like Margaret Thatcher and Ronald Reagan have accelerated the inequality within Western countries such as the US and UK. For example, in the US, between 1973 and the later 1990s wages have fallen since compared with inflation and as a proportionate share of GDP (Cox & Alm 1999, pp. 14–15). In spite of this increased inequality within the Western nations, the very poor actually live a better life than in the 1970s.[2]

How did this happen? In agriculture, commercial farming in peripheral countries designed and financed by the transnationals from the rich Western countries on the one hand, together with generous subsidies by the Western countries of their own farming industries on the other, means that the prices of daily necessity products have gone down. The real benefits, therefore, are for the working class in the West, with lower incomes for those on the farms in those countries that could not afford subsidization (Mehmet 1995). The same kind of beneficial effect for the poor working class in the Western countries also occurs in other industries. Poor working conditions and very low wages for the workers in non-Western countries mean cheaper imported consumer goods for consumers in the West. According to one estimate, 'between 1980 and 2003, real terms of trade adjustment wages of unskilled workers in the US increased by 14%' and 'around half of this improvement resulted from falling prices of imported consumer goods' (Smith 2008, pp. 10–11). Furthermore, 'three quarters of the total inflation-lowering effect of cheap imports is accounted for by cheap Chinese imports' and 'the rise of Chinese trade ... alone can offset around a third of the rise of official inequality we have seen over this period' (Smith 2008, pp. 10–11).

Clearly the Western hegemony of world affairs and its dominance over the arrangements of global economic structure have a huge impact on learning and teaching in Western universities. In particular, a university education tends naturally to have certain features. One of these is that courses of history, philosophy, literature, ideas, war and peace, values and ethics are Western-centred. Another feature is that from the perspective of the curriculum, everything tends to be judged by Western norms, be it religion, or political or educational systems. Other cultures and values are either exotic or deviant. Still another feature is the dominance of economic rationalism, particularly in the fields of economics, commerce and management. The fact that peripheral countries are poor is often interpreted by the mainstream discourse, which has been perpetuated by university teaching, as the result of market forces or poor management by undemocratic, 'rogue' or corrupted governments, rather than understood through an examination of the situation in the big picture of the unjust and unfair system of Western dominance as a result of colonialism and imperialism. I will present and discuss concrete examples of these features later in the chapter. There have been many attempts in Western universities to break this dominant discourse, for instance, by feminist, post-colonial, and post-modernist scholars. However, the effect of breaking the complacency of moral superiority in Western education will remain minimal unless and until there are forces emerging from outside the education sphere. There are now signs of that. And this is what I call centre-shifting.

Signs of centre-shifting

The major location of centre-shifting seems to be happening in Asia, especially in China, and this chapter's focus will be here. Since 1949, when the Chinese Communist Party (CCP) took over mainland China and set up the People's Republic of China (PRC), China has embarked on ambitious programs for modernization. However, by the Western standard of two spheres of modernity — political democracy and material affluence — China is not yet there. Even though the GDP total of China might have reached second in the world, overtaking Japan some time in 2010, China is not a wealthy society by any means. Nor is China a democratic society by the normal standard. However, this is precisely the point: China might be on the road to being a modern society but it has done so by bypassing the two defining criteria of modernity: prevailing material wealth on a per capita basis and a political system that is supposed to be democratic. China is on the edge of becoming a power to be reckoned with precisely because it is different from all the Western powers, and from those who have tried, or are trying, to copy the West. It is this difference that poses challenges and that makes the centre shift. But are there signs of this shifting?

Recently, statements like the following seem to attract intellectual attention worldwide:

> **We are entering** a new era of world history marked by two distinct features. First, after 200 years, we will see the end of Western domination of world history (but not, of course, the end of the West). Second, we will see the return of Asia. From the year 1 to 1820, China and India were consistently the two largest economies of the world. Hence, by 2050 or earlier, when they once again become the two largest economies of the world, we will return to the historic norm of the past 2000 years. And, in history, it is easier to return to historical norms than to deviate from them. (Mahbubani 2008, bold in original)

Or in the words of another thinker:

> In sum, if the early demise of Western enlightenment dominance is to be avoided, it is time for all concerned to take a proper look at the true direction of international power — towards East Asia. An examination of East Asian Confucian values must be front and centre of this analytic realignment. … there must be a determined attempt to understand the culture that underpins East Asian economies. (Little 2010)

High profile think tank personalities like Joshua Cooper Ramo would argue that the sign of centre-shifting is the gradual abandonment of what is called the Washington Consensus, which in a nutshell says that every country will and should take the market mechanism for its development, and will and should have the same political system, that is, Western-style democracy. The success of China seems to suggest that not only does a country not have to follow the Washington recipe but also, he argues, that it is the wrong one. Instead, there is now something called the Beijing Consensus (Ramo 2009) and it is the Beijing Consensus that has made China successful. The Beijing Consensus dictates that what a nation needs is hard work and innovation initiatives, based on that country's history and characteristics. Safeguarding of state sovereignty is necessary, instead of subjection to transnational companies or world organizations like the IMF and the World Bank, which were organized for the convenience of the world order dominated by the West. Other nations, like China, have to develop their society in connection with their own past and their concrete conditions. That is, in a word, the 'path dependence framework' (Mahoney 2000).

The West used to see China as a bike or even a rickshaw on a highway. To the West, then, there was no threat; China was cute and laughable. Now China is a truck on a highway. You would be worried when a bike suddenly turns into a huge truck that is trying to pass you. In 2012, Australia particularly acutely feels the rise of China because it is widely understood that Australia almost bypassed the 2008 Global Financial Crisis because of the economic factor of China. Asia is now two-thirds of Australia's total export market and provides just under half of Australia's import needs (Melbourne Institute Asialink Index 2009, p. 10); China is the largest and Japan the second largest trading partner of Australia.

As a result, the impact of these transformations in Asia has not passed without notice in Australia. Politicians, academics and public discussions in Australia have spoken of 'the Asia Century' and therefore of the need for Australians to be 'Asian literate' (Asialink and Asia Education Foundation 2010). 'Asia literacy' has become a fashionable term. And while I think it is an overstatement to say that there is going to be an Asian Century, the fact that the world will no longer be West-centred is written on the wall. This is only reasonable and just, though it is still not inevitable.

In any case, the evidence for centre-shifting is quite convincing. Consequently, partly in anticipation of the outcome of this shift and partly out of the necessities of economic well-being and national security, there has been some top-down and élite-led policy to make Australians 'Asia literate', at least since the Keating Labor government (Lo Bianco & Wickert 2001). However, despite these efforts, the success of which can be seen by the fact that Australia records the highest levels of Japanese teaching of any country in the world (Liu & Lo Bianco 2007), the bleakness of Australia's engagement with Asia is evident. As Callick (2010) summarises: by 2008 Australia's investment in Asia comprised just 18 per cent of its total investment overseas; Australia's investment in Italy was close to that in India; China's investment in Luxembourg was close to that in Australia; and Australia had less investment in all 10 ASEAN countries combined than in France. The Australian mass media employs fewer full-time journalists in Asia than they did a decade ago. Moreover, according to Asialink and the Asia Education Foundation (2010), no Australian (state-based) education system requires schools to teach about the Asian region, 50 per cent of schools teach very little about Asia, only six per cent of Year 12 students study an Asian language, and just three per cent pursue these studies at university. From the same source we also learn that only 2.5 per cent of Year 12 students study Chinese. In one state only two per cent of Year 12 Modern History students choose to study China, while 65 per cent choose Germany and 19 per cent choose the Soviet Union, and this trend applies nationally.

The need for change: From the Other to us

There are several possible reasons for this lack of interest in learning about Asia and its languages. One is that English is the lingua franca of the world and therefore native speakers of English feel that there is no need for them to learn any other language. But a more fundamental reason is that many Australians still think we, the West, we the democratic 'Us', are superior, and that China, the undemocratic and unChristian 'Other', is inferior. China is taken typically as the Other that is totally different from us, physically, politically, culturally and linguistically. Based on this mental framework, how do we deal with a China that is rising fast? At the moment there seem to be two schools of thoughts in the West. One is that we — 'we' being the West — should contain China so that it cannot rise. But that school of thought is losing ground because Western powers are recognising that they are not powerful enough to contain China any more. The other school is that we will accept China if they are like us. This school of thought is still developing, though recent events at the Copenhagen summit on climate change seem to suggest that China is not going to join the West in the way the West wants it to.

In my view, this dualism of either 'the Other' or 'us' should be abandoned. Instead, we should establish a framework to replace the confrontation or Cold War mentality of mechanical framing. The new framework should be organic, using intrinsically Confucian but very traditional Chinese philosophy: *qiu da tong cun xiao yi*, that is, seek common ground to work and live together while allowing differences to be maintained. China, or India for that matter, is not simply going to join the West. China wants and will have to participate in the shaping of the new world order. Of course, China needs to change; it has been changing all the time and very often too fast. But the West cannot just expect China to change in its own image.

What is going to happen, or rather what *needs* to happen, is a change in the attitude that the Other is inferior and insignificant, the kind of change that is not much different from what has recently happened in Australian or British politics. The traditional big and powerful parties have gradually lost much of their power base and find it necessary to work with the small parties, even the independent MPs. Take recent British politics as an example. The British Conservative leader, David Cameron, had to work together with the minority Liberal Democratic Leader, Nick Clegg, after the 2010 election. Cameron said that he had moved on from partisan rancour and was looking at 'the bigger picture'. He added, 'And if it means swallowing some humble pie, and if it means eating some of your own words, I cannot think of a more excellent diet' (Lyall 2010).

Australia, although a small country, feels superior enough to lecture countries like China because it is a nation of Western values, and because it is allied with the

Big Brother, the US. Maybe it is now time, or the time will soon come, to accept China as it is, and to acknowledge that other cultures and languages have their own intrinsic values. Reflecting the change of political landscape in the UK, immediately after the 2010 election Prime Minister Cameron said:

> We are announcing a new politics — a new politics where the national interest is more important than party interest, where cooperation wins out over confrontation, where compromise, give and take, reasonable, civilized grown-up behaviour is not a sign of weakness but of strength. (Lyal 2010)

The unthinkable in UK party politics seems to be happening in front of our eyes, though many political commentators have looked on with open-mouthed incredulity.[3] If we replace Cameron's party politics with international politics, Australians have now to think the unthinkable, as Ramo (2009) tries to tell us to do. Maybe we should think that the peace and prosperity of humankind are more important than one nation's interest, in a kind of new international politics where cooperation wins out over confrontation, and where China is one of Us instead of just one of the Other. Are Australian universities ready for that? To do that, even history has to be rewritten.

History has to be rewritten

Every government and most scholars of any given nation would assume that their writing of history is the most accurate version, and that their values and beliefs are on the right side of history. This is particularly true of the countries and peoples that are in dominant positions. For example, James Loewen, a sociologist who spent two years at the Smithsonian Institution surveying 12 leading high school textbooks of American history, finds that American history texts, weighing in at an average of 888 pages and almost five pounds, is an embarrassing blend of bland optimism, blind nationalism, and plain misinformation. As a result he has written a best-selling book, *Lies My Teacher Told Me: Everything Your American History Textbook Got Wrong*. Loewen thinks the best way to address this problem is to outsource history writing: ask the Chinese to write American history and visa versa and the outcome will probably be more balanced accounts (Loewen 1995).

If the centre of the world is shifting, away from complete Western domination to an order in which there are multiple-competing powers, such as the US, Europe, India and China for instance, then the narratives of the world need to change accordingly. History can no longer be Western-centred. Students, especially academics and teachers at Australian universities, have to realize that Australia cannot be the outpost of a superior Western civilization. As Professor Tim Lindsey, Director of the Asian Law Centre at the University of Melbourne, observes, 'Together, ASEAN,

China and Japan make our Western partners seem almost insignificant ... our future is tied to our region' (Lindsey 2009, p. 57).

History has to be re-written because history writing is not just a construction of the past but also an act of identification with a particular narrative that has specific values and beliefs. In other words, the Chinese and Indians would like to have narratives of the world that respect their own value and belief systems. The 'making of history', as Certeau (1992) terms it in the title of a chapter in *The Writing of History*, deals with the present as much as with the past. It is what is required of the present as a framework for constructing the past. If the present, or the context, changes, so does the past.

Because of its dominance of the world in every sphere of life in modern history, history writing in the West has been propagating its superiority. Precisely for the same reason, most of the 'enlightened' Chinese, whether communists or liberals, feel inferior towards the dominant West and therefore have been, for at least since the beginning of the twentieth century, critical of their own values and beliefs. This is what I call the tradition of anti-China's past, a tradition carried on so as to identify with modernity and persisting until very recently.

To the Japanese, the Chinese have been anti-Western and anti-modern because the Chinese did not change fast enough towards the end of the Qing Dynasty (Sun Ge 1999), and the 'enlightened' Chinese agree with this assessment. But that assessment was widely accepted only when China was weak and the Chinese people felt that they were inferior. That was how the Chinese felt even as recently as immediately after the end of the Mao era and throughout the 1980s, a sentiment comprehensively and vividly portrayed in the documentary film *He shang (River elegy)*. *River elegy* attacks China's Yellow River as a symbol of ancient Chinese culture. It uses the river's silt and sediment as a metaphor for Confucian beliefs and the significance of the traditions that the creators believe caused China to stagnate. The filmmakers hoped that the Chinese traditional culture of the 'yellow' river would be replaced by the Western culture of the 'blue' ocean. The film also takes the Great Wall as representing an isolationist, conservative and incompetent defence (Su & Wang 1991).[4]

However, since the late 1990s the narrative in China has started to change. This is partly because of the intellectual efforts made by what is called the New Left in China, which keeps reminding the Chinese of the pitfalls of cold-blooded capitalism on the one hand, while, on the other hand, it tries to rescue modern values from China's remote tradition (Wang Hui 2003, 2004, 2009) as well as from their recent past (Cui 1996; Gao 2008; Wang Chaohua 2005). In addition, the narrative about China and its relation to the West has started to change because of China's leap forward in economic and material development. The Chinese do not feel inferior anymore, and can face their past.

Implications for Asian cultural studies

If Australia is to keep pace with these accelerating developments, its own self-narratives will have to change accordingly. In Australian universities, the mainstream curriculum and ideologies of the past will have to give way to some alternative perspectives. University academics have to educate the public that not everything technologically and scientifically wonderful was or is Western. This point can be illustrated by two anecdotal examples from my own experience. Some years back when I was in the UK, I once showed some Chinese money to some curious guests. One school teacher, upon seeing the Chinese notes for the first time in her life, commented, 'So you use Western numbers as well'. I said quietly, 'Actually these are Arabic numbers'. The teacher blushed and was very apologetic. Another example is very recent. One of my colleagues teaches an Asian Studies subject that includes an introduction to Ancient Chinese civilization, and the technological and scientific inventions that benefitted humankind. My wife, who is of Anglo-Saxon heritage, was tutoring the students who took this course. One day my wife told me that one student in the class was very angry, and I asked why. It turned out that the student could not believe this so-called 'bullshit' about Chinese inventions so long ago. Any suggestion contrary to her belief actually made her angry. What is interesting is that this student probably would not have shown her anger to me if I had been the tutor, because I obviously look Chinese.

These two isolated examples are only anecdotal but they nevertheless provide some insight into the comfortable assumption that we in the West are superior, modern and possess the best of everything. The shifting of centre away from the West means that this comfortable assumption will be challenged. The public will have to know, for instance, that China was not always the backward, barbarian and inhumane country that they assume. They will have to know that not everything that is supposed to be good and advanced or progressive originated from the West; that Egyptian civilization, which is African, played a central role in the formation of Ancient Greece (Bernal 1987, 1991; 2006); and that the Aryan Model of the West and its connection with Ancient Greece were results of European racism.[5]

The implications are, therefore, not only that the contents of history writing, for instance what to include and what not to exclude, have to be changed, but also the perspectives and interpretations have be different. History should be historical but not historicist. It should be historical in the sense that technological advance at certain times in certain places is not only not racially-intrinsic but also not value-intrinsic, and it should avoid historicism in the sense that political values and cultural features are not history-specific but transcend time and space.

Asia literacy or cultural change?

In other words, coping with centre-shifting in international politics requires paradigm shifting in narratives of the world that requires change of culture that in turn requires what has been called a change of mentalité (Clark 1993; Godelier 1991). In Australian universities, the idea of Asian literacy is currently being entertained. But this idea is already out of date. The curriculum should reflect and go along with the changes of the times; it is not enough today to just advocate Asian literacy. There is now a need to go beyond just knowing something about Asia, the Other. We need to be wired with the mentality that there is no divide between 'us' and 'them', that no one is superior to the other and that we are all of us together on this planet.

Unless there is a cultural change, Australians will continue to find life too comfortable to do anything different or to think anything differently. In my perception, there is a lack of divergent thinking among the Australian public, which can be viewed in two ways. One is an indifference to the outside world. Australian apathy towards the world outside can be illustrated by Australians' lack of interest in taking up scholarships to study overseas. Recently, there have been various kinds of scholarships to study in Asia. China, for example, has made many scholarships available in recent years through the China Scholarship Council and the headquarters of the Confucius Institute. However, it is very difficult to get Australians to take up these generous scholarships. One student in the Centre for Asian Studies at my fairly typical Australian university even declined a scholarship because he would lose his part-time job at McDonald's if he went to China.

The other way to view Australian lack of divergent interest is that there is little challenge to established truths. One can think of many examples of the comfortable truths that we cherish but which are actually not the whole truth. A good example relates to World War Two. The Australian curriculum of history on this topic focuses on the Pacific War starting from the Japanese bombing of Pearl Harbour. However, it tells us very little about Chinese resistance against the Japanese invasion of China. There is also a lot of scholarship and documentation of the Holocaust, and tracking down of its perpetrators, but very little about the Japanese atrocities in China and about how the US protected Japanese war criminals because of the Cold War. There are also many uncomfortable facts about Australia's support of the Suharto regime in Indonesia that are not uncovered. Another example concerns early Chinese migrants to Australia and the White Australia policy (Price 1974). Again, the accepted wisdom and mainstream narrative is that the Chinese were sojourners who came to Australia to make quick money to send back to China, and those Chinese did not intend to become Australian settlers (Siu 1952; Williams 1998). In fact, the Chinese wanted to settle down as much as any other migrants (Skeldon 2004). The construction of the sojourner Chinese was a convenient discourse for European colonialism and for racial exclusion against the Chinese (Chan 1981; Petty 2009; Hsu 2000). These are just a few examples, which are nonetheless sufficient to show that there is a real need for an Australian cultural change of mentality. If this change does not occur, history writing in Australia will continue to ignore such facts as these, and will continue to interpret history purely from its own Western perspective.

It is not easy to make this kind of culture change happen, though. First, there is a need for policymakers to be aware of the necessity of change, and that takes a long time. Secondly, even if the élite were to see the need to change, it would take a long time to persuade the vast majority of the people to see that necessity. Logically one would think that Australia needs visionary leaders who care about more than their political careers. However, the system of democracy practised here is such that, in order to implement their beliefs and values, a politician has to be in office. But in order to win and maintain office, a politician very often has to hide or even change his or her priorities in relation to values and beliefs, because the public is not on side. Historically, renowned leaders are the ones who could lead the public even when it was against their own political survival. But it is rare to find politicians who have vision and care for the future rather than for immediate political power, especially today when political parties are managed by faceless power manipulators. Therefore, the process of transformation has to take us back to basics: the public has to be inspired to consider key issues for the future differently and to change their way of thinking, not by politicians, nor the commercial media, but by educators.

It is in this respect that learning at Australian universities can play an important role: to get students to question the comfortable assumptions that we all take for granted, and challenge the existing 'truths' that we all cherish. In other words, universities in Australia have to do the very opposite of what the former Prime Minister John Howard wanted, for us to be relaxed and comfortable. Textbooks and course materials have to include contents that problematise our history and critique our assumptions rather than being designed to make us feel so great and superior. Furthermore, our understanding of the history of Asian centres such as China should not only include but also be more reliant on the perspectives of that country. With regard to China, for instance, Chinese academics should be invited to give lectures on China, not just for occasional seminars but integrated into the normal course lectures. Students should be directed to be global citizens, and part of being a global citizen is to know that Australian history is only a small percentage of human history, and to know that there is no such thing as an intrinsic, Australian way of life, because every way of life is a result of changing dynamics, at all times and in all places.

Conclusion

Let us start this conclusion with one basic assumption. The assumption is that as a group, all human beings, whether their sub-groups are called Chinese, Japanese, Indian, German, African or British, are equally intelligent and equally human. If we do not accept this assumption then there is no basis on which to talk about intercultural or international issues rationally. Based on this assumption, then, we need to explain why what is called the West has been so dominant in the last few hundred years. We have to remember that in the history of humankind on this globe, other peoples, for instance, the Chinese, the Egyptians and the Persians, had previously been dominant in military power, material wealth and human values. So the fact that Western nations have more recently been dominant cannot be explained on the basis of their ethnic superiority, nor that they are more human, a kind of implicit assumption taken by some when the issue of human rights is debated. Once we accept this basic assumption, the rise of Asia in general and China in particular should not be surprising. Once we accept this as fact, then the loss of centre position by the West should not be unthinkable. And once the centre-shifting is thinkable, then we can think of changing our thinking so as to be tuned to the idea that human values and beliefs (of what is right, what is wrong, what is good and what is bad) are historical in time and place. There is always a sense of what is right and what is wrong at any given time in any community, but none of these ethical values is universal in the sense that they can be applied at all times and to all places. Once we accept this, we should be able to understand that there cannot be any sense of transcendental superiority by any community.

Learning at Australian universities should inspire this kind of cultural change. To do that, the curriculum in many fields has to change dramatically. For instance, in the fields of history, philosophy, politics, literature, arts, anthropology, sociology, economics, law, commerce and music, content other than just European and Western should be included in textbooks, teaching materials, and required readings and assessments. Furthermore, assessment criteria should require perspectives other than Australian or Western. Students should be directed to know how the Vietnamese, Chinese or Russians analyse the Vietnam War or the Korean War. How do the Chinese, or indeed the Japanese, view World War Two?[6] How do we settle issues of dispute together peacefully? How do we interpret and understand our different values and cultural experience? How might we resolve differences without wars? How might we live together as global citizens, not as political, cultural or economic enemies? University learning should prepare Australians for the change we are all part of, instead of transmitting historically established truths and knowledge. This is the fundamental implication of the shift of the centre of the world towards Asia.

Notes

1. Currently most of the 31 members of the OECD are European countries except Turkey, Mexico, Japan and Korea. Chile joined the OECD in 2010.
2. According to Cox and Alm (1999, pp. 40–41), between 1970 and 1997 the real price of a food basket containing one pound of ground beef, one dozen eggs, three pounds of tomatoes, one dozen oranges, one pound of coffee, one pound of beans, half a gallon of milk, five pounds of sugar, one pound of bacon, one pound of lettuce, one pound of onions and one pound of bread actually fell and by 1999 it took 26 per cent less of the worker's time to buy it.
3. Martin Farr, a senior lecturer in contemporary British history at Newcastle University, said: 'Today, everything is sunny and rosy. But there are so many divisions between the parties on so many issues that I can't see how it can be anything like as polished and harmonious as they project. It has the recipe for being a complete mess' (Lyall 2010).
4. The Japanese, who wanted to identify with the West (out of Asia and into Europe), took their departure from the ugly Asia, exemplifying Michel de Certeau's conceptualisation of 'place'; the Chinese, who now want to identify with liberal democracy and market capitalism values, take their departure from 'time', especially their very recent ugly past. To the Japanese then, 'to kill the Chinese is throwing off Asia in every conceivable way' because China was anti-West and anti-Modern (Dower 2006). To the Chinese now, to condemn the Cultural Revolution is throwing off the ugly past in every conceivable way (Gao 2008, p. 32).
5. For a debate on this issue, and a critique of Bernal and Bernal's response, see Mary Lefkowitz ed., *Not out of Africa* (1996, Harper Collins, New York), and *Martin Bernal's Post to the Athena Debate* (viewed 10 June 2010 at http://asiapacificuniverse.com/pkm/bern.htm).
6. This approach is explored in detail in relation to the teaching of Asian Studies in Pak (Chapter 9, this volume).

References

Abbot, T 2010, May 25, 'Mapping our future in the Asian century, speech delivered at the Aisalink and Asia Society National Forum, Parliament House, Canberra.

Asialink and Asia Education Foundation 2010, *Statement of the business alliance for Asia literacy*, viewed 10 August 2010, <www.asialink.unimelb.edu.au> and <www.asiaeducation.edu.au>.

Bamford, James 2002, 'Clandestine air war: the truth behind Cold War US Surveillance Flights', *Harvard International Review*, Winter, pp. 86–88.

Bernal, M 1987, *Black Athena: the Afroasiatic roots of classical civilization*, Rutgers University Press, New Jersey.

Bernal, M 1991, *Black Athena: the Afroasiatic roots of classical civilization: the archaeological and documentary evidence*, vol. 2 (paperback), Free Association Books, London.

Bernal, M 2006, *Black Athena: The Afroasiatic roots of classical civilization: the linguistic evidence,* vol. 3 (hardcover), Rutgers University Press, New Jersey.

Callick, R 2010, May 24, 'Growing need to sharpen focus on Asia', *The Australian,* Sydney.

Chan, A B 1981, '"Orientalism" and image making: the sojourner in Canadian history', *The Journal of Ethnic Studies,* vol. 9 no. 3, pp. 37–46.

Chang, G 2001, *The coming collapse of China,* Random House, New York.

Clark, C 1993, 'Mentalité and the nature of consciousness', in MK Cayton, EJ Gorn & PW Williams (eds), *Encyclopaedia of American social history,* Scribner, New York, pp. 387–95.

Cui, Z 1996, 'Particular, universal, and infinite: transcending Western centrism and cultural relativism in the third world', in Marx and B Mazlish (eds), *Progress: fact or illusion?,* University of Michigan Press, Ann Arbor, MI, pp. 141–152.

De Certeau, M 1992, *The writing of history,* Columbia University Press, New York.

Dower, JW 1994, 'Throwing off Asia: Woodblock prints of the Sino-Japanese War (1994–95) & Russo-Japanese War (1904–5)', MIT visualizing cultures website, viewed 15 May 2006, <http://www.encyclopedia.com/topic/Japan.aspx>.

Friedman, T 2005, *The world is flat: a brief history of the twenty-first century,* Farar, Straus & Giroux, New York.

Gao, M 1992, 'Democracy, what democracy? China's road to modernization', *China Report,* vol. 28 no. 1, pp. 13–25.

Gao, M 2007, *Gao village: rural life in modern china,* Hawai'i University Press, Manoa, HI.

Gao, M 2008, *The battle for China's past: Mao and the cultural revolution,* Pluto, London.

Godelier, M 1991, 'Is the West the model for humankind? The Baruya of New Guinea between change and decay', *International Social Science Journal,* vol. 43 no. 2, pp. 387–399.

Hsu, M 2000, *Dreaming of gold, dreaming of home: transnationalism and migration between the United States and South China, 1882–1943,* Stanford University Press, Stanford, CA.

Hutton, W 2008, *The writing on the wall: China and the West in the 21st Century,* Little Brown, New York.

Kan, Shirley A. (Coordinator) et al., *China-U.S. Aircraft Collision Incident of April 2001: Assessments and Policy Implications,* CRS Report for Congress Received through the CRS Web, Updated October 10, 2001.

Lefkowitz, M 1996 (ed.), *Not out of Africa,* Harper Collins, New York.

Levathes, L 1997, *When China ruled the seas: the treasure fleet of the Dragon Throne, 1405–1433,* Oxford University Press, Oxford.

Lindsey, T 2009, *Melbourne Institute Asialink Index 2009 Report*, Pricewaterhouse Coopers, Melbourne, viewed 11 August 2010, <pwc-mi-asialink_index2009[1].pdf>, p. 10.

Little, R 2010, 'The 21st century global order — time for enlightenment countries to take proper look at Confucian values', East Asia Forum, viewed 12 May 2010, <http://www.eastasiaforum.org/2010/05/01/the-21st-century-global-order-%E2%80%93-time-for-enlightenment-countries-to-take-proper-look-at-confucian-values>.

Li, X 2005, 'Live coverage of lies or truth?', viewed 24 May 2005, <http://www.tbsjournal.com/Archives/Spring04/paper.htm>.

Liu, G & Lo Bianco, J 2007, 'Teaching Chinese, Teaching in Chinese, and Teaching the Chinese', *Language Policy*, vol. 6 no. 1, pp. 95–117.

Lo Bianco, J & Wickert, R 2001, *Australian policy activism in language and literacy*, Language Australia Publications, Melbourne, Vic.

Loewen, J 1995, *Lies my teacher told me: everything your American history textbook got wrong*, Touchstone, New York.

Loewen, J 2010, 'Not Aesopian enough: a Chinese publishing fable', *Japan Focus*, viewed 05 July 2010, <http://japanfocus.org/-JamesW-Loewen/3371>.

Lyall, S 2010, May 13, 'New hybrid British Cabinet holds first meeting', *New York Times*.

Mahbubani, K 2008, The New Asian Hemisphere: *the irresistible shift of global power to the East, Public affairs*, viewed 14 August 2010, <http://americanreviewmag.com/articles/The-Chinese-century>.

Mahoney, J 2000, 'Path dependence in historical sociology', *Theory and Society*, vol 29 no. 4, 507–548.

Mehmet, O 1995, *Westernizing the third world: the Eurocentricity of economic development Theories*, Routledge, New York.

Melbourne Institute Asialink Index 2009 Report. Pricewaterhouse Coopers, Melbourne, viewed 11 August 2010, <pwc-mi-asialink_index2009[1].pdf>.

Petty, AA 2009, *Deconstructing the Chinese sojourner: case studies of early Chinese migrants*, Unpublished PhD thesis, University of Tasmania, Hobart.

Price, C 1974, *The great white walls are built: restrictive immigration to North America and Australasia 1836–1888*, Australian National University Press, Canberra, ACT.

Ramo, JC 2009, *The age of the unthinkable: why the new world disorder constantly surprises us and what we can do about it*, Little Brown, London.

SIPRI Yearbook 2011: Armaments, Disarmament and International Security. Stockholm International Peace Research Institute, Stockholm.

Siu, PCP 1952, 'The sojourner', *American Journal of Sociology*, vol. 58 no. 1, pp.

34–44.

Skeldon, R 2004, 'China: from exceptional case to global participant,' *Migration Information Source: Country Profiles*, Migration Policy Institute, K. Kalia, Washington, DC.

Su, X and Wang, L 1991, *Death song of the river: a reader's guide to the Chinese TV series*, Heshang, East Asia Program, Cornell University, Ithaca, New York.

Sun, Ge 2001, 亚洲意味着什么：文化间的日本 (what does Asia mean: Japan among cultures), 巨流图书公司 (Juliu Books) 北京 (Beijing).

Time, 1962, January 19, 'South Africa: honorary whites', viewed 15 June 2010, <http://www.time.com/time/magazine/article/0,9171,895835,00.html>.

Wallerstein, I 1974, *The modern world system: capitalist agriculture and the origins of the European world economy in the sixteenth century*, Academic Press, New York.

Wang, C (ed.) 2005, *One China, many paths*, trans. C Wang, Verso, London.

Wang, H 2004, *Xiandai zhongguo sixiang de xingqi* 現代中國思想的興起 (*The rise of modern Chinese thought* [4 vols]), SDX Joint Publishing, Beijing.

Wang, H 2003, *China's new order: society, politics, and economy in transition* (trans. Ted Huters), Harvard University Press, Cambridge, MA.

Wang, H 2009, The end of the revolution: China and the limits of modernity, Verso, London.

Williams, M 1998, *Brief sojourn in your native land: Sydney's Huaqiao and their links with South China during the first half of the twentieth century*, University of New England Press, Armidale, NSW.

Zhang, S(E) 2007, *The impact of ELT on ideology in China (1980–2000)*, Central China Normal University Press, Wuhan.

Zhang, S(E), & Gao, M 2001, 'The Trojan horse of English language teaching: contribution of ELT to the de-radicalization of political discourse in China', *China Information*, vol. xv no. 2, pp. 114–130.

3

(Post) Modern times: Transcultural exchange and the circumstances of postgraduate social science research

Greg McCarthy

> Men make their own history, but they do not make it as they please; they do not make it under self-selected circumstances, but under circumstances existing already, given and transmitted from the past. The tradition of all dead generations weighs like a nightmare on the brains of the living. (Karl Marx, *The Eighteenth Brumaire of Louis Bonaparte*, 1852).

This chapter is a reflection on the pedagogic circumstances in which postgraduate research students, especially from China, find themselves when studying in Australia. These students coming from China to Australia are, in a manner of speaking, living through a maelstrom of change, where the dead weight of the past weighs heavily on the present. These students have almost certainly experienced an education system where the Marxism-Leninism educational tradition sits uneasily with the market modernization model of China, where continual change dominates Chinese students' lives and shapes their identities. On arrival in Australia, these students enter into an Australian academic milieu where poststructuralist and postmodernist thinking has challenged the master-narrative of Marxism, resulting in a series of competing mini-narratives. Moreover, in the Chinese social sciences a somewhat positivist model predominates, which has great strength in empirical research but is largely unchallenged by reflective thinking on the methodology underpinning this research approach. In contrast, in the Anglo-Celtic world, the after-effects of the postmodern and post-structural debates have made 'scientific' inquiry open to constant challenge and methodological multiplicity. As such, Chinese students studying in the Australian academy have to confront a quite distinct pedagogical world from the one they have experienced in China. Likewise, the pedagogic challenge for any Australian supervisor is not to denigrate Chinese models of scientific learning. In contrast, the soundest pedagogic mode is to respect Chinese methodologies whilst showing these students that Western social science models also offer unique opportunities for them to analyze their own society through a different investigative lens.

In this chapter I will outline elements of this supervisory challenge by tracing out how an awareness of the poststructuralist tradition, especially as it applies to Marxism, can be of great benefit to Chinese students in the formulation of their research projects. However, I also show that this awareness cannot be based on the supervisor's assumption that this is superior to other forms of learning. For the benefit of both the postgraduate student and the supervisor, there must be reciprocity in the exchange of knowledge from the Western to the Eastern traditions of learning, including that of Marxism. I will argue that this reciprocal exchange of knowledge is best achieved when there is mutual respect for the learning circumstances under which the knowledge has been produced in the East and the West. To this effect, I will outline the specific circumstances of the Western Marxist debate on modernisation before turning to the current circumstances of the Chinese debates on modernisation. The aim will be to reveal how this understanding can contribute to the exchange of ideas between supervisor and social science postgraduate from China on a mutually considered basis. This will not only help Chinese postgraduate students developing their arguments but also enrich the awareness and thereby the effectiveness of the supervisor in the process.

Western Marxism and industrial change

When Marx analyzed the industrial revolution in nineteenth century Europe, he was seeking to find an overarching theory to explain the whole process, including socialisation. There is a parallel occurring today in China where the extent of its rapid industrialisation is equivalent to that of Marx's day but even more concentrated and rapid in its transformation of an economy and of subjectivity. As such, students coming from China have to deal with this maelstrom and discover means by which their educational training equips them to understand the momentous change in China. In this regard, it is useful to consider how the debates on Marx's theory open up different pedagogic approaches, which can be of benefit to an understanding of China from these different paradigms.

In reflecting on the current social science research environment in the West, contemporary postgraduate students have to come to terms with what Marshall Berman terms the 'maelstrom of modernization' (1983,159), where the certainties of the past, notably Western supremacy, are now under challenge from China's economic rise, and this presents unique and exciting pedagogic challenges. In today's

China, one finds one's worlds in continuous change, regeneration, uncertainty and contradiction between capitalism and state-socialist modernisation. In Australia, moderniation produces subtle changes, where its settler-colonial-democratic history is now at a moment of unease with its integration into a neo-liberal global market of trade, commerce and the movement of people, including refugees. These conditions place pressure on social science theory to find a coherent way to explain the ever-changing world and yet understand the local specificities (Hardt & Negri 2000).

In explicating the clash of pedagogic and lived worlds that confronts these postgraduate students, I will compare and contrast debates over modernization, modernism and postmodernism in the West and the East. I will show how the debate on these three seminal but perplexing concepts is built on a sense of cultural superiority that has its origins in the European Enlightenment and its 'Orientalist' vision of the East, which is now under serious challenge from the economic rise of China and India (see Gao, Chapter 2, this volume). The argument will then relate this superiority-inferiority binary to the intellectual discourse and political passion in contemporary China, symbolised by the 'man versus the tank' syndrome (Dutton 1998, p. 17), the symbolic picture of the massacre in Tiananmen Square in May 1989. I will then bring the debates on modernisation in Europe and China to the issue of how to translate this experience for Chinese postgraduate students, who are likely to be living in their current circumstances dislocated from the past in theory and practice, and from the political passion of the Cultural Revolution, in a society of governmental control and marketisation.

The demise of the Marxist and its affects on research

To explore the relationship between different cultures and educational understandings between the Australian research environment and that in China, the discussion will take the reader back to 1983 to a debate between two Marxists, the American Marshal Berman and the Englishman Perry Anderson. This debate, on modernity and modernism, was occurring at the very moment when the Marxist paradigm was dissolving into mini-narratives. The exchange is remarkable as this was a debate about modernity and revolution but it occurred on the cusp of momentous changes in China as the country broke from its Maoist past to create a socialist-market economy (Jameson 1991). In 1983, Marshall Berman's book, *All that is solid melts into air: the experience of modernity*, was published globally to international acclaim. Berman took the title from Karl Marx's *Manifesto* to depict, as Berman expresses it, the dialectic between modernisation and modernism. According to him, being modern was to experience personal and social life as a maelstrom, to find one's world in perpetual disintegration and renewal, trouble and anguish, ambiguity and contradiction, to be part of a universe in which all that is solid melts into air. To be modernist is to make oneself somehow at home in this maelstrom. (Berman 1983, p. 15)

For Berman, to be modernist was to capture the spirit of modernity, to be aware of life's opportunities and its perils, an experience he associates as worldly but is more specifically Western. Men and women change the world (have agency) but are changed by the world. As such, they are both subjects and objects of modernisation.

Perry Anderson assails Berman's notion of an eternal modernist spirit, arguing that it is far more conjunctural, and that it is tied to the nineteenth and not the twentieth century. But here Anderson is more culturally rooted in Eurocentric ideas of modernisation than Berman, whose sensibilities are a mixture of the cultural superiority of the American century and positive adaptation of European culture. Anderson argues there was limited modernist literature emanating from the UK in the early decades of the twentieth century. He notes that Berman's maelstrom is comprised of 'scientific discoveries, industrial upheavals, demographic transformations, urban expansions, nation states, mass movements — all propelled, in the last instance, by the ever-expanding, drastically fluctuating capitalist world market' (Anderson 1984, p. 1). For Anderson, what Berman depicts is the destruction of feudalism and a fundamental transformation of Europe from around 1790 to the nineteenth century. It would seem to me that Anderson's claims for Europe are too sweeping and miss the shift in modernist spirit from Europe to Japan and then China. He argues that World War Two destroyed the modernist spirit, replacing it with a certain anomie and nihilism. He writes that:

> After 1945, the old semi-aristocratic or agrarian order and its appurtenances was finished, in every country. Bourgeois democracy was finally universalized. With that certain links with pre-capitalist past were snapped. At the same time Fordism arrived in force. Mass production and consumption transformed the Western economies along North American lines. There could be no longer be the smallest doubt as to what kind of society this technology would consolidate, an oppressive stable, monolithic industrial capitalist civilization as now in place. (Anderson 1984, p. 7)

Anderson rejects Berman's notion of a 'permanent revolution', arguing that a revolution is the overthrow of a State from below. As such, it is conjunctural and specific not everlasting and spectral. For this reason he dismisses the 'ideology of Maoism, with its proclamation of a Cultural Revolution' as but a 'moral conversion' that has no potential to be a revolutionary force to overthrow any State within the European context (Anderson 1984, p. 10).

What underlies this Marxist debate is its Western-centricity, occurring paradoxically at the very moment when China was creating its own form of modernisation that has come to be conjuncturally significant. In the exchange between these two eminent Marxists, Europe and then America become the end points of modernity and modernisation. For them, Asia may have been the starting point of modernity but 'oriental despotism' prevented it from becoming modern (Anderson 1979, p. 7). Here both Berman and Anderson echo Marx and his notion of an Asia being outside of the European modernist teleology (Hindess & Hirst 1975, p. 207). Marx's theory of Asian society (the Asian mode of production) was in effect a product of European intellectual thought of his day. It was, in short, a synthesis of both Hegel's belief that Asia was barbarous and Adam Smith's notion of a hierarchy of productive patterns with Europe at the apex.

Berman and Anderson both regarded Asia as the opposite to European modernisation and believed it could only become modern by following the teleology of the capitalist West, principally through political and economic integration. Yet this debate is of significance for China and for students' understanding of China, as it brings together the ideas of capital accumulation and industrialisation with subjectivity and epoch change. To all of these aspects, which Chinese students routinely face in their lives and now in their research, these students are striving to bring knowledge in their postgraduate studies in the Social Sciences.

The Berman and Anderson debate on modernisation was in its own way seeking to revive Western Marxism in an epoch where in the Anglo-Celtic academy, Marxism was being challenged by poststructuralist claims that it could not explain other forms of oppression that went beyond the economic to include gender, race and sexuality. Expressed more broadly, in response to the challenge of the social movements, the social sciences and humanities in the West opened their doors to radical debates and the challenges emanating from the re-thinking on the history of knowledge. In this move during the 1970s and 1980s, poststructuralist and postmodernist thought influenced the social science research agenda and in turn the postgraduate research environment. In the process, the methodologies of these new forms of inquiry significantly affected the traditional empirical modes of investigation associated with both Marxist class analysis and market models in the 1980s.

Post-structuralism and the research environment

The early 1980s was notable for the emergence of poststructuralist and postmodernist debates in the Western academy. In particular, Foucault's work filled the void created by the demise of Marxist research. Foucault was not only prolific but also highly provocative. Many of his writings have been published since his death and edited by others so it is not always clear that they actually constitute Foucault's thoughts. Moreover, there is a degree of inconsistency in his thinking with regards to power, the nation and sovereignty. What is clear, however, is his widespread influence in Western thought and how this has spawned many insightful postgraduate dissertations in the fields of political science, anthropology, sociology, legal studies, criminology, geography and cultural studies.

By breaking with the metanarratives of Marxism and Liberalism, Foucault freed up theoretical inquiry, and by doing so provided new insights into the multiple natures of power, knowledge and discourse across cultural and national divides. Academics and postgraduate students in the Western academy freely dipped into Foucault's 'toolbox' to explore power in its multifarious settings. The most cited example is Edward Said's *Orientalism*, which shows how the discourse of the 'orient' was set on the epistemological and ontological binaries of West/East, Superior/Inferior, Master/Slave, the Civilized/Other (Said 1978).

However, 25 years after Foucault's death, there has been a substantial re-evaluation of his body of work. Scholars have noted the inconsistency between his earlier and later writings on power and his one-sided notion to sovereignty (governmentality), which was made apparent after 9/11 when State power emerged into the open to override governmental power against the designated 'enemies' of the State (Hindess 2010; Dutton 2010). Moreover, there has been a reassessment of Foucault's depictions of colonialism.

This later point is made by Ian Goodwin-Smith, who notes that in one of Foucault's critical books, *The Order of Things*, his anti-foundationalism was inspired by a reading of a Chinese encyclopedia, where he recognized a completely different but subordinated taxonomical discourse (Goodwin-Smith 2010, p. xv; see also Yoneyama, Chapter 10, this volume). Foucault's unreflective borrowing is apparent in the following passage, where he depicts Chinese taxonomy as 'exotic' from that of the dominant European discourse: 'The wonderment of this taxonomy, the thing we apprehend in one great leap, the thing that, by means of fable, is demonstrated as the exotic charm of another system of thought, is the limitation of our own, the stark impossibility of thinking that' (Foucault 1970, p. xv).

Barry Hindess (2010, p. 670) takes this argument further by noting that in *The Order of Things* Foucault seems to accept Western culture in teleological terms as 'pure theory' (Foucault 1970, p. 36). The issue for Hindess is whether Foucault was merely reporting the seventeenth century liberal views that Europe was superior to all other cultures or unconsciously reproducing this position of superiority. For Hindess, Foucault, like Friedrich Hegel, Karl Marx and John Stuart Mill, fails to challenge the dividing of societies and cultures into higher and lower orders, with the West being at the pinnacle (Hindess 2010, p. 699). A tradition of 'othering', he argues, continues to this very day with the division of cultures along a Western divide with the US and Western Europe at the top and the East, especially Islam, at the bottom (p. 674).

The second argument that Hindess advances is that Foucault's account of the liberal art of governance is one based not on the principle of freedom, as claimed by its supporters, but on pragmatic grounds, where anti-liberal violence and suppression of freedom could be endorsed in the colonies, against 'inferior beings'. Foucault failed to address the historic record that liberalism had a different form of governing in the colonies from that in the metropoles of Europe. As such, his theory of biopolitical government (governing the population via 'make-life' rather than 'take life') is mainly applicable to the countries of the colonisers not the colonised. According to Hindess, in the colonies the techniques of governing were repression rather than the supposed promotion of freedom central to Foucault's paradigm (2010, p. 674).

For social science research, this questioning of Foucault's foundational principle has importance for those seeking to apply his research toolbox to non-Western countries, including those in Asia. In particular, the assumption underlying the Foucault project was that it was applicable to all societies and could replace traditional forms of research. There is in Foucault, as Goodwin-Smith and Hindess note, a form of research that, when applied to countries such as China, contains a tendency for a sense of superiority to unconsciously enter into its methodological approach, which can denigrate the research methods in those Non-Western countries. However, Foucault's research methodology, when combined with other methodologies, can add to rather than supplant the research approaches in non-Western countries such as China. In this regard, Michael Dutton's work is significant as it seeks to adapt Foucault's theory to governance in China but he also opens up the research agenda to include both anti-Marxist theories such as that of Carl Schmidt, together with Marxists such as Raymond Williams, combined with Chinese scholars investigating their own society using their own learnt research methodologies (Dutton 1992, p. 4).

In the first instance, Dutton sees Foucault's disciplinary power as a useful set of ideas that can explain how the Chinese State systematically disciplines citizens. Nevertheless, Dutton sees this notion of a disciplinary society as only a partial explanation for governance in China, as its research methodology fails to take account of the persistent 'friend-enemy' distinction in Chinese politics and the resort to 'states of exception' when the CCP-Government feels threatened (Dutton 1998, 48, re: Schmitt 1996). This he argues was the case on 4 May 1989 in Tiananmen Square when the State repressed the population in the name of defending the population (Dutton 2010, p. 636). He writes that:

despite the claims that liberal governmentality relies upon the deployment of disciplinary power and focuses this collectively upon data collection and deployment techniques of the bio-political that ascertains the 'correct disposition of people and things', it is the contention of this paper that it is still, inevitably, haunted by the ever-present spectre of Sovereign power exercised through political 'decisionism'. In the language of Michel de Certeau, one might say that the Sovereign exception reveals the way in which disciplinary power never 'flies solo'. (Dutton 1988, p. 48)

The critical note that Dutton makes about poststructuralist thought as characterized by Michel Foucault is that it had a series of modernist assumptions on (State) power hidden beneath its stress on layers of governance, and that it fails to see how elements of colonial rule can apply to countries such as China. In this condition, the disciplinary power is always open to a reversion to 'states of exception', which is the underlying power of Chinese governance. Dutton brings a transcultural analysis to his use of Foucault's biopolitics and biopower, where Chinese culture is read through critical theory lenses that give due respect to both Western and Chinese cultures. This combination is important as Dutton shows how by adopting pedagogy that combines insights from across cultures, it is possible to have an enriched research environment, whilst respecting and engaging the learning practices of both cultures.

Transcultural theory: Bringing poststructuralist and Chinese thought together

In his deconstruction of power relations, Michael Dutton brings to the research agenda insights from British New Left tradition, notably Raymond Williams, with continental theory from authors such as Michel Foucault, Michael de Certeau, Carl Schmitt, Theodor Adorno and Max Hokheimer with a wide range of Chinese collaborators. His books are notable for their transcultural dialogue with his colleagues in China between Chinese political thought and contemporary radical Western thought. For example, Dutton's first book, *Policing and Punishment in China* (1992), whilst known as a Foucauldian analysis of Chinese politics, is as much a conversation between Carl Schmitt and the Chinese interpretations of Mao Zedong in terms of the friend-enemy distinction (p. viii). Moreover, Dutton uses Hannah Arendt's (1958) modernist concept of moral action to explain the debates with the CCP, known as the two-line struggle, and by doing so he escapes the Cold War paradigm of totalitarian power from above, whilst noting how Chinese scholars responded to the isolation caused by the Cold War.

In his second book, *Streetlife in China* (1998), Dutton collaborates with a wide range of China scholars to account for how the spirit of communist modernisation was quashed by the 'man versus the tank' in Tiananmen Square. The loss of revolutionary spirit (a la Berman) was replaced from above via the CCP leaders' promotion of the market, and by below by the commodification of everyday life. In presenting this momentous historical change, where everything that is solid is melting into air, Dutton (in the manner of De Certeau) tells tales of people 'making do' in the maelstrom of rapid industrialization. In developing his own pedagogy, Dutton takes on the persona of Walter Benjamin's *flaneur*, touring the Chinese city streets capturing the flavour and the plight of the people caught in forces that they cannot control. He seeks to be both Western and yet tell the story from a Chinese point of view.

For him, the contemporary Chinese 'make-do society' is the result of the dismantling of the pillars of the communist system, which had all-round protection of workers and peasants at the point of production, sometimes known as the 'iron rice bowl'. As well, the work unit was a political agency for articulating the mass-line politics of the day. Dutton sees the depoliticisation of the Communist Party units in the workplaces as akin to the subaltinisation (Spivak 1998) of the population under colonialism. By this he means that under the old-system the workers and peasants had a voice from the basic public unit in society that could rise upward to the CCP leaders, while under the new system it was now a disaggregated voice that was not being heard by the CCP. Dutton is borrowing from post-colonial theory to bolster his argument that post-1989, China was a distinctly different society in both political and economic terms, akin to a colonial power, and this was markedly different from the Mao period. Dutton argues that to understand this change requires different research methodologies and close collaboration with Chinese scholars on the ground. The pedagogic point is that Western researchers can borrow from a wide range of theorists and research toolboxes to analyse society but that this is insufficient without due respect for the research being carried out in the respective country.

Dutton's turn to post-colonial theory combined with collaboration with local scholars to explain everyday life in the maelstrom of industrialisation is highly effective because it illustrates China's unique modernisation path. In contrast to those Western theorists who merely depict China as catching up with the West from an inferior position, Dutton's theory creates a space for a different conceptualisation of China as having its own unique path to modernisation. He notes, however, that China's modernisation uses some of the worst aspects of European industrialisation, along with colonial forms of governing, to control the population. This social-controlling governance is most clearly felt by the marginalised, the immigrant workers who have lost their rights and welfare protection held in the Mao period.

These immigrant workers are a 'floating' ('manglin') population who exist in a 'bare life', with little protection even in terms of their wages and ignored in the Government-sponsored research agenda in China (Dutton 1998, p. 282). This floating population of migrant workers, moving from the countryside to the cities, is on a scale never witnessed before in human history. As Dutton notes, this subaltern group have no political voice: they are not represented by the CCP and nor do provincial governments offer them rights. Their dialogue with the powerful is not by political dissent but rather by forms of market subversion, through such means as cheating and embezzling (Dutton 1998, p. 284).

By the time of his third book, *Beijing Time* (2008), written in collaboration with Hsiu-ju Stacy Lo and Dong Dong Wu, Dutton's poststructuralist theoretical now blends with postmodern sensibilities. He observes how Beijing's architecture has borrowed from around the world and created a commoditisation of its historic monuments, such as the Great Wall and the Forbidden City, along with the newly built Olympic buildings such as the Beijing Airport and the Bird's Nest stadium to be consumed as much by local tourists as overseas visitors. Dutton looks behind the postmodern architectural of the Olympic City to the backstreet markets, where high and popular culture merge as commodities, in a manner matching Fredric Jameson's claim that postmodernism is the logic of 'late capitalism' (Jameson 2000). In China, however, for Dutton, this logic becomes cross-class as high fashion rubs shoulders with pirated Hollywood blockbuster movies, bootlegged DVDs and distorted versions of Western culture consumed by the poorer classes. In *Beijing Time*, Dutton writes:

> An entire generation has now grown up on these things and developed its own unique mentality based on the world of which it is a part. While only a few have had access to 'authentic' top brands, just about every city kid on the street has had a chance to buy a knockoff CD. (2008, p. 11)

Here Dutton reveals how even the poorest consumer is ever-ready to partake in Western culture, whilst transforming it in a unique Chinese manner. What Dutton and his colleagues find is that consumerism has fundamentally transformed the city and everyday life but the political system remains seemingly unchanged. For example, the three loyalties of the communist era, that of loyalty to Mao, to the Party and to Socialism, have been replaced by the 'four haves, an apartment, a car, a good facial and a great body' (Dutton 2008, p. 10). However, the CCP retains political control throughout society. Moreover, in this consumer-driven city, the vacuum left by the socialist ideology is filled by a nationalism that both pre-dates and post-dates Mao. In this transformation of nationalism, Maoist thought and Marxism-Leninism come to students as a postmodern artefact, a consumer fetish in a variety of Mao paraphernalia, therein commodifying and depoliticising this past.

Yet every Chinese student must pass Marxist-Leninist studies to obtain university entry. This examination and the lived experience of the students in a marketised China are paradoxical. In this regard, the pedagogy of Chinese political studies sits uneasily with the lived experience of the students and yet almost simulacra-like Chinese students need to incorporate this Marxist-Leninist learning in their studies but act as market citizens outside the classroom. They do so, moreover, unexposed to the revisionist forms of Marxism as articulated by Dutton, which, when combined with Chinese scholarship, can throw a unique light onto Chinese society. Dutton shows that the research environment in the West is distinct from that existing in China but this does not mean it is somehow superior. Rather, it offers a different paradigm from that experienced by Chinese students and one that they could combine with their own knowledge of their society to everyone's benefit.

Postmodernism and post-colonialism

The strength of Dutton's analysis of China is its reflection on the circumstances under which one can know the present through the past via diverse theoretical frames. To explore contemporary China, Dutton brings modernist, post-structuralist, post-colonial and then postmodern sensibilities to his investigation, skilfully integrated with Chinese sources. In less assured hands, this theoretical blending would confuse rather than illuminate. The strength of this transcultural appraisal is made possible by Dutton's command of two languages, Chinese and English, and by his ability to bring together diverse methodologies guided by the insight he develops through his collaborative work with a wide range of Chinese scholars living and researching in China.

As such, Dutton has avoided the danger so prevalent for postgraduate research students of forgetting the past and simply concentrating on a present that has been emptied of its historic content. This danger is ever so evident in contemporary China, where the past is as much denigrated by the current leadership as it is in the anti-communist (dominant strand) of the Western academy. Both views all too readily dismiss both Mao and the Cultural Revolution (for example, Chang and Halliday 2005; Qin 2006) without any sense of historical balance or awareness of the debates in China. For postgraduate students in the Social Sciences, whether studying inside or outside China, the official ideology and its Western reinforcement have to be made transparent to them in shaping their research projects. These Chinese students can gain from an exposure to Western debates on Marxism, such as those of Berman and Anderson, or to Foucault's poststructuralist thinking. Equally, Chinese students' evaluations of their own societies via the research environments they have been trained in can strengthen any proposal, especially when it blends knowledges gained from both the diverse research environments.

Post-colonialism

This is the very point Pal Ahluwalia (2010) makes in regard to post-colonial theory, where he argues that the experience of colonial power in Algeria shaped the thinking of French poststructuralists to create new forms of knowledge. He argues that post-structuralist and post-modernist French theorists, such as Foucault, Jacques Derrida, Helene Cixous and Jean-François Lyotard, were profoundly affected by their colonial experiences in Algeria and the oppression and racial discrimination experienced by the Algerian people, and that they used this experience to rewrite research projects analysing Western society. In turn, this blending of knowledge opened up a whole new research agenda that critiqued traditional notions of modernity and the Enlightenment. On this, Ahluwalia writes that

> postcolonialism is a counter-discourse that seeks to disrupt the cultural hegemony of the West, challenging imperialism in its various guises, whereas post-structuralism and postmodernism are counter discourses against modernism that have emerged within modernism itself. It is my contention that, in order to understand the project of French post-structuralism, it is a imperative both to contextualize the African colonial experience and to highlight the Algerian locatedness, identity and heritage of its leading proponents. (2010, p. 3)

The political point that Ahluwalia makes is that Algerian colonialism had the effect of a radical cultural experience on these intellectuals, who on return to France challenged the very spirit of the Enlightenment project. They became the key writers of this new research agenda. Imbued by their first-hand knowledge of the subordinated colonial discourse, they deconstructed France's claim to being the centre of civilisation. For these theorists, there had to be alternative discourses that not just critiqued the colonial oppression of Algeria and Indochina but offered counter-perspectives to understand the world across cultural divides and become the basis of a whole different research environment and pedagogy that analysed power from a race-based-colonial perspective.

This new research environment has become the subject of dispute in developing countries, where paradoxically it exposed the power relations in those societies but only to reinforce them as legitimate forms of decolonisation by copying the colonial power practices (Ahmad 1993; Hutcheon 1994; Juan 1998). Moreover, the theoretical basis of this debate is that the West is imposing this new theory from outside in a new form of superiority at the expense of local knowledge, pedagogy and power. This raises the question of whether postmodernism and post-colonialism can be characterised as a discourse only of Western intellectuals, and not a discourse of intellectuals in the developing South. For example, the eminent China scholar

Arif Dirlik (1994) is highly critical of post-colonial theory, arguing that it erred in borrowing too much from Northern/Western sensibilities, notably the postmodern trend of thought, rather than using the material analysis offered by those living in developing countries, such as China. By doing this, he argues, the theory has a depoliticising effect as it explores, from an elitist point of view, cultural imperialism and its afterglow rather than the lived conditions of the population, as expressed by them in their own academies (Dirlik 1994, p. 352). Similarly, Aijaz Ahmad regards the exchange between postmodernism and post-colonialism as divorced from the material reality of the developing world and therein reinforcing the very power these theories claim to destabilise (1992, p. 94). The important point here is that by applying new supposedly radical Western intellectual research foci to non-Western countries, the research conducted may well not escape from an innate sense of superiority. The research project may be radical in the North/West but regressive in the South/East due to the lack of cultural respect for the intellectual traditions of the Southern/Eastern communities.

Postmodernism and post-colonialism in China

Another way of thinking through the dialogue between post-colonialism and postmodernism is that for many countries, such as China, Western modernisation has become the model to aspire to, whereas in the developed West it is being reconstructed around a form of chaotic flux (for example, the Global Financial Crisis), where terms such as post-industrial or postmodern capitalism have come into vogue (Harvey 1990, p. 9; 2005, p. 5). In post-Mao China, the terms modernism and postmodernism have now taken on a distinctly different meaning. According to Wang Hui (2009), the dominant thinking amongst Chinese intellectuals is that Western modernism is the standard to emulate and communist modernisation (in the Mao period) is akin to traditionalism and therefore pre-modern. Likewise, he argues, postmodernist thinking in China is not a critique of consumer capitalism as in the West (see Jameson 2000) but a celebration of commoditisation (Wang Hui 2009, p. 79).

In Wang Hui's view, there is a significant tension between modern and postmodern thought in China that hampers any critical debate on these terms. He writes:

> China's postmoderns read history as developing linearly from modernity to the Chinese, while the defenders of 'modernity' believe that Chinese sentiments have not yet evolved to the same degree that Western sentiments have. As a result, they think that we shouldn't discuss or study the question of modernity. (p. 79)

Wang Hui argues that China had its own unique modernity and modernisation, which were based on shared learning rather than hierarchy. He believes that this historical foundation offers both a sound intellectual and material basis for constructing a modern Chinese society quite distinct from that of the Western model. Wang Hui traces this alternative modern history to the Song dynasty, which he argues was founded not on a single teleology but an interactive relationship between East and West. In his book *The end of the revolution: China and the limits of modernity* (2009), Wang Hui takes issue with Chinese modernists for their uncritical adoption of Western modernism as a tensionless process. Likewise, he criticises Chinese postmodernists for an assumption that China will pass from modernity to postmodernity in a Western linear form. He regards the celebration of postmodern consumerism as neglecting the plight of those caught in the industrialisation maelstrom, as well as erasing China's long of history of anti-traditionalism and anti-imperialism (Wang Hui 2009, p. 80).

The 'state of exception' of June 1989, when Wang Hui witnessed the State repression first hand, sharpened his reflections on Chinese modernity. He laments the loss of life but also the loss of political passion for socialist equity. As such, the notion of the free market leading inextricably to democracy is for Wang Hui merely an obfuscation that hides the lack of economic democracy in China. He deconstructs the dominant thinking in China by both the intellectual-liberal dissidents and the Communist Party leaders, who, for quite opposite reasons, support market reforms. That is, there are vocal liberal critiques of the CCP who argue that an expansion of the market will cause new forces of power to arise that will bring down the CCP. Wang Hui, in contrast, argues that the market will cause too high a price on the poor whilst not weakening the rule of the Party, as the middle class will not challenge the CCP because they are economically benefitting from the flow of wealth.

For his part, Wang Hui, like Mobo Gao (2008), has a different research project. Whilst previously supporting socialist-market reforms of the kind implemented by Deng Xiaoping, Wang Hui and Gao both now express disappointment that the market process has gone too far in creating gross inequalities and by doing so has betrayed the spirit and the intent of market-socialism. They both express the view that if the CCP could be reformed then it might revive the socialist project of equitable redistribution from above. As such, they differ fundamentally from liberal dissidents who want to accelerate marketisation so as to dismantle CCP power. The critical point to note here is that there is a highly developed and diverse research environment in China, with the researchers seeking to explain the maelstrom that their country is experiencing. Western scholars have to understand and respect this search for knowledge within China's academy if there is to be a true transcultural research agenda in the West that comprehends China in a fuller research frame.

Unreflective science paradigms

This research agenda in China is charged with controversy and intellectual energy. For instance, reflecting on the failure of the Democratic Movement, Wang Hui is highly critical of the students' and intellectuals' approach to science. He argues that the students in Tiananmen Square were mistakenly enamoured with the scientific paradigm, as were the CCP leaders, and this was a mistaken research approach. Instead, they should have adopted a more poststructuralist framing of science to destabilise the existing power relations tied to scientific truth claims. That is, following the repression, the dissidents looked to science as the means of promoting the market (business studies, engineering and computer science), seeing these approaches as advancing the cause of democracy. Paradoxically, Wang Hui argues, such a move mirrored the Party leadership, who looked to science to promote the market and to reinforce their power. For their part, the CCP leaders, having rejected 'scientific socialism', embraced new forms of positivist science. They moved from Soviet-based science to Western scientific paradigms to guide the reforms. Wang Hui argues that both approaches to science fail to appreciate community thinking and lead to a closed rather than an open system of knowledge (2009, p. 169). In this light, he is advancing a claim that echoes the positive potentials of transcultural pedagogy, where the benefits of reflective social science as it emerged in the West are blended with local knowledge to challenge the truth claims of both the scientists and the CCP leaders.

Equally, Wang Hui is concerned that Chinese social science is of little benefit to the plight of the poor, bewailing the liberal-research agenda that has arisen in the Chinese academy, which stresses political democracy at the expense of economic democracy. Wang Hui is critical of the manner by which the new social science research environment has little regard for broad-based equality. Western governments read and fuel this tension in the Chinese intellectual community; they also stress political freedom rather than economic equality. As such, any social science research approach toward China has to chart a difficult course between these intellectual and political controversies to create dependable knowledge of the contemporary Chinese conditions.

Postgraduate student research and the postmodern turn

This chapter began in the year 1980 with a debate about revolutionary changes between Marxists across the Atlantic. It then took a journey through post-structuralism, post-colonialism and postmodernism to contemporary China, where I argued that these Western intellectual concepts have taken on different cultural meanings when they fully engage with knowledge generated in China. The chapter then highlighted how minority or subordinate discourses, such as that articulated by, say, Foucault, can shine the spotlight on the normalising effects of the dominant modernisation discourse but the danger is that this research paradigm can take on a Western form of superiority when applied to developing countries. It is important to remember that these subordinate discourses have also taken on new meaning in the postmodern turn in the West where their once radical elements have been muted by incorporation into a plethora of discourses (for example, gender, race and ethnic studies) or ignored by others in the case of natural science and business studies (Lyotard 1984).

This is an important point of contrast: by the 1980s the postmodern challenge to scientific positivism had had a significant impact in the Western academy and a whole new range of research projects were generated in the social sciences. Postmodern thought led to a wide range of journals and book series, profoundly influenced cultural and gender studies, and made a major impact in the disciplines of anthropology, the law, fine art, architecture and planning, sociology, international studies and political science. Paradoxically, however, it impacted far less on discourses directly geared to the postmodern consumer market, such as economics, business studies, accountancy and commerce (Rosenau 1992, p. 11). However, the appearance of postmodern thought in the humanities and social sciences in the West, once seen as a liberating force in gender, race, ethnic and cultural studies, became isolated in disciplinary corners of the academy (Rosenau 1992, p. 12).

In general, the diversity of theoretical directions and methodologies is a profound challenge for international students (as it is for domestic students), who cross the barriers between social, natural and business science courses. It is often claimed that the difference between, say, Australian postgraduate students and Chinese international students is the former's understanding and use of critical thinking and the latter's adherence to positivism and empiricism. However, this view is too simplistic. It fails to recognise the critical thinking of these Chinese students shaped by their own knowledge paradigms. It also contains the kernel of superiority, claiming that critical thinking defines the Western academy whereas the Easter academy is unreflective (see Yoneyama, Chapter 10, this volume). This is an unsustainable proposition, as the postgraduate research students coming from the South/East to the metropolitan North/West are critical thinkers. It is just that they are critical thinkers in different paradigms. Supervisors in the dominant pedagogic roles must be both respectful and make a genuine effort to blend the research environments in a transcultural manner.

Moreover, in Australia the combination of mass enrolments in higher education with disciplinary specificities has meant that even domestic students who enter postgraduate studies in the social sciences (who have typically studied an undergraduate degree for three years and then completed a one-year Honours degree) are often not the ideal-type critical thinkers the Western model claims they have been trained to be. Rather, these students also struggle to engage in broad-ranging critical theory. Under the pressure to complete on time, they tend to conduct research along a mini-narrative and single language pathway, and have limited time for wide-ranging critical analysis. The high cost of higher education exacerbates this situation, creating a certain utilitarian attitude to study aimed at the job market rather than life skills in analytical and cultural thought.

In the case of international students, their postgraduate studies are predominantly in the disciplines least exposed to critical thinking (for example, Feyerabend 1975; Harding 1990; Kuhn 1970) or the postmodern turn. Rather, international students coalesce in courses where positivism prevails, notably Business Studies, Commerce, Accountancy and Engineering. Martin Davies estimates that in 2008, international students comprised 39 per cent of all students studying in Australian universities and that 74 per cent of these international enrolments were in Business/Management, Computer Science and Engineering-related courses (2010, p. 1). The incentive for international students in doing these courses is that the broad area of business studies carry higher residency points but this is only part of a complex picture. For instance, only 10 per cent of overseas students currently obtain residency, so this is only a partial explanation for the preference by international students for Commerce or Engineering degrees. A more obvious explanation is that these courses are geared to capitalist modernisation in China, India, Malaysia, Indonesia, just as they are in the West. Such courses serve both the market in the student's homeland as well as the global capitalist diaspora of international business students.

These degrees, however, offer little space for subordinate discourses (Foucault 2008; Gordon 1991) or mini-narratives (Lyotard 1984) to emerge and give voice to these international students. Moreover, as Michael Singh argues, there is minimal dialectical space for reciprocity of learning, when the mini-narratives of the students are given limited opportunity to be shared with either their class-mates and peers or their supervisors (2009, p. 195). Singh's research on Chinese students in Australia shows that there is a form of 'orientalism' at work, where these students are aware of the Western canon but their supervisors (and Australian students) have little or no understanding of Chinese culture or history (p. 196). He calls for a dialogue, following Ranciere, where the supervisor/professor assumes a veil of ignorance to bring out the many subordinated narratives carried by the students to the Western research environment (p. 199). He argues it is essential that the supervisor/postgraduate student relationship be destabilised by the supervising academic's adoption of a pedagogic posture of 'cross-cultural ignorance' so as to provide a space for transcultural reciprocity (p. 196).

Such reciprocal and respectful learning is highlighted in this book and forms the foundation of Xianlin Song and Kate Cadman's teaching practice. They offer a sophisticated methodology that goes far beyond the usual learning practices espoused for teaching international students (see Song & Cadman, Chapter 12, this volume). They give a fresh perspective to a somewhat orientalist paradigm, clearly exemplified by Jude Carroll and Janette Ryan's metaphor that international students are like 'canaries in a coalmine': if they die from poor learning practice so do the lecturers (Carroll & Ryan 2005, p. 9). In addition, Song and Cadman's transcultural pedagogy gives due respect and appreciation for knowledge and cultural exchange on an equal footing between the cultures. A critical aspect of this learning exchange is that it is cross-languages as well as across culture.

In this chapter I have argued that for effective cross-cultural and cross-language pedagogy, it is important to understand the history of ideas as they play out in different practices. The unfolding of these diverse histories, whether it is Western Marxism or Chinese modernity, creates the research circumstances in which transcultural exchange can occur. This exchange can enrich both overseas students and their supervisors alike, whilst producing original knowledge.

Conclusion

International students, especially those from China, studying in the humanities and social sciences, will be confronted by a research environment with many subordinate discourses and mini-narratives as they seek to explore their society and its rapid modernisation. Faced with this challenge, they need to find the space and the research environment where the knowledge they have gained can merge with the new paradigms they confront. In explaining the need for a transcultural pedagogic environment I have here highlighted the different research agendas in the West and in China and called for the blending of these schemas. This chapter has drawn parallels between the Marxist debates on the industrial revolution in Europe in the seventeenth to nineteenth century and the lived experience in China today. It has taken the reader on a cultural journey into Western and Chinese debates on revolutionary change through the prisms of modernism, post-structuralism, post-colonialism and postmodernism. The chapter has then shown how the application of these theories to China can be heuristically informative, but only if such an application respects the culture and pedagogy of the Chinese academy and its traditions. This journey has carried readers from Europe to China, and to the conundrum of postgraduate study and supervision, where Australian and Chinese students alike are constrained by the tendency to forget the past, and to respond only to mini-narrative or to succumb to the danger of accepting the Western research environment as superior.

The task of transcultural pedagogy is to create a learning zone where it is possible to find intercultural research that respects the knowledge held by the student and then to open a dialogue within the Western research environment. In the social sciences, I have noted that this dialogue should raise the issues evoked by poststructuralism, postmodernism and post-colonialist thought. I have argued that the role of the supervisor is to ensure that this Western-derived form of knowledge is raised with students from China in a manner that compliments their knowledge to create a truly transcultural pursuit of truth.

References

Adorno, T & Horkheimer M 1979, *Dialectic of enlightenment*, trans. J Cumming, Verso, London.
Ahluwalia, P 2010, *Out of Africa: poststructuralism's colonial roots*, Routledge, Abingdon, Oxon.
Ahmad, A 1992, *In theory: classes, nations, literatures*, Routledge, London.
Anderson, P 1984, March–April, 'Modernity and revolution', *New Left Review I*, vol. 144, pp. 1–11.
Arendt, H 1958, *The human condition*, Chicago University Press, Chicago, Ill.
Berman, M 1982, *All that is solid melts into air: the experience of modernity*, Verso, New York.
Berman, M 1984 March–April, 'The signs in the street: a response to Perry Anderson, *New Left Review I*, vol. 144, pp. 1–6.
Carroll, J & Ryan, J (ed.) 2005, *Teaching international students: improving learning for all*, Routledge, Abingdon, Oxon.
Chang, J & Halliday, J 2005, *Mao: the unknown story*, Jonathon Cape, London.
Goodwin-Smith, I 2010, 'For cutting: an introduction to Foucault, 25 years on', *Social Identities* vol. 16 no. 5, pp. 583–587.
Davies, M 2010, 'The permanent residency rort", *Quadrant Online*, viewed 30 October 2011, <http://www.quadrant.org.au/magazine/issue/2010/3/>.
De Certeau M 1984, *The practice of everyday life*, trans. S Randall, University of California Press, Berkeley, CA.
Dirlik, A 1994, 'The postcolonial aura: third world criticism in the age of global capitalism', *Critical Inquiry*, vol. 20, pp. 529–544.
Dutton, M 1992, *Policing and punishment in China*, Cambridge University Press, Cambridge, MA.

Dutton, M 1998, *Streetlife China*, Cambridge University Press, Cambridge, MA.

Dutton, M 2005, *A history of policing Chinese politics*, Duke University Press, Durham, NC.

Dutton, M, Hsiu-ju, SL & Dong Dong, W 2008, *Beijing time*, Harvard University Press, Cambridge, MA.

Dutton, M 2010, 'The paradoxical after-life of colonial governmentality', *Social Identities*, vol. 16 no. 5, pp. 635–651.

Foucault, M 1970, *The order of things*, Tavistock, London.

Foucault, M 2008, *The birth of biopolitics: lectures at the College de France 1978–1979*, Palgrave Macmillan, Basingstoke & New York.

Gordon, C 1991, 'Governmental rationality: an introduction', in G Burchell, C Gordon & P Miller (eds), *The Foucault effect: studies in governmentality*, University of Chicago Press, Chicago, Ill, pp. 1–52.

Feyerabend, P 1975, *Against method: outline of an anarchist theory of knowledge*, New Left Books, London.

Goa, M 2008, *The battle for China's past*, Pluto Press, London.

Harding, S 1990, 'Feminism, science, and the anti-enlightenment critique', in LJ Nicholson (ed.), *Feminism/postmodernism*, Routledge, New York, pp. 83–107.

Hardt, M & Negri, A 2000, *Empire*, Harvard University Press, Harvard, MA.

Harvey, D 1990, *The condition of postmodernity: an inquiry into the origins of cultural change*, Blackwell, Cambridge MA.

Harvey, D 2005, *A brief history of neoliberalism*, Oxford University Press, Oxford, UK.

Hindess, B and Hirst, P 1975, *Pre-capitalist modes of production*, Routledge and Kegan Paul, London.

Hindess, B 2010, 'Liberalism: rationality of colonial governmentality', *Social Identities*, vol. 16 no. 5, pp. 669–675.

Kuhn, T 1970, *The structure of scientific revolutions*, Chicago University Press, Chicago, IL.

Jameson, F 1991, *Postmodernism or, the cultural logic of late capitalism*, Verso, London.

Lyotard, J-F 1984, *The postmodern condition: report on knowledge*, trans. G Bennington & B Massumi, University of Minnesota Press, Minneapolis.

Qin, J 2006, *An introduction to intercultural communication studies*, Shanxi People's Press, Taiyuan, PRC.

Rosenau, PM 1992, *Post-modernism and the Social Sciences: insights, inroads, and intrusions*, Princeton University Press, Princeton, NJ.

Said, E 1978, *Orientalism*, Routledge and Kegan Paul, London.

Schmitt, C 1996, *The concept of the political*, trans. G Schwab, Chicago University Press, Chicago, IL.

Singh, M 2009, 'Using Chinese knowledge in internationalizing research education: Jacques Rancier, an ignorant supervisor and doctoral students from China', *Globalization, Societies and Education,* vol. 7 no. 2, June, pp. 185–201.

Spivak, GS 1988, 'Can the Subaltern Speak?' in C Nelson & L Grossberg (eds), *Marxism and the interpretation of culture,* University of Illinois Press, Chicago, IL, pp. 271–313.

Wang H 2009, *The end of the revolution: China and the limits of modernity,* Verso, London.

Williams, R 1973, *The country and the city,* Oxford University Press, Oxford, UK.

Part III

Transforming curriculum in Asian language teaching

4

Teaching Asian languages from an intercultural perspective: Building bridges for and with students of Indonesian

Anthony J Liddicoat and Michelle Kohler

Introduction

The teaching and learning of Indonesian in the Australian context represent both a unique opportunity and challenge for developing Australians' capabilities to engage with Asia and Australia's place in the region. The place of Indonesian in Australian education has usually been justified in terms of the importance of developing a better understanding of the culture and religion of our nearest neighbour (Kohler & Mahnken 2010). This justification is based on a belief that the learning of a language forms a fundamental part of the development of intercultural understanding. However, language teaching approaches have not traditionally made intercultural understanding a central part of programs and have instead focused primarily on the acquisition of the language system. Where cultural understanding has been included in such programs it has typically been separated from the learning of language (Byram 1988). This means that there has often been a disconnection between a stated aim of language learning and the language learning experience offered to students. More recently, however, much attention has been given to pedagogical responses that integrate language learning with intercultural understanding (for example, Byram 1991; Byram and Morgan 1994; Crozet and Liddicoat 1999; Kohler 2010; Kramsch 1993a; Liddicoat 2002, 2005b, 2008; Liddicoat et al. 2003; Papademetre and Scarino 2000). In this chapter, we will extend these initiatives, and examine some of the issues that emerge for understanding language education as an endeavour focused on the development of intercultural understanding using the teaching and learning of Indonesian as a starting point.

Intercultural language teaching and learning: Some basic assumptions

Intercultural language teaching and learning is a perspective of languages education that is based on particular ways of understanding the nature of language and culture as these are involved in the processes of learning.

Conceptualisations of language

An understanding of language is fundamental to language education, and how language is conceptualised is a significant feature of how it is taught. In intercultural language teaching language is understood primarily as a culturally contexted meaning-making system (Kramsch 2006; Papademetre and Scarino 2000), and understands language teaching as engagement with and participation in the practices of a community of language users (Kern and Liddicoat 2008). This view of language, and of language education, involves a problematising of language as a central construct rather than considering the nature of language as self-evident, as has usually been the case in language education. This problematising stands in contrast to ways in which language has sometimes been treated as a conceptual notion in education.

In many contexts language educators have tended to define the substance and scope of their work through a process of labelling particular languages (Chinese, Japanese, Indonesian, and so on). This named entity then becomes the de facto conceptualisation of what is to be taught. The act of naming a language has typically invoked a view of language as a set of prescriptive linguistic structures of an ideal, standardised variety, and knowledge of a language as the knowledge of these structures (Odlin 1994). In other words, pedagogical grammar has been equated with prescriptive grammar (Liddicoat and Curnow 2003). This is an understanding of language-as-code that views language as a fixed and finite system that exists independently of speakers and contexts of use.

Language has also been understood in languages education as a human communication system (Davies 2005). This again can be seen as a labelling — in this case of the purpose of language — rather than a theorisation of the nature of language or the nature of communication, and this too has tended to be seen as unproblematic and unproblematised (Haugh and Liddicoat 2009; Eisenchlas 2009). In fact, communication-oriented views of language may not differ much from code-based views. For Saussure (1916), for example, communication was a simple process in which an active speaker encodes a message for a passive listener — an unproblematic exchange of meaning through language. In this view, communication involves a straightforward transfer of thoughts from one mind to another (Harris 2003). The focus here tends to be placed on the linguistic resources available for expressing thought, and successful communication is seen as resulting from access to these linguistic resources and the arrangement of them. What tends to be missing in this focus is the idea that communication itself is a creative, cultural act in its own right through which social groups constitute themselves (Carey 1989). Moreover, it is a complex performance of identity in which the individual communicates not only information but also a social persona that exists in the act of communication (Sacks 1975). Such complexities of communication have often been ignored in the theories of language that underlie language education, even those that have privileged communication.

In understanding language education and an intercultural endeavour, it is necessary to begin with an enlarged theory of language, seeing language as 'open, dynamic, energetic, constantly evolving and personal' (Shohamy 2007, p. 5), and viewing communication as interactionally-grounded and involving 'participants' contingent, emergent and joint accomplishment' of meaning (Kasper 2006, p. 22). This involves issues of voice, identity and co-construction between participants, and the expression of self through language (Kramsch 2008b). Shohamy (2007) argues that language should be a vehicle for the expression of the self not a constraint on self-expression because the self is fundamental to language use: each choice that an individual makes from their language repertoire is a portrayal of personality. The student cannot simply be seen as a student, as deficient in their command of language (Kern and Liddicoat 2008). From the beginning of their learning, students are users of language, in fact users of languages through which they present themselves, and construct and explore their worlds.

Language is not so much a thing to be studied, as a way of seeing, understanding and communicating about the world, and each language user uses his or her language(s) differently to do this. In this sense, language is both personal and communal. Individuals use language for social purposes within social contexts. Language use is a process of adaptation, negotiation and accommodation (Shohamy 2007). Knowing a language means more than knowing the code; it means engaging in social practices using that code in order to participate in social life. Such processes exist wherever two individuals communicate across their own personal versions of a language. However, when such communication happens across languages or in contexts where multiple languages are at play, there are different needs and possibilities for negotiating and adapting language choices (Kramsch 1999). Just as language use is an engagement in and with social practices, so too is language learning (Kramsch 1994). Language is something that people do in their daily lives, something they use to express, create and interpret meanings, and to establish and maintain social and interpersonal relationships.

Conceptualisations of culture

A core belief in intercultural language teaching is that language does not function independently from the context in which it is used (Byram 1988; Kramsch 1993a). Language is always used to communicate something beyond itself and is at the same time affected by the context in which it is found. The cultural context therefore affects the ways in which participants shape language in a particular interaction, at a particular time, and in a particular setting. People who share the same general set of cultural practices share an understanding of the meanings that are associated with language as it is used for communication, and their language use is shaped by these shared understandings. Successful communication happens because of a shared understanding of context, regardless of how well individual participants know each other (Heath 1986). Culture provides for this shared knowledge, which, because it is so deeply embedded in processes of meaning-making through language, typically comes invisible in intracultural communication (Crozet 2003). Thus, as a process of developing intercultural understanding, students need to be able to decentre from their own culture (Kramsch 1993a; Byram 1989). This can only happen as the result of a deliberate process of teaching that brings to the students the sorts of exposure they need to begin the decentring process, and the skills and knowledge to understand and interpret these experiences in order to achieve decentring. In this way, the study of language exposes students to another way of viewing the world as it develops flexibility, and independence from a single linguistic and conceptual system through which to view the world (Kramsch 1993a; Byram 1989).

At its most global level, culture constitutes a frame in which meanings are conveyed and interpreted, and it is at this level that culture is least apparently attached to language (Liddicoat 2009). Culture as context consists of the knowledge speakers have about how the world works, and how this is displayed, and understood, in acts of communication. This form of cultural knowledge has probably been the best covered in most approaches to culture in work on intercultural communication (see, for example, Fitzgerald 2002; Levine & Adelman 2002; Thomas 1983, 1984). However, the linguistic dimension of world knowledge is often ignored, although such knowledge of the world is integrally associated with and invoked by language (and other semiotic systems). This means that the message itself is not simply the sum of the linguistic elements of which it is composed but also includes additional elements of meaning that are invoked by, but not inherent in, the linguistic elements. Culture gives specific, local meanings to language by adding shared connotations and associations to the standard denotation of terms. In this way, culture can be understood as a form of community of practice (Eckert & McConnell-Ginet 1992; Holmes & Meyerhoff 1999), in which certain meanings are privileged above other possible meanings in ways that are relevant to the purposes and histories of the communities of practice. World knowledge is by its nature embedded and complex, but its operations can be seen through specific instances of communication in which assumed, shared world knowledge is fundamental to the message being communicated. As Bakhtin (1981) argues, discourse always represents a worldview — when language is used in communication, it is used within and for this worldview, and the worldview is as much constitutive of the message as are the linguistic forms and their agreed meanings.

Culture is not simply a body of knowledge but rather a framework in which people live their lives and communicate shared meanings with each other. In seeing culture in this way, it becomes fundamentally necessary to engage with the variability inherent in any culture. This involves a movement away from the idea of 'national' culture, and recognition that culture varies with time, place and social category, and for age, gender, religion, ethnicity and sexuality (Norton 2000). People participate in different groups and have multiple memberships within their cultural group, each of which affects the presentation of self within the cultural context (Tajfel & Turner 1986). This variability is not limited, however, to membership of sub-cultures but also to the ways in which the individual participates within his/her cultures. People can resist, subvert or challenge the cultural practices to which they are exposed, in both their first culture and in additional cultures that they acquire. Moreover, individual members of a culture enact that culture differently and pay different levels of attention to the cultural norms that operate in their society; interactions within a cultural context have the potential to reshape the culture (Paige et al. 1999). Culture in this sense is dynamic, evolving and not easily summarised for teaching. Rather, it is the complexity of culture with which the student must engage (Liddicoat 2002).

The implication of such ideas for language education is that culture needs to be studied as a process of meaning-making in which students engage, rather than as a closed set of information that they will be required to recall (Liddicoat 2002). Viewing culture as a dynamic set of practices rather than as a body of shared information engages the idea of individual identities as a more central concept. Culture is then seen as a framework in which the individual achieves his/her identity using a cultural group's understandings of choices made by members as a resource for the presentation of self. Jayasuriya (1990) suggests that to understand the relationship between culture and individual behaviour one needs to think of it only as a blueprint for action, as 'the manifest culture revealed in individual behaviour is selective, and not necessarily representative of a historical cultural tradition in its abstract form' (p. 14). Individuals select from such a blueprint in order to act appropriately, but not reductively, in different social contexts within the same culture. This notion of selective cultural behaviour recognises that although individuals' use of language is to a certain extent 'bound' by their native cultural blueprint, they are also capable of creating a personal, unique expression in communication. This reflects Sacks's (1984) notion of 'doing being ordinary': who we are is an interactionally accomplished product not an inherent quality, and the culture provides a reference point for this interactional accomplishment. Such a view implies an orientation to the individual as a semiotic system, that is, as a set of meaningful choices about the presentation of self. Culture provides a context in which this semiotic is to be read, and choices will be understood differently in different cultural contexts (Kramsch 1993a, 1995a, 1995b). This means that for the second language user, doing being ordinary involves presenting a self within a different framework of conventions for reading the individual.

In order to learn about culture, it is necessary to engage with the linguistic and non-linguistic practices of the culture and to gain insights into the way of living in a particular cultural context (Kramsch 1993a; Liddicoat 1997). Cultural knowledge is not, therefore, limited to knowing information about a culture; it is about knowing how to engage with that culture. Thus, it is important that the scope of culture learning moves beyond awareness, understanding, and sympathy, and begins to address the ways in which students will practise culture learning. Carr (1999) argues that students need to become 'interculturally competent players as well as sensitive observers' (p. 106) and the role of culture learning is to provide a framework for productive dialogue between old and new understandings. A dynamic view of culture sees cultural competence, therefore, as intercultural behaviour. It is the ability to negotiate meaning across cultural boundaries and to establish one's identity as a user of another language (Kramsch 1993b). As a result, cultural knowledge is not limited in its use to a particular task or exercise, but instead it is a more general knowing that underlies how language is used, and how things are said and done in a cultural context.

The intercultural in language learning

In language education it is possible to distinguish two broad orientations to the teaching of culture. The first of these can be termed a cultural orientation. This term implies the development of knowledge about culture that remains external to the student and is not intended to confront or transform the student's existing identity, practices, values, attitudes, beliefs and worldview. It is about the acquisition of a body of knowledge about a culture (Liddicoat 2005a). Beacco (2000) finds this to be the dominant approach to culture in much language teaching material, and remarks that the body of knowledge taught is often limited and overgeneralised and subordinated to the teaching of linguistics structures. Cultural orientations have a long history, especially in the European context where *civilisation* in the teaching of French and *Landeskunde* in the teaching of German have focused on a presentation of cultural information judged to have been of national significance, with particular focus on literature, art, history and geography (Byram 1989). Both *civilisation* and *Landeskunde* have the goal of developing a better knowledge of salient aspects of the national culture of the relevant country among language students. However, the cultural emphasis is by no means uniquely European. In Japanese teaching, 日本事情 *Nihonjijou* (lit. 'the Japanese situation') (Toyota 1988) represents a similar approach to the teaching of culture.

The second orientation is to privilege the intercultural. This orientation implies a transformational engagement of the student in the act of learning. Here learning involves the student in oppositional practice (Kramsch & Nolden 1994) that seeks to decentre the student and to develop an intercultural identity as a result of an engagement with another culture. Here the borders between self and other are explored, problematised and redrawn. In teaching language from an intercultural perspective, developing a static body of knowledge is not seen as the equivalent of developing an intercultural capability (Zarate 1983). Rather, the student needs to engage with language and culture, and elements of a meaning-making system, that influence and are influenced by each other. This means that language learning becomes a process of exploring the ways language and culture relate to lived realities — the students' own as well as that of the target community.

The view of the intercultural presented here relates to an understanding of the language student as a language user who mediates between languages and cultures. An intercultural mediator is a person who is able to build bridges between understandings developed and communicated through different languages and cultures (Byram 2002). Such mediators are people who are able to interpret cultures for themselves and for others. This means that they are able to articulate their own understandings in ways that those who do not share their linguistic and cultural starting points can understand. They are also able to articulate the linguistic and cultural understandings of others for members of their own culture (cf. Gohard-Radenkovic et al. 2004). That is, they stand between cultures and provide a bridge between them.

In developing language learning experiences to facilitate the development of intercultural mediators, the pre-existing culture and identity of the student is an important element, as mediation places the language student in contact with oppositions between their own cultural positioning and that of the new group with whom they are seeking to engage. This means that, within an intercultural perspective, culture learning engages with issues of identity and existing cultural memberships, and seeks to involve the student in decentring from these in the process of engaging with a new culture (Liddicoat 2005a). Mediation also involves reacting to encounters with diverse others in constructive ways. It is not a passive, observational approach to difference but rather an active 'being in diversity', in which diversity is not an external reality but rather is experienced as communities in which one lives and acts (Liddicoat and Scarino 2010). The 'intercultural' is developed through becoming aware of linguistic and cultural diversity and one's own place within that diversity. Becoming a mediator involves developing insights both into one's own 'intracultural' positioning and how this is shaped by one's language, and into culture as part of the process of coming to understand the cultural situatedness of others (Papademetre 2000). This means that mediators need to decentre from their own culture and to see their own positioning from the perspective of another (Kramsch 1993a; Byram 1989). This decentring is a process of varying the perspective one takes in understanding the world, not simply seeing the other as an object of study, but seeing their perspective as a valid understanding and exploring the consequences of diversity. This can only happen as the result of a deliberate process of teaching that exposes the students to the decentring process, and helps them to gain the abilities and knowledge to understand and interpret these experiences. The study of language, therefore, has the potential to develop students' flexibility and independence from a single linguistic and conceptual system (Liddicoat 2005a; Kramsch 1993a; Byram 1989). This can be characterised as a dynamic approach to culture (Liddicoat 2002), seen as sets of variable practices that are continually created and re-created by participants in interaction. Culture, then, is not about information and things; it is about actions and understanding. In order to learn about culture, it is necessary to engage actively with linguistic and non-linguistic practices and to gain insights about the way of living in a particular cultural context (Kramsch 1993a; Liddicoat 1997).

The intercultural, therefore, involves an understanding that one's knowing is always informed by the past and present of a particular language and culture and that, in intercultural contacts, it is necessary to recognise the same in others (Liddicoat & Scarino 2010). This means understanding the impact of such situatedness on communication and relationships. The relationship between awareness and knowing is, however, not a unidirectional one in which awareness precedes knowledge, but a multidirectional one in which knowing contributes to expanded awareness and awareness contributes to expanded knowing. Through experiences of and engagement with languages and cultures, the intercultural student develops an increasingly complex sense of self as a user of language and as a cultural being acting on and in the world. The intercultural in this sense also involves the ability to analyse, explain and elaborate one's awareness. That is, it involves a meta-level of awareness (or meta-awareness) that needs to be captured in the elicitation of the intercultural.

For the intercultural language student, the development of this awareness and knowing is achieved through the experience of another language and, through this language, another culture. It is through exposure to and engagement with culturally situated text — whether spoken or written, intrapersonal or interpersonal — that the student comes to appreciate the manifestation of diversity through language as a communicative process.

Interculturality is, however, not simply a manifestation of awareness and knowing, it also involves acting — in other words, it involves active mediation, and so demands an understanding of the student as both participant and analyser in interaction, that is, as both student and user of language and culture (Kern & Liddicoat 2008; Liddicoat & Scarino 2010). The intercultural mediator does not simply communicate in contexts of diversity but also monitors, reflects on, and interprets what is occurring. While it is not true that the participant and analyser roles are always present to the same degree in any act of communication, the capacity to draw on, combine, and move between these interactional identities is a fundamental element of the intercultural.

The interpersonal and interactional nature of the intercultural as it is conceived here requires that the language user is able to decentre form his/her own cultural and linguistic framework in order to see the world from alternative perspectives, or what Byram et al. (2002) describe as the 'ability to make the strange familiar and the familiar strange' (p. 14). Such decentring is a capacity to understand multiple perspectives and a willingness to search for and accept multiple possible interpretations of the same message. As an interpersonal phenomenon, interculturality is predicated on the development of reciprocity in interaction, which recognises one's own multiple roles and responsibilities and is sensitive to, and accommodating of, those of one's interlocutors. This means that, for us, to be intercultural involves continuous intercultural learning through experience and critical reflection. There can be no final end-point at which the individual achieves the intercultural state, but rather to be intercultural is by its very nature an unfinishable work-in-progress of action in response to new experiences and reflection on the action.

Realising intercultural language teaching and learning in practice

The following discussion explores the nature of Indonesian language teaching, from an intercultural perspective. The data presented in this section were collected as part of a larger study designed to investigate the ways in which teachers of Indonesian mediate the intercultural in their classroom interactions with students. The data were collected using ethnographic methods of interview, collaborative planning and observation of classroom practice during a one-year period in three secondary school

Indonesian classes. The class interactions were audiotaped and the tapes transcribed.

Here, the extracts below show how the teachers and students themselves mediate from an intercultural perspective as they engage with otherness and build bridges between the known and the new. The first two examples focus in particular on students as analysts, while the latter two focus on students as performers. Students' names have been replaced with pseudonyms in all cases.

Representing culture as dynamic

One way in which teachers develop the capacity of students to be intercultural mediators is to work with culture as dynamic and variable. In doing this, teachers depict culture in ways which mediate the dynamic, contingent nature of culture with students. The representation of culture in interaction with students is a source both of input about the specific culture, and of ideas about the nature of culture and its relationship to language. The following extract provides an example of how a teacher simultaneously mediates the nature of the specific target culture and of culture in general through discussion of a particular text and the cultural context underlying it.

Extract 1[1]

Teacher:	What would we put alongside here? Freedom of Press? Media? What about in Indonesia? Or here [teacher points to centre of Venn diagram]?
Jaxson	Indonesia tends to be stricter.
Teacher	Stricter laws, policies on *apa* (what)?
Jaxson	It's too broad to narrow it down.
Teacher	*Ya*, OK. On media? What issues …? How did you come up with this? What impressions … what led you to believe … to come up with a statement like this?
Jaxson	The article on Inul Daratista.
Teacher	What can you tell me about Inul?
Jaxson	She's a *dangdut* (pop music with Arab and Indian influence) dancer.
Teacher	She's a *penari dangdut* … she's a *dangdut* dancer, So, what's the problem?
Jaxson	The way she dances. It's very controversial for some Islamic leaders.

	leaders.
Teacher	So, controversial … *kontroversi* exists in Indonesian.
Jaxson	They're trying to ban her from doing it.
Teacher	Right. So, *melarang dia* (forbade her) … *pemerintah* (government)? Or *tokoh* (prominent figures) …
Jaxson	*Tokoh Islam.* (Islamic leaders)
Teacher	*Tokoh Islam ingin melarang show Inul Daratista karena dia sangat … tariannya sangat erotis menurut pendapat mereka … menurut pengalamannya …* (Islamic leaders wanted to ban Inul Daratista's show because she's very … her dancing is very erotic in their view … according to their experience) from their perspective. Do we have anything like that here? Have we heard of anything like that here?
Jaxson	No.
Teacher	So, we're *bebas* (free)?
Jaxson	No. I can't say, not to that degree. We're less strict on stuff like that.
Teacher	Is there anything that had come up in the news like that … that you know that could be put on a par or that could say something about how we feel about that sort of thing?
Jaxson	I don't know but on a par like that you'd see stuff like on Video Hits on Saturday mornings.
Teacher	*Ya*, mm. Good point. *Bagus* (Good). *Bagus sekali* (Very good).
	[Discussion continues]
Teacher	What do you see on those Video Hits?
Jaxson	Women dancing half naked.
Teacher	Right, OK. So, do you think it's caused any controversy? If there were controversy, where would it come from? *Dari mana?* (from where?) Do you think it would come from the government?
ALL	No.
Teacher	Or from political groups?
Jaxson	*Mungkin.* (Maybe)
Teacher	But what sort of political groups?
Mark	Maybe like local government.

Jaxson	I don't think they'd be too upset with it. It's not an issue I think they'd deal with. I reckon it would cause more outrage with the public than it would at a higher level.
Mark	That's like when … was it Madonna who brought out that film clip when someone got shot in a car park and they completely banned it? They made her remove the film clip. They were like a parents' committee on like a local level who took it higher and it got banned.
	[Discussion continues]
Teacher	But isn't that interesting? That video is to do with violence … not really sex or eroticism. So, perhaps controversy can be caused by … maybe we can conclude by saying violence is more of an issue on television than it is … not an issue but not a concern on Indonesian television as much as it is on our television. But you're right then to say that a lot of the controversy that may come out of these Video Hits comes not from a political party but from … *orang tua* (parents) … or maybe from a political party such as Family First … maybe … *partai Kristen* (a Christian party) that have foundations that have some religious connection. *Apakah kamu setuju?* (Do you agree?)

From the outset of this interaction, culture is framed within a comparative perspective in which both the target culture and the students' own cultural positioning are relevant, with the use of a Venn diagram as a tool for considering similarities and differences. This comparative view enables the teacher to relate students' developing understanding of Indonesian culture to their own reality, through specific scaffolding of their thinking: 'Do we have anything like that here?' The effect is that culture is referenced against students' understanding of their own culture and there is an experiential basis for explaining opinions, represented by turns such as: 'Stricter laws, policies on *apa* (what)?'; 'How did you come up with this?'; 'What do you see …?'; 'If there were controversy where would it come from?' The teacher is constructing a paradigm in which culture is represented as open to interpretation and challenge, and in which aspects of culture can be seen as resonating across contexts. That is, the interaction develops the idea that there is a basis for moving beyond the specifics of otherness found in any given culture to a more universal concept of culture. This more generalised concept of culture is portrayed as belonging to self and others. In addition, the text chosen is recent and the discussion focuses attention on the internal dynamics of cultures by exploring the power of sub-groups to influence political change and social values. Therefore, culture is represented here as immediate and interconnected.

The teacher's discourse reflects the dynamic nature and internal diversity of culture through the ways she refers to sub-groups within an overarching national culture. She identifies religious groups and parent groups, and uses caveats such as '(according to their experience) from their perspective', which convey the idea that culture is personalised and at times conflicted. This sense that culture is variable and open to individual interpretation is reflected also in the teacher's questioning techniques in which she uses referential questions to encourage personal perspectives, such as 'What impressions … what led you to believe…?', and to seek explanations: 'Do you think it's caused any controversy?', 'What sort of political groups?'. When the teacher adds her own perspective, she does so with qualifications, 'perhaps', 'maybe', or 'not an issue but not a concern', modelling an open interpretation of experience subject to ongoing exploration, rather than representing her cultural knowledge as authoritative and finalised. In drawing to a close, the discussion emphasises the provisional nature of the conclusions when the teacher states, 'Maybe we can conclude by saying …', signalling a loosely agreed position. However, this is qualified by her use of 'maybe' and the follow up question, '*Apakah kamu setuju?* (Do you agree?)', suggesting that the view is contestable. By qualifying and moderating her comments in this way, the teacher creates a sense that culture is layered, multifaceted and open to interpretation.

The ways in which this teacher guides the interaction helps to construct a narrative around the ideas and, in doing so, builds bridges between students' existing knowledge and new insights. The teacher begins by revisiting what is familiar using open-ended questions, 'What can you tell me about …?', which she follows with 'So, what's the problem?' In doing this, she provides opportunities for students to decentre from their own cultural perspectives. She uses the comparative question, 'Is there anything … that could be put on a par?' to develop points of connection, and the deliberately provocative question, 'So, we're *bebas* (free)?', challenges implicit assumptions about students' own perspectives. She affirms students' connections ('Good point') and then probes these further ('What do you see …?'). She asks students to notice, compare and reflect (Crozet & Liddicoat 1999) on their own culture ('Where would it come from?') and in doing so, she is constructing a basis for comparison of specific cultures while also developing a meta-awareness of the nature of culture itself. She concludes the interaction with a summary connecting social practices and religious values: 'Controversy can be caused by … *orang tua* (parents) or maybe a political party …'. Throughout, the teacher is constructing a narrative of connection, developing students' capability to decentre (Liddicoat 2005a) and make connections for themselves as mediators between their existing and new cultural worldviews.

Analysing culture in language

Understanding the interconnection between language and culture is a basis for developing an intercultural perspective in language teaching and learning, which, in turn, forms a basis for intercultural mediation. The following extract reveals how the teacher purposefully mediates this integration, and furthermore how this relationship influences and reflects social mores.

Extract 2

Teacher	What about the use of the language? How can you determine today if you were to explain to a tourist or a student going over there … just from the short experience we've had yesterday and a little bit today what would he or she need to know to recognise the severity of a sign?
Jaxson	I would say just to get a rough image like a nice sign or something that would be the least severe would have words like *Selamat datang* (Welcome) or *terima kasih* (thank you) which are nicer words but something more severe would have words like *jangan* (don't) or *dilarang* (It's forbidden). Yeah, harsher words.
Teacher	What about the use of the subject pronoun like *kamu* (you), *Anda* (formal you), *kami* (exclusive we), *kita* (inclusive we). Um, anyone … now this is broad … but just from what you've seen …
Jaxson	Maybe signs that use *Anda, kamu* are more detailed, might be addressing you personally and would probably mean that they might be nice signs of course this is very general … Something might be the most severe probably would just say, 'Don't do this' and address you specifically yes but there's exceptions …
	[Discussion continues]
Teacher	Perhaps government type messages. Messages that promote certain behaviour that perhaps are not as seen here in public. What about signs like *Apakah bapak sudah pakai kondom hari ini?* (Have you (men) worn a condom today?) Now have you ever seen a sign like that out in the open, say going down King William Street? Have you ever seen a sign like that? No, I haven't either because I'm sure a lot of brakes would go on! Um. *Apakah bapak sudah pakai kondom hari ini* or *Apakah ibu sudah pakai*

	obat hari ini? (Have you (women) taken your pill today?) Have you taken the pill? Because it could go both ways couldn't it? But that leads us to another discussion, doesn't it? That's a different sign isn't it? Generally what could it fit under?
Jaxson	I reckon it could be *diumumkan* (announced) but it's also saying it's not telling you … it's recommended. It's implying it.
Teacher	Yeah. Excellent. That's true. It's a bit like that *Mari kita* (let us) … Going back to that *Apakah bapak* … it doesn't say *Pakailah kondom* (Wear a condom) … maybe there are signs like that around but I haven't found them as yet but if I'm ever back in Indonesia I'll certainly be doing research on this.
Jaxson	It would be a very aggressive sign! I wouldn't like a sign shouting at me, telling me to wear a condom. Like the whole Uncle Sam thing …
Teacher	Actually that's a very good analogy. That's a very good analogy. It gives you an idea of what people think; what they prioritise. So, let's come up with some ideas, some observations of the signs we've looked at. So, what does the language tell us about the culture? And I use this very, very carefully because when you talk about a culture it's never one and I don't think so anyway because as you know Indonesia is an archipelago and it's made up of many, many … and relatively recently it's become a united country so it's made up of many cultures.

(Students choose a public sign text and discuss their observations)

Jaxson	It really reminds me of … you're doing something everybody pitches in … you're doing it for the good of the nation. Fresh, beautiful. Start today …
Mark	It looks like a primary school poster.
Jaxson	Yeah. It does. I can't really describe it but …
Phung	I suppose he's putting rubbish in the bin.
Teacher	Yeah. All … I find that all the posters regarding the city talk about this clean *bersih*. *Jagalah kebersihan* (Take care of cleanliness). Those ways of communicating and who's in control … who has an influence on society. Who do you think …?
Jaxson	Maybe the local council. It's put up by local council or government.

Here, the teacher directs students' attention to the ways in which the target language functions in creating meaning as her starting point: 'What about the use of the language?' Language is immediately positioned as significant and potentially powerful. The teacher refers to the potential emotional impact of language on people, the 'severity of a sign', and this is echoed by students: 'a rough image', 'a nice sign', 'the least severe', and 'harsher words'. There is a shared understanding, expressed by the students themselves, that language can be used deliberately to create an emotional effect, 'addressing you personally' and 'the most severe', and therefore meaning is represented as not simply communicated by language but constructed as interpersonal practice. The discourse being created here is that language is a way of rendering relationships between participants in the communication. It can position, frame and represent relationships between people, and in this way language shapes and reflects culture.

The teacher narrows the focus to a specific example, 'What about signs like …?', in order to show how language and culture are operating together to create a particular text. She then detaches from the specific and shifts to more general principles by making a statement that connects language and people's behaviour: 'messages that promote certain behaviour'. The way in which the teacher talks about language and culture provides a representation for students that enables them to notice this interconnection of language and social action and explore it in their own language and culture: 'Now have you ever seen a sign like that…?'. The teacher moves the students' reflection between the specific and the abstract, drawing attention to specific examples developing a metalanguage and framing for considering the relationship itself. When a student observes that modifying the linguistic structure (from a question to an imperative) impacts on the emotional content of a sign and makes an analogy to military recruitment posters, the teacher praises his interpretation and highlights the more abstract idea that 'it gives you an idea of what people think'. Here language becomes a vehicle for seeing deeper social and cultural information. The teacher creates a *leitmotiv* of the relationship between language and culture throughout the interaction, constantly drawing attention to it: 'What does the language tell us about the culture…?'. At one point, she qualifies the term 'the culture', and cautions students to be mindful of diversity within a national culture — 'I use this very, very carefully' — reflecting the provisional nature of conclusions about culture drawn through such experiential practices. Culture is represented as multidimensional, 'many, many'.

The teacher mediates the idea that language and culture are integrally related in a number of ways. She explicitly states integration as the nature of the relationship. She problematises language in text, encouraging interpretation and questioning meanings. In addition, the teacher invites students to notice the integration of their own language and culture, as a way of making the strange familiar and the familiar strange (Byram, Girbkova & Starkey 2002). As a result, she is modelling ways to understand language and culture as well as developing students' skills in mediating these concepts for themselves. The practice of deconstructing authentic Indonesian texts positions students as analysts and invites them to build their own connections between their existing and their new linguistic and cultural frameworks.

Problematising language

An intercultural orientation draws into focus the context dependent nature of language and highlights the intrapersonal dimension of meaning making across languages and cultures. The following extract shows how an intercultural perspective influences the teacher's explanation as she contextualises and personalises the response to a student's question.

Extract 3

Jodie	Miss, what's the word for 'singlet'?
Teacher	I think it's just a *baju kaus*. The reason I don't … that I've got to really think about that is because a singlet in Indonesia is not something you'd walk around in. It would be a bit …
Jodie	But what would you say for it then?
Teacher	Guys, that's another really good question. See this picture here OK some things when you translate … when you ask me something I have to think long and hard about it. It was like the woollen jumper … *baju wol* … you can say … but you really don't very often walk around Indonesia in a big woolly jumper because it's too hot. This is another classic example … you would not walk around Indonesia like this because you wouldn't want to send … If you were in Bali in Kuta Beach and there's hundreds of tourists sitting around you may choose to be dressed a bit more what I would call ultra informal in Indonesia OK. And if you're in the privacy of your own home and there was no-one else around then possibly but you wouldn't want to send this message to an Indonesian by walking around like this and why wouldn't you?
Charlotte	Like in Hong Kong I walked around in shorts and then everyone looked at me funny.
Teacher	And what … then what message do you think you were sending?

Charlotte		Um, I'm a prostitute?
Teacher		Well, possibly that you're fairly carefree with your values. And why?
Charlotte		Um, because they don't wear shorts.
Teacher		When you go to Indonesia you've got to think about that and think about if you're getting a certain reaction because of your appearance and you're not happy with that reaction then what do you need to do?
Charlotte		Don't go outside in shorts.
Teacher		Yeah, because you're actually sort of … and I'm not saying if I was in Indo I'd never wear something like that but I would never walk outside in Indonesia … because the message I'm sending is that this really isn't … an Indonesian person, a male in Indonesia or even a female, would be quite embarrassed about where to look because you're revealing … that's like you're in Australia coming to school in a top where every time … like if I was a teacher and I leaned over and every time you saw everything, you wouldn't really know where to look. That's the kind of message you're sending. OK. So, that's why I have trouble translating this because in a way it is a *baju kaus* because I don't think they've got a special word for 'tank top' or loose top. To an Indonesian it is probably like wearing a bra.

What initially appears to be unproblematic (a word for word equivalence in meaning, i.e. singlet = *baju kaus*) on reflection by the teacher becomes an opportunity to problematise the relationship between language and culture. The word 'singlet' becomes an instance for reflection on the complexities of the relationship between language, culture and meaning, and she declares, 'I've got to really think about that', 'I have to think long and hard', positioning herself as an analyst of language and culture as part of her own mediation of these to her students. The emphasis is on the inappropriateness of using a word that does not have an equivalent sensibility or usage in an Indonesian context. The teacher uses the opportunity to explore how, even at an individual word level, meaning does not translate directly due to the culturally constructed nature of language: 'some things when you translate…'. She represents meaning as linguistically and culturally situated, and she models the practice of critical reflection and interrogation of meaning.

Another way in which this teacher builds connections is through her creation of scenarios in which students are imagined participants. She draws students' attention to an image from a magazine, 'See this picture here', and offers her view:

'you would not walk around Indonesia like this'. She is signalling an alternative cultural perspective on modesty and she then positions students as participants: "if you were in Bali ... you may choose to be dressed ... ultra informal'. She then contrasts this with another scenario, 'in the privacy of your own home'. She is constructing an imagined world where students can project what it may be like to participate in another cultural context. She is also demonstrating through these scenarios that cultural appropriateness is context-dependent and that as mediators of languages and cultures, students need to develop sensitivity to context. The teacher follows her explanation with a question in order to confirm students' understanding of her point: 'why wouldn't you [walk around in a singlet]?' She is depicting an alternative worldview for her students, and modelling the need to navigate linguistic and cultural difference sensitively.

The teacher in this dialogue is moving between students' familiar culture and the unknown culture, inviting them to move into the new world whilst bringing awareness of the potential impact of their own cultural frame on an Indonesian one.

To construct a bridge between students' existing and new cultural perspectives, the teacher reinforces the idea that language is culturally determined and context dependent. She supports students' understanding by offering an analogy drawn from their own cultural frame, 'if ... I leaned over and every time you saw everything' and in this way is scaffolding by using equivalent notions and behaviours. She restates the inadequacy of word-for-word translation, 'that's why I have trouble translating this ... I don't think they've got a special word for "tank top"', highlighting the need to navigate meaning beyond the linguistic code. She emphasises that language may have equivalent words but not necessarily equivalent meanings. Through problematising meaning at the level of a word, the teacher models how, as language students and users, students need to make meaning against their existing and their new linguistic and cultural frames.

Expressing personal identity

A further way in which teachers build bridges for and with students is to use the target language as a vehicle through which students can express their personal identity. That is, the target language becomes a tool for mediating one's sense of self.

Extract 4

Teacher   *Mengapa Jaxson tertarik pada menjadi ahli hukum? Karena banyak tugas...* (Why do you want to become a lawyer? Because they have lots to do...)

Jaxson	*Ya. Banyak tahun saya suka dan saya selalu pikir bahwa ahli hukum pekerjaan yang bagus untuk saya.* (Yes. For a long time I have liked it and have always thought that being a lawyer would be a good job for me.)
Teacher	*Uang gajinya penting untuk Jaxson atau tidak?* (Was the money an important thing for you or not?)
Jaxson	*Tidak. Karena pada tahun awal ahli hukum, gajinya tidak bagus.* (No. Because at first lawyers' salaries are not that good.)
Teacher	*Bagaimana agama tradisional mempengaruhi mungkin pilihan karir Jaxson atau mungkin tidak ada hubungan?* (How has religion affected your choice of career or maybe there isn't a connection?)
Jaxson	*Ya. Agama mempengaruhi banyak aspek dari kehidupan saya. Putusan dan perspektif …* (Yes. Religion affects many aspects of my life. My decisions and my perspective …)
Teacher	*Perspektif terhadap apa?* (Your perspective towards what?)
Jaxson	*Perspektif terhadap ahli hukum.* (Towards being a lawyer.)
Teacher	*Dan perspektif terhadap keadilan?* (And towards justice?)
Jaxson	*Ya. Yesus mengajar saya banyak pelajaran.* (Yes. Jesus has taught me many lessons.)
Teacher	*Dan Edmund Rice juga?* (And Edmund Rice too?)
Jaxson	*Ya.* (Yes.)

This exchange follows a formal oral presentation task in which students used Indonesian to describe significant symbols or influences in their lives. In this case, the student, Jaxson, presents his family, education and interest in music as the major influences in his life. There is a smooth transition from the formal presentation, in the target language, to the informal discussion following the teacher's question, '*Mengapa Jaxson tertarik pada menjadi ahli hukum?*' (Why do you want to become a lawyer?) The teacher delves further into Jaxson's reasons by playing devil's advocate, '*Karena banyak tugas …*' (They have lots to do) and prompting him to move deeper into his personal perspective. She forms a question based on her assumption, 'Was the money an important thing for you or not?' and then responds to his answer with a shift in focus to religious values. At each exchange, the teacher responds and creates an additional question that requires more insight into the student's perspective. Her questioning processes assist him to articulate his interpretation of his own cultural frame of reference. She is creating a space in which the student becomes a participant in the new language and its culture using them to express his own reality.

The exchange reflects how the teacher creates a culture of language learning in which the target language is a legitimate medium for students to express their own ideas and identities. This is a spontaneous discussion, albeit led by the teacher, with an interest in exploring the student's identity and building relationships; they are jointly constructing an intercultural experience, in which the student's own personalised culture represents the focus of the discussion. There is no predefined grammatical point or structure being practised and no correction or stepping out of the target language to instruct or make a point. The questions are exploratory, including 'Why …?', 'How has religion affected your choice …?', 'Your perspective towards what?', reflecting the importance of the student's identity and not his language use. At this moment, the student is more than a student learning Indonesian; he is an intercultural language user, articulating his own views, in his own context, and with Indonesian as part of his own linguistic make-up. The teacher has created an opportunity in which the student uses Indonesian as part of who he is. Moreover, the extract reveals how the teacher has created an opportunity for the student to mediate himself to others through the target language. The teacher has here decoupled the target language from any construction of Indonesia and Indonesians only, and in doing so she has positioned the student as an insider, a participant in this alternative linguistic and cultural world. She has helped the student build his own bridge and move between the worlds on both sides.

Conclusion

The chosen extracts show the ways in which teachers of languages build bridges for and with students, from an intercultural language learning perspective. The teachers construct relationships between students' existing languages and cultures and the target culture and its language. They offer representations of the target language and culture, by selecting and depicting particular texts and images and through their own talk with students. In addition, the teachers create opportunities for students to engage in critical analysis of target language texts, deconstructing the language-culture relationship in a process of interpreting meaning. These teachers successfully make connections between students' own language and culture and those of the target community, requiring students to decentre, compare and abstract from the particular to general concepts of language and culture. Furthermore, students are invited to be participants in otherness through the teachers' constructions of imagined worlds and scenarios, enriched with examples from their own experiences as models of ways to operate from an intercultural perspective. Through their own personal facility in intercultural dialogue, the teachers here represent ways to construct bridges and ways to move across bridges that span alternative linguistic and cultural worlds.

The act of building bridges through language teaching and learning involves teachers working for students in designing interculturally focused programs, mediating cultures and designing specialised learning experiences. Teachers make the intercultural present for students through an engagement that makes language, culture and their relationship a visible and sustained focus. This not only involves presentation of language and culture to students but also involves selected representation of these. That is, the teacher, through the act of teaching, makes particular understandings of language and culture available for students and opens them up for student critique. Language teaching from an intercultural perspective is not simply a perspective adopted by a teacher but one that frames how language and culture can be understood and integrated into learning. A view which is founded on an understanding of both as elements in meaning making, therefore, not only presents a particular version of language and culture for learning but also develops a representation of what these broad concepts may mean and how they can be understood, developed and used. Teachers also provide for students particular experiences that involve treating language use, whether written or spoken, productive or receptive, as opportunities for reflection on how language can be made meaningful, and what needs to be done to discover meaning in language. Finally, as we have seen in these extracts, teachers act as mediators of language and culture for students. That is, teachers have a role in interpreting the other for students and in developing their capacity for interpretation. As mediators, therefore, teachers work in multiple ways. They make sense of language and culture for the learner because they have already had to make sense of it for themselves as part of their own intercultural engagement, and they provide scaffolded assistance for students to become mediators themselves as they engage with a new language and culture.

An intercultural perspective also involves teachers in working with students in dialogue, personalising learning opportunities, drawing on students' identities, and positioning them in relation to the language and culture they are learning. Teachers and students together work to analyse the meanings made present through language in collaborative ways. Meaning is always situated so the process of teaching meaning (Kramsch 2008a) needs to recognise that meanings are created and personal, and that learners' interpretations themselves are not only valid but also indispensible to the learning process. Language learning builds bridges between cultures on the basis of personalised interpretation understanding rather than through the transmission of 'correct' and often stereotyped interpretations. Teachers therefore work with students to elicit, clarify and question interpretations rather than to provide them. Such work recognises the necessity of integrating the students' lived realities into the process of learning about others, as a pre-requisite for this learning. In working with students, therefore, teachers are engaging with their students in the processes of mediation to create new ideas and understandings about language and culture and their interrelationship.

If language education is to achieve the goals of intercultural understanding that it sets for itself, it is important that the intercultural takes a central place in practice. This requires a move to ways of teaching and learning that engage teachers and learners in the processes of meaning-making and interpretation. In this paper we have examined some of the ways that teachers have engaged with such a focus in their teaching and pointed to ways in which language education can achieve its intercultural goals.

Notes

[1] In these Extracts, an ellipsis indicates a pause, the curved brackets indicate translation and the square brackets indicate explanation of context (i.e. not part of spoken interaction).

References

Beacco, J-C 2000, *Les dimensions culturelles des enseignements de langue*, Hachette, Paris.

Byram, M 1988, 'Foreign language education and cultural studies', *Language, Culture and Curriculum*, vol. 1, pp. 15–31.

Byram, M 1989, *Cultural studies in foreign language education*, Multilingual Matters, Clevedon, UK.

Byram, M 1991, 'Teaching culture and language: An integrated model', in *Mediating languages and cultures*, ed D Buttjes & M Byram, Multilingual Matters, Clevedon, UK, pp. 17–30.

Byram, M 2002, 'On being 'bicultural' and 'intercultural'', in G Alred, M Byram & MP Fleming (eds), *Intercultural experience and education*, Multilingual Matters, Clevedon, UK, pp. 50–66.

Byram, M, Gribkova, B & Starkey, H 2002, *Developing the intercultural dimension in language teaching: A practical introduction for teachers*, Council of Europe, Strasbourg.

Byram, M & Morgan, C 1994, *Teaching and learning language and culture*,

Multilingual Matters, Clevedon, UK.

Carey, JW 1989, *Communication as culture: essays on media and society*, Routledge, New York and London.

Carr, J 1999, 'From 'sympathetic' to 'dialogic' imagination: cultural study in the foreign language classroom', in J Lo Bianco, AJ Liddicoat & C Crozet (eds), *Striving for the third place: intercultural competence through language education*, Melbourne, Vic, Language Australia, pp. 103–112.

Crozet, C 2003, 'A conceptual framework to help teachers identify where culture is located in language use', in J Lo Bianco & C Crozet (eds), *Teaching invisible culture: classroom practice and theory*, Language Australia, Melbourne, Vic, pp. 39–49.

Crozet, C & Liddicoat, AJ 1999, 'The challenge of intercultural language teaching: engaging with culture in the classroom', in J Lo Bianco, AJ Liddicoat & C Crozet (eds), *Striving for the third place: intercultural competence through language education*, Language Australia, Canberra, ACT, pp. 113–126.

Davies, A 2005, *A glossary of applied linguistics*, Edinburgh University Press, Edinburgh.

Eckert, P & Mcconnell-Ginet, S 1992, 'Think practically and look locally: language and gender as community-based practice', *Annual Review of Anthropology*, vol. 21, pp. 461–490.

Eisenchlas, S 2009, 'Conceptualising "communication" in second language acquisition', *Australian Journal of Linguistics*, vol. 29, pp. 45–58.

Fitzgerald, H 2002, *How different are we? Spoken discourse in intercultural communication*, Multilingual Matters, Clevedon, UK.

Gohard-Radenkovic, A, Lussier, D, Penz, H & Zarate, G 2004, 'La médiation culturelle en didactique des langues comme processus', in G Zarate, A Gohard-Radenkovic, D Lussier & H Penz (eds), *La médiation culturelle et didactique des langues*, Council of Europe Publishing, Strasbourg, pp. 225–238.

Harris, R 2003, 'On redefining linguistics', in HG Davis & TJ Taylor (eds), *Rethinking linguistics*, Routledge, London, pp. 17–68.

Haugh, M & Liddicoat, AJ 2009, 'Examining conceptualisations of communication,' *Australian Journal of Linguistics*, vol. 29, pp. 1–10.

Heath, SB 1986, *Beyond language: social and cultural factors in schooling language minority students*, California State Department of Education, Sacramento, CA.

Holmes, J & Meyerhoff, M 1999, 'The community of practice: theories and methodologies in language and gender research', *Language in Society*, vol. 28, pp. 173–183.

Jayasuriya, K 1990, *The problematic of culture and identity in cross-cultural theorising*, Department of Social Work and Social Administration, University of Western

Australia, Nedlands, WA.

Jayasuriya, L 1990, 'The problematic of culture and identitiy in cross-cultural theorising', in M Clare & L Jayasuriya (eds), *Issues in Cross-Cultural Practice*, University of Western Australia, Nedlands, WA.

Kasper, G 2006, 'Speech acts in interaction: towards discursive pragmatics', in K Bardovi-Harlig, C Félix-Brasdefer & A Omar (eds), *Pragmatics and language learning*, National Foreign Language Resource Center, University of Hawai'i at Manoa, Honolulu, pp. 281–314.

Kern, R & Liddicoat, AJ 2008, 'De l'apprenant au locuteur/acteur', in G Zarate, D Lévy & C Kramsch (eds), *Précis de plurilinguisme et du pluriculturalisme*, Éditions des archives contemporaines, Paris, pp. 27–65.

Kohler, M 2010, 'Intercultural language teaching and learning: policy and practice', in AJ Liddicoat & A Scarino (eds), *Languages in Australian education: problems, prospects and future directions*, Cambridge Scholars, Newcastle upon Tyne, pp. 179–192.

Kohler, M & Mahnken, P 2010, *The Current State of Indonesian Language Education in Australian schools*, Department of Education, Employment and Workplace Relations, Canberra.

Kramsch, C 1993a, *Context and culture in language education*, Oxford University Press, Oxford.

Kramsch, C 1993b, 'Language study as border study: experiencing difference', *European Journal of Education*, vol. 28, pp. 349–358.

Kramsch, C 1994, 'Foreign languages for a global age', *ADFL Bulletin*, vol. 25, pp. 5–12.

Kramsch, C 1995a, 'The cultural component of language teaching', *Language, Culture and Curriculum*, vol. 8, pp. 83–92.

Kramsch, C 1995b, 'Introduction: making meaning visible', in C Kramsch (ed.), *Redefining the boundaries of language study*, Heinle and Heinle, Boston.

Kramsch, C 1999, 'The privilege of the intercultural speaker', in M Byram & M Fleming (eds), *Language learning in intercultural perspective: approaches through drama and ethnography*, Cambridge University Press, Cambridge, pp. 16–31.

Kramsch, C 2006, 'The multilingual subject', *International Journal of Applied Linguistics*, vol. 16, pp. 97–110.

Kramsch, C 2008a, 'Ecological perspectives on foreign language education', *Language Teaching*, vol. 41, pp. 389–408.

Kramsch, C 2008b, 'Voix et contrevoix: l'expression de soi à travers la langue de l'autre', in G Zarate, D Lévy & C Kramsch (eds), *Précis de plurilinguisme et du pluriculturalisme,* Paris, Éditions des archives contemporaines, pp. 35–38.

Kramsch, C & Nolden, T 1994, 'Redefining literacy in a foreign language', *Die*

Unterrichtspraxis, vol. 27, pp. 28–35.

Levine, DR & Adelman, MB 2002, *Beyond language: cross-cultural communication*, Prentice Hall, Upper Saddle River, NJ.

Liddicoat, AJ 1997, 'Everyday speech as culture: implications for language teaching', in AJ Liddicoat & C Crozet (eds), *Teaching language, teaching culture*, Applied Linguistics Association of Australia, Canberra, ACT, pp. 55–70.

Liddicoat, AJ 2002, 'Static and dynamic views of culture and intercultural language acquisition', *Babel*, vol. 36, pp. 4–11, 37.

Liddicoat, AJ 2005a, 'Culture for language learning in Australian language-in-education policy,' *Australian Review of Applied Linguistics*, vol. 28, pp. 1–28.

Liddicoat, AJ 2005b, 'Teaching languages for intercultural communication', in D Cunningham & A Hatoss (eds), *An international perspective on language policies, practices and proficiencies*, Editura Funda iei Academice Axis & Fédération Internationale des Professeurs de Langues Vivantes, Belgrave, Vic, pp. 201–214.

Liddicoat, AJ 2008, 'Pedagogical practice for integrating the intercultural in language teaching and learning', *Japanese Studies*, vol. 28, pp. 277–290.

Liddicoat, AJ 2009, 'Communication as culturally contexted practice: a view from intercultural communication', *Australian Journal of Linguistics*, vol. 29, pp. 115–133.

Liddicoat, AJ & Curnow, TJ 2003, 'Language descriptions', in *Handbook of applied linguistics*, ed A Davies & C Elder, Oxford, Blackwell, pp. 25–53.

Liddicoat, AJ, Papademetre, L, Scarino, A & Kohler, M 2003, *Report on intercultural language learning*, DEST, Canberra, ACT.

Liddicoat, AJ & Scarino, A 2010, 'Eliciting the intercultural in foreign language education', in A Paran & L Sercu (eds), *Testing the untestable in foreign language education*, Multilingual Matters, Clevedon, UK, pp. 52–73.

Norton, B 2000, *Identity and language learning: gender, ethnicity and educational change*, Longman, London.

Paige, RM, Jorstad, H, Siaya, L, Klein, F & Colby, J 1999, 'Culture learning in language education: a review of the literature', in RM Paige, DL Lange & YA Yeshova (eds), *Culture as the core: integrating culture into the language curriculum*, University of Minnesota, Minneapolis, MN, pp. 47–113.

Papademetre, L 2000, 'Developing pathways for conceptualising the integration of culture-and-language', in AJ Liddicoat & C Crozet (eds), *Teaching languages, teaching cultures*, Language Australia, Melbourne, Vic, pp. 141–149.

Papademetre, L & Scarino, A 2000, *Integrating culture learning in the language classroom: a multi-perspective conceptual journey for teachers*, Language Australia, Melbourne, Vic.

Sacks, H 1975, 'Everyone has to lie', in M Sounches & BG Blount (eds), *Sociocultural dimensions of language use*. Multilingual Matters, Clevedon, UK, pp. 57–80.

Sacks, H 1984, 'On doing "being ordinary"', in JM Atkinson & J Heritage (eds), *Structures of social interaction*, Cambridge University Press, Cambridge, pp. 413–429.

Saussure, F 1916, *Cours de linguistique générale*, Payot, Paris.

Shohamy, E 2007, *Language policy: hidden agendas and new approaches*, Routledge, London & New York.

Tajfel, H & Turner, JC 1986, 'The social identity theory of intergroup behaviour', in WG Austin & S Worchel, *The social psychology of intergroup relations*, Nelson-Hall, Chicago, IL, pp. 220–237.

Thomas, J 1983, 'Cross-cultural pragmatic failure', *Applied Linguistics*, vol. 4, pp. 91–112.

Thomas, J 1984, 'Cross cultural discourse as unequal encounter: towards a pragmatic analysis', *Applied Linguistics*, vol. 5, pp. 226–235.

Toyota, T 1988, '日本語教育における日本事情 [Japanese way of life in Japanese language education]', 日本語教育 [*Japanese Language Education*], vol. 63, pp. 16–29.

Zarate, G 1983, 'Objectiver le rapport culture maternelle/culture étrangère', *Le français dans le monde*, vol. 181, pp. 34–39.

5

A Study Skills Action Plan: Integrating self-regulated learning in a diverse higher education context[1]

Kayoko Enomoto

Introduction

In recent years, there has been a dramatic increase in international student enrolments in language programs in Australian universities, accelerating the diversity of the language student cohort in the classroom. This increasing student diversity presents many challenges for language lecturers, necessitating both a review of pedagogical strategies and new engagement in innovative teaching practices to enhance learning for all students. As this chapter will show, this is a particularly pressing issue in the context of the first-year Japanese course at an Australian research-intensive university.

Japanese 1A is a beginners' course for non-native speakers with no or little previous knowledge of Japanese. Since 2008, the student numbers in this course have more than doubled (n=120, 2008; n=190, 2009; n=260, 2010) and in 2010 it became the largest foreign language course at the University. In Semester 1, 2010, this student cohort was diverse in terms of cultural, linguistic and disciplinary backgrounds. Around 60 per cent were international students from a variety of cultures and first language backgrounds, and 90 per cent of them were enrolled in various non-Arts degrees.[2]

Such a unique student group inevitably has profound implications for pedagogy in this large first-year course. It is imperative to create and deliver learning environments where all students feel equally able to succeed both in and beyond their first year at university. One way to create such an environment that maximizes each student's chance of success is through curriculum revisions that integrate study skills development into the curriculum of the mainstream courses/subjects that students are studying for their degree (DEEWR 2008; Wingate 2006). Furthermore, course curriculum is one common platform that all students do share and that, therefore, can be effectively used to influence the learning process of individual students. Such an integrated approach to developing generic academic/study skills leads to high quality learning (Enomoto 2011) and a high degree of equity, mitigating the likelihood that student success is left to chance.

In the first-year Japanese course, it was identified that study skills development could be enhanced through the educational process known as 'self-regulated learning' (SRL) (Zimmerman & Schunk 2001). As a result, a new pedagogical initiative, a feedback-based Study Skills Action Plan (SSAP) was developed, embedded and integrated systematically into the first-year language curriculum, actively integrating two new focuses for learning: 1) the process of understanding and using feedback, and 2) opportunities to practise regulating aspects of learning and to reflect upon that practice. Thus, the feedback-based SSAP was piloted and evaluated as a key component of the first-year Japanese course. A research project then examined the effectiveness of SSAPs for enhancing students' proactive use of feedback, and for developing their study skills through SRL.

This project was framed not only to investigate the impact of integrating study skills through SRL, but also to contribute to the understanding of students' perceptions of learning and of their learning process, which ultimately informs pedagogy. It was also aimed that this feedback-based SSAP would offer pragmatic value and potentially broader applications for pedagogy beyond this Japanese course and into other contexts in higher education. In order to contextualise the goals of the project, this chapter will first review relevant scholarship on the key issues of self-regulated learning and 'deep' and 'surface' approaches to learning, with particular focus on students' study skills development, and their understanding and use of feedback. It will then outline the study objectives and methods before presenting the research findings and the implications those findings have for the integration of study skills action planning into assessable curriculum in higher education.

Self-regulated learning

Many studies on first-year experience report that facilitating students' course engagement is crucial for successful completion of subsequent studies at university, as it improves student retention, success and learning outcomes (Krause & Coates 2008; Krause, Hartley, James & McInnis 2005; McInnis, James & Hartley 2000). Other studies (Crosling, Heagney & Thomas 2009; Long, Ferrier & Heagney 2006) also point out that one reason why students drop out of university is due to insufficient preparation and readiness for higher education. These findings lend support to the hypothesis that, given learning environments where students' course engagement and study skills development are specifically targeted and facilitated, it is possible for students to take control of their learning and improve their chances of succeeding at university.

Similarly, some studies show (Butler & Winne 1995; Schunk & Zimmerman 1994; Zimmerman & Schunk 2001) that SRL can enhance students' course engagement and study skills development, with SRL defined as:

> an active, constructive process whereby learners set goals for their learning and then attempt to monitor, regulate and control their cognition, motivation, and behavior, guided and constrained by their goals and the contextual features in the environment. (Pintrich 2000, p. 453)

In other words, SRL involves learners' regulation not only of their cognition, but also their behaviour and motivation, according to their self-set goals. Importantly, self-regulation refers to the degree to which students can regulate aspects of their thinking, behaviour and motivation while they are learning (Pintrich & Zusho 2002). Therefore, self-regulation models recognise that individual students are already assessing their own performance to varying degrees, whilst generating their own self-feedback.

To build upon this existing ability in students, Nicol and MacFlane-Dick (2006) propose two effective ways to facilitate and develop students' self-regulation. One is through effective feedback practice, because, when it is effective, feedback can help develop students' sense of control over their own learning. The other is through provision of opportunities for students to practise regulating aspects of their learning and to reflect upon that practice. Drawing upon these findings, in order to facilitate the development of SRL, we integrated both these strategies into the design and implementation of specially targeted SSAPs, forming a cycle of feedback-based active planning (Figure 1). The Methods section discusses this further.

Promoting deep learning through SSAP

It was important in the SSAP design to create contexts that facilitate students' adoption of 'deep' learning methods and processing strategies to develop long-term quality learning outcomes. The concept of a deep approach to learning is framed within Biggs's early 3-P model of learning (1989), which conceptualises the learning process in terms of three sets of variables: the learning environments (Presage), students' approaches to learning (Process), and learning outcomes (Product). Within this model, the approach that students use to process their academic tasks is operated during the Process phase and can be broadly conceptualized as a deep or surface approach (Entwistle 1991; 2009).

A deep approach to learning is described as striving for improved understanding by applying and comparing ideas, involving an intention to understand the material to be learnt, using such strategies as reading widely and relating parts to a whole (Lizzio, Wilson & Simons 2002). In contrast, a surface approach to learning involves an intention to reproduce the material to be learnt, using reproductive strategies, such as rote learning with little attempt to integrate information (Lizzio et al. 2002). The following excerpts from students' personal reflective commentaries exemplify a deeper strategy for learning vocabulary in Japanese 1A:

- Another study method that I found very useful was writing out lists of vocabulary and arranging them by topic [=relating parts to a whole]. I found this arrangement good, as it allowed me to have a systematic way of remembering words.
- I have my own way to remember vocabulary. Firstly, I try to write those words on paper times and times [=rote learning]; secondly, I put those words into sentences [=integration of new information]. It's easier to remember the meaning of words this way.

According to Biggs (1999), students with developed academic skills come to class with relevant background knowledge. Because they have previewed for that class, they come with questions they want answered in that class, using a deep approach to learning. On the other hand, students with less developed academic skills come to class with limited background knowledge and with no questions to ask. This is because they do not preview the material, nor automatically review to consolidate or integrate information, thus often adopting a surface approach to learning to prepare for assessments (Biggs 1999). In summary, students who are at various stages of an academic skills development continuum, process new information and academic tasks differently from each other, as they exercise varying degrees of conceptual involvement in their approaches to learning.

Importantly, previous studies have argued that deep/surface approaches to learning are not inherent cognitive attributes of those students, but are elicited and shaped by particular contexts/situations that those students perceive and experience as individuals (Wilson, Lizzio & Ramsden 1997; Biggs 1999). Yet, with regard to the assumed 3-P relationships between learning environment, learning approaches and learning outcomes, Haggis (2003) has critiqued such a model for being a broad description of élite goals, which do not relate to the reality of many students. Similarly, Malcolm & Zukas (2001) have also critiqued the dominance of psychological, quantitative approaches for examining such relationships.[3]

Nevertheless, researchers have usefully identified learning environments that could or could not help learners to develop a deeper approach. For example, earlier studies by Trigwell and Prosser (1991a; 1991b) found that perceptions of good teaching were associated with both surface and deep approaches to learning. Further, Lizzio et al. (2002) ascertained that student perceptions of having clear goals and good teaching led to a deep approach, whereas Kember and Leung (1998) found that a perception of a heavy workload was associated with a surface approach. Furthermore, Wilson and Fowler (2005) reported that students who were typically deep in their approach to learning were consistent in their approaches across two contrasting learning environments (lectures/tutorials vs projects/learning groups), but that students who typically used surface approaches could be influenced to shift to deeper processing strategies.

Therefore, the challenge has been to ascertain how we can encourage students with less well-developed deep academic skills to adopt deeper processing strategies to achieve long-term learning outcomes. As Biggs (1999, p. 2) states,

> Good teaching is getting most students to use the higher cognitive level processes … The problem is to describe a technology of teaching that maximizes the chances of engaging students' learning processes in this way.

To respond to this challenge in the Japanese language-teaching context, we designed the feedback-based SSAP to encourage students to experiment with and practise deep learning methods and processing strategies.

Using an Action Plan to develop study skills

Despite the large body of literature on developing generic study skills and learning strategies in higher education (Leggett et al. 2004; Leveson 2000; Sumison & Goodfellow 2004), few studies examine the use of SSAPs or their equivalents to enhance study skills, and none describe the use of SSAPs in university language teaching. Discussions on the use of action plans, or their equivalents, appear in only a limited number of studies. For example, Cheek and Campbell (1994) proposed that, to help students use what they learn, an action plan exercise can be utilised, and such an exercise must reflect individual rather than group needs. In a problem-based learning context, Connell (2003) adopted an action plan exercise as one of the core learning strategies. Her study used an action plan form to help new students apply what they had learned during an orientation workshop, so students could produce a concrete and practical personalised plan of action.

More recently, using a small sample of 15 students, Selby (2007) piloted the use of Action Planning Statements (APS) to develop medical students' clinical skills. After the students had examined one Standardised Patient, they completed five statements (for example, 'One thing I am going to do is…', 'In future I am not going to…', 'One idea I am taking away is…'). While acknowledging the need for further research to evaluate the place of APS in developing students' clinical skills, the study reported that 'effectiveness of teaching' significantly increased with the use of such APS in tutorials. However, it was inconclusive as to whether or not APS improved the students' learning. One reason for these inconclusive results could be due to a lack of active integration of the process of understanding and using feedback into the APS. In light of this gap, the current project intended that its findings shed light on the potential pragmatic value of actively integrating the process of feedback into the action plan.

Understanding and using feedback

The importance of providing effective feedback is long established. At its best, feedback can positively influence learning experience, playing a positive role in developing, improving, and directing student learning, and sustaining motivation (Duncan 2007; Hounsell et al. 2008; Warner 2010). Timeliness of feedback is central to its success in that students need to have sufficient time both to understand and to act upon it (Crisp 2007; Race 2001). Apart from a minority of students who appear to take little notice of feedback, there are those who do not understand it, and those who understand it but do not know how to use it strategically to prepare for subsequent assessments (Race 2001). Therefore, to facilitate SRL, it is crucial to make feedback understandable and usable for students, enabling them to translate their understanding of responses into concrete action.

Understanding feedback necessarily involves students' ability to perceive the existence of a gap between their current and their desired level of knowledge, understanding, or skills, as well as their ability to identify the action/s they can take to lessen that gap (Furnborough & Truman 2009). However, as Furnborough and Truman (2009) point out, student perception of how teacher feedback may be interpreted and used to identify and bridge gaps remains relatively under-researched. This is particularly true for the paucity of studies dealing with students of non-English languages, and with students at a beginner level.

Likewise, there has been little exploration of best practice feedback strategies for a culturally and linguistically diverse cohort, mostly consisting of international students (Roberts 2009). According to Johnson (2008), the international students in her survey reported that they often did not understand why they had received a particular grade, largely because they received insufficient teacher feedback, especially feedback they could use for subsequent assessments. Indeed, students' positive or negative perceptions of teacher feedback necessarily influence this issue of understanding. This is because such perceptions can determine to what extent a student will actually exploit that feedback, or monitor and evaluate their progress to sustain motivation. To be effective, teacher input must be perceived positively and interpreted as part of an ultimately successful learning process in the first place.

In the context of the first-year Japanese course, because of the cultural diversity therein, some students' initial reactions to feedback revealed that teacher feedback could be interpreted very differently. For example, the following unsolicited emails from two students of non-Australian cultural backgrounds show marked differences in perceptions of teacher feedback.[4] They wrote to the course coordinator after receiving their first teacher feedback (a personalised feedback form filled in by their tutor) on their performance in the first formative test:

- I am so sorry i got a bad mark on the first test ... This is the first [sic] I was nervous to have the test and i will do my best to study Japanese and relax when am [sic] testing. (Thursday, 22 April 2010 9:27 PM)
- Enomoto-sensei ... so much work to do, but I will do my best to work hard, because I don't want to disappoint you and Hayashi-sensei [=the student's tutor]. (Saturday, 24 April 2010 12:55 PM)

No such messages had been received in previous Japanese 1A courses in which no personalised feedback forms had been provided to individual students. The first student apologises to the teacher for getting a bad mark and the second student does not want to disappoint the teachers. These responses to feedback could suggest that these students saw the teacher feedback as a sign of their failure to meet teachers' expectations, and such negative interpretations might prevent them from fully utilising feedback in subsequent learning.

Thus, to investigate the effectiveness of SSAPs for enhancing students' proactive use of feedback, and for developing their study skills through SRL, this project addresses the following research objectives:

i. to examine the effect of feedback-based SSAPs on students' understanding and use of teacher feedback

ii. to examine the effect of feedback-based SSAPs on students' study skills development through SRL

iii. to examine whether students would experiment with and practise deeper learning methods and strategies through the feedback-based SSAP exercises.

In addressing these objectives, the present analysis uses a combination of qualitative and quantitative evaluations. This is to determine not only whether the SSAP was effective, but, if so, what actually happened in the process. This process-focused approach is concerned with students' perceptions of how they were learning and, thus, enables us to explore learning processes, which quantitative acquisition/ product data (for example, test scores and final grades) alone cannot address. On this point, second language acquisition researchers have long been aware of such limits of product research:

> Product research sets out to answer questions about the effectiveness, reflected in achievement scores of one program (approach or 'treatment') ... [R]esearchers are required to be as process-oriented in their evaluations as possible, that is, to find out what actually transpires ... under each treatment ... [T]here is a need for some balance. (Lambert 1991, p. 59)

Methods
Participants

A total of 92 students in Japanese 1B (J1B) in 2009 and 238 students in Japanese 1A (J1A) in 2010 participated in the project at The University of Adelaide.[5] In J1A, around 60 per cent of the participants were international students from a variety of cultures and countries: China, Korea, Singapore, Malaysia, USA, Canada, France and South Africa. This diversity was also reflected in the fact that 57 per cent spoke English as an Additional Language (EAL), with the majority being Chinese speakers. J1B was equally diverse, with 53 per cent being EAL students. In addition, as Table 1 shows, the vast majority of participants were enrolled in various non-Arts degrees.

There were also two control groups (CG) in this project. One CG consisted of students in J1B (2008, n=60), and the other consisted of students in J1A (2009, n=162). No students in the CGs experienced the SSAPs, as they were not implemented in these two courses. Table 2 summarizes the numbers of participants in this project.

J1B 2009			J1A 2010		
B.Commerce	24	26%	B.Commerce	92	36%
Other programs	14	15%	Other programs	58	23%
Cross-Institutional UG	13	14%	B.Arts	25	10%
B.Teaching/B.Arts	9	10%	B.Medicine & B.Surgery	17	7%
B.Arts	8	9%	B.Psychological Science	15	6%
B.Computer Science	6	7%	B.Finance	13	5%
Diploma.Languages	6	7%	B.Computer Science	9	4%
B.International Studies	5	5%	Cross-Institutional UG	8	3%
B.Design Studies	4	4%	Diploma.Languages	8	3%
B.Science	3	3%	B.International Studies	8	3%
Total (as of 27/11/2009)	92	100%	Total (as of 6/4/2010)	253	100%

Table 1: Academic programs of student participants[6]

	J1A : Semester 1	J1B: Semester 2
2008		60 (CG without SSAPs)
2009	162 (CG without SSAPs)	92 (with SSAPs)
2010	238 (with SSAPs)	

Table 2: Total numbers of student participants, with and without SSAPs

Materials and procedure

Three steps were developed and implemented to help students develop study skills through SRL: 1) Teacher Feedback, 2) Study Skills Action Plan (SSAP), and 3) Personal Reflection (PR). These steps were embedded cyclically in the curriculum for each assessment (Tests 1, 2 & 3)[7] (Figure 1). Students completed two SSAPs (1 & 2) and two PRs (1 & 2) during one semester[8] in the following order: Test 1 → Feedback 1 → SSAP 1 → Test 2 → PR 1 → Feedback 2 → SSAP 2 → Test 3 → PR 2.

After Test 1, students received their marked papers accompanied by both a Feedback 1 form (already filled out by their tutors; Appendix A) and an empty SSAP 1 form (Appendix B). They were then required to create their own personalised

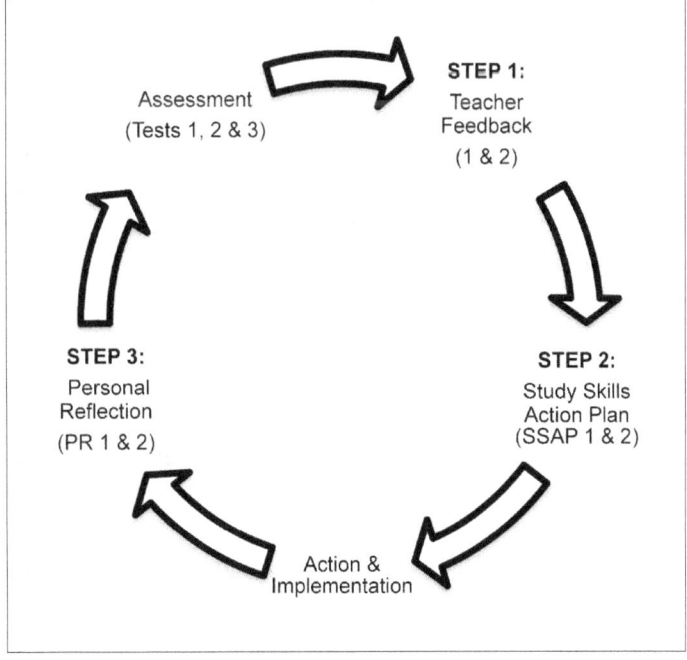

Figure 1: Cycles of feedback-based SSAP

SSAP 1, and within one week, submit a copy of this to their teacher as a signed study contract. Students kept the original to follow through with SSAP 1, and for their subsequent self-reflection practice (PR 1). They wrote their PR 1 on the last page of the Test 2 paper (Appendix C). Because students needed to write their PR 1 during Test 2, they were advised to practise reflecting upon how they had been learning and following through after their SSAP 1. Both Test 2 and Test 3 papers were set so that a majority of students had a minimum of 15 minutes to write their PR 1 and PR 2 respectively. Submissions of two SSAPs (0.5 per cent x 2) and two PRs (1 per cent x 2) counted towards the final mark (3 per cent in total).

Step 1: Teacher feedback

The feedback form was designed to make feedback timely, simple, concise and clear, as the majority of students were first-year and EAL (Appendix A). This form consists of all the relevant study areas (for example, *kanji*, vocabulary, grammar) covered in a particular formative assessment; each study area shows the specific skills tested in that assessment. All areas of weakness for a student to work upon for the next assessment were marked in the appropriate boxes on each student's feedback form by a tutor. Then, individual students received formative test papers with the personalised feedback form attached.

Step 2: Study Skills Action Plan (SSAP)

The SSAP form is written in clear and concise English (Appendix B). In order to help students establish a clear link between their feedback form and their SSAP form, the latter replicates the same study area sections (for example, *kanji*, vocabulary, grammar) as the feedback form. Each study area section presents a list of possible area-specific learning methods and strategies. Importantly, such a list contains learning methods and strategies likely to facilitate a combination of both a surface approach (for example, a simple memorisation of a textbook vocabulary list) and a deep approach (for example, previewing, reviewing, learning new words in meaningful contexts).

To devise their own SSAPs, after having understood the given feedback, students then chose which study methods and strategies to adopt for the next assessment, by ticking boxes on a list containing a wide range of study methods and strategies in each study area. We adopted this method of ticking boxes intentionally, because, without being made aware of a range of study ideas available in language learning to begin with, some students might have become overwhelmed.

Step 3: Personal Reflection (PR)

As discussed previously, while good feedback practice facilitates SRL, students' ability to monitor, evaluate and reflect on their learning process contributes equally to their success. Consequently, the personalized SSAP is followed by each student's personal reflective commentary. To emphasise student accountability for their submitted SSAP as a study contract, this commentary involves each student's personal reflective analysis of how far they have followed through with their chosen study methods and strategies (Appendix C). Thus, the PR writing process provides students with opportunities to reflectively evaluate their own behaviour, motivation and achievements, as well as the relevance of different language learning methods and strategies to their own needs.

Students were notified in advance of two marking criteria for the PR: 1) length (200-250 words in English), and 2) ability to reflect upon their learning. Importantly, students were told that no marks are deducted for English grammar mistakes. This is to ensure that the students do not see the PR exercise as an 'English essay' assignment, and to encourage students to practise self-reflection by focusing on the content of their commentary.

Data collection and analysis

Quantitative data

The project used the extended standard Student Experience of Learning and Teaching (SELT) course survey[9] to fulfill research objective (i), as follows:

i. To examine the effect of feedback-based SSAPs on students' understanding and use of teacher feedback.

The survey took place in classes during the eleventh week (out of 12 weeks) of semester in J1B (2009) and in J1A (2010).[10] This extended SELT survey[11] included the following three statement questions (Q6, Q16 and Q18), specifically relating to 'feedback on work' and one open-ended question (Q22) on 'feedback', as follows:

Q 6: I received adequate feedback on my work.

Q16: The feedback on my work includes clear suggestions for further improvement.

Q18: The feedback on my work is helpful to my learning.

Q22: Please comment on the feedback that you received regarding your work.

Participants indicated degrees of their agreement/disagreement for each statement question on a 7-point-Likert scale (from 7='strongly agree' to 1='strongly disagree') and the three statement questions also had 'not applicable'. The project then calculated Broad Agreement (BA) percentages on a basis of responses where students indicated their 'agreement' as 5–7, and then compared between the groups. For Q6, the project collected responses from the CG participants in J1B (2008) and in J1A (2009), using the standard SELT.[12] The project compared the obtained BA percentages for Q6 between J1B CG (2008) and J1B (2009), and between J1A CG (2009) and J1A (2010).

Qualitative data

Qualitative content analysis was conducted on the data derived from the participants' PR 1 and PR 2 (n=564),[13] to fulfil research objectives (ii) and (iii), as follows:

ii. To examine the effect of feedback-based SSAPs on students' study skills development through self-regulated learning.
iii. To examine whether students would experiment with and practise deeper learning methods and strategies through the feedback-based SSAP exercises.

As Table 3 shows, the vast majority of students submitted both assigned SSAPs. The majority of those who did not submit two SSAPs, did not sit for the subsequent tests to write the PRs. Among those participants who wrote PR 1 and PR 2 during Test 2 and Test 3 respectively, 20 per cent in J1B and 24 per cent in J1A wrote brief/scant reflections that did not satisfy the two marking criteria. Therefore, such PRs were not given full marks. The following section discusses this further.

	N of participants who submitted both SSAP 1 & SSAP 2	N of participants who wrote both PR 1 & PR 2	N of brief/scant reflections
J1B 2009	88/92 (96%)	80/92 (87%)	32/160 (20%)
J1A 2010	223/238 (94%)	202/238 (85%)	97/404 (24%)

Table 3: Percentages of completed SSAP, PR and brief/scant reflections

Phenomenographic research methods strongly influenced the qualitative method of analysis for the PR commentary. Phenomenographic research aims for a collective analysis of individual experiences, that is, to explore the range of experiences, conceptualizations and understandings within a group, rather than to capture any particular individual's understanding within that group (Åkerlind 2005). This is achieved by categorising perceptions of individuals that 'emerge' from the (transcribed) data into specific 'categories of description' (Åkerlind 2005). Such an analysis continuously involves grouping and re-grouping of data and comparing between data and the developing categories of description, and among the categories themselves. In support of this phenomenographic qualitative method, Gustafsson and Fagerberg (2004, p. 278) argue that

> Qualitative methods do not have the purpose of finding generalizable results; instead, they aim at understanding the lived experience of others. The lived experience can have similarities with how other experiences are understood and therefore help us to understand the other.

The qualitative analysis in this project derives from the participants' written PRs, not from interview transcripts,[14] following the phenomenographic study by Niemi (1997) who used learning logs written by medical students (n=110) to examine the quality of their self-reflection during the preclinical year. The present analysis first entailed the reading and re-reading of participants' PR 1/PR 2, to group the excerpts into the categories of experiences, conceptualisations and understandings in line with research objectives (ii) and (iii). This process also involved searching for the key themes and issues widely recognised by the participants.

Results and discussion
SELT course surveys

Table 4 shows the obtained BA percentages for Questions 6, 16 and 18. Overall results show that, in all three questions, very high (92 per cent or above) BA percentages were obtained in the two SSAP courses (J1B 2009 & J1A 2010).

Firstly, regarding Question 6, the comparisons between J1B CG (2008) and J1B (2009) and between J1A CG (2009) and J1A (2010) reveal that the courses with

Q6	N of Responses/Total Enrolled	BA (%)	SD	Mean	Median
2008:1B(CG)	53/60 (88%)	92%	1.0	6.0	6.0
2009:1B	65/92 (71%)	97%	0.7	6.3	6.0
2009:1A(CG)	116/162 (72%)	86%	1.0	5.6	6.0
2010:1A	165/238 (69%)	95%	0.8	6.2	6.0
2009	44186 (University wide)[15]	62%	1.6	4.8	5.0
Q16					
2009:1B	65/92 (71%)	97%	0.8	6.2	6.0
2010:1A	166/238 (70%)	92%	0.8	6.1	6.0
Q18					
2009:1B	65/92 (71%)	97%	0.7	6.3	6.0
2010:1A	165/238 (69%)	96%	0.8	6.2	6.0

Table 4: Results of the SELT course surveys

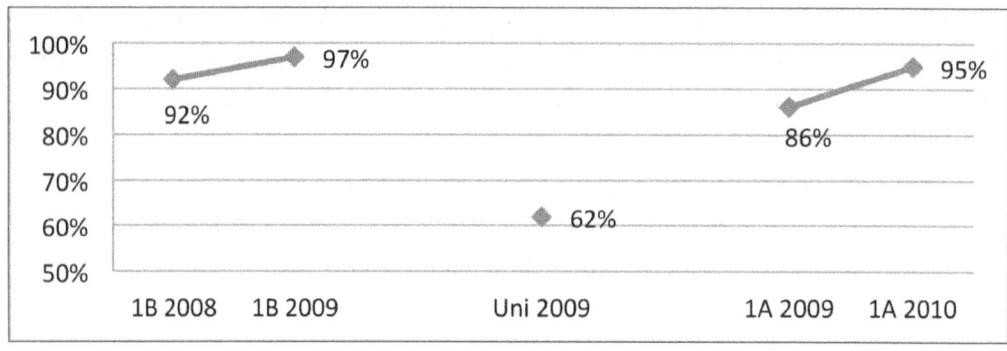

Figure 2: Comparisons of BA percentages for Question 6

the SSAP obtained consistently higher BA per cent with shifts from 92 per cent to 97 per cent in J1B and from 86 per cent to 95 per cent in J1A (Table 4). This means that higher percentages of students noted that they received adequate feedback in the SSAP courses than in the non-SSAP courses. The student numbers in the two SSAP courses were larger than those in the two non-SSAP courses (Table 2). Taking into consideration that it is generally harder to provide adequate feedback to individual students' work in larger courses than in smaller courses, such BA percentage increases strongly point to the SSAP implementation as a key contributing factor.

Indeed, further analyses using a Mann-Whitney U test[16] revealed that the difference in obtained ratings for Q6 was highly significant between the two J1A groups ($p<0.001$), but the difference was not significant between the two J1B groups ($p>0.05$). In other words, these results indicate that the provision of feedback embedded as part of the SSAP cycles significantly improved between the two large J1A courses ($n>100$), but this was not the case between the small J1B courses ($n<100$). This is largely due to the fact that the rating scores obtained from the J1B CG were already high prior to the SSAP implementation (BA per cent=92 per cent; Figure 2), indicating that it was relatively easier to provide adequate feedback to the small J1B CG than the large J1A CG, prior to the SSAP implementation. Consequently, the impact of the inclusion of the SSAP on the J1B group did not prove significant, despite its BA percentage reaching 97 per cent with the implementation. In summary, while the feedback-based SSAP improved the provision of feedback in both J1A (large) and J1B (small) courses, the results strongly suggest that the SSAP can improve the provision significantly with a large ($n>100$) course.

Secondly, regarding Questions 16 and 18, the obtained BA percentages reveal that between 92–97 per cent of students noted that the feedback included clear suggestions for further improvement, and was helpful to their learning. Notably, these high BA figures compare very favourably with those obtained in the aforementioned

Selby's study (2007, p. 11) on the use of APS with medical students. Selby (n=15), using the same measurement in a special SELT survey, reported 73 per cent BA for the Question, 'APS improved feedback', and 53 per cent BA for the Question, 'APS improved learning'. Although the statement questions used in Selby's study and this project were not identical, the obtained BA percentage gaps between the two studies strongly point to the effectiveness and benefits of integrating the process of understanding/using teacher feedback into an action plan, to improve both feedback and learning.

Finally, the students' SELT comments obtained from the open-ended response question (Q22) further support the above interpretations of the quantitative results. These comments (with emphases and underlining added) provide direct evidence that students interpreted receiving feedback as a helpful step to improve their learning, while positively responding to the speed, amount and clarity of feedback they received:

- It was usually received quite <u>fast and gave detailed suggestions as to how work could be improved</u>.
- It has all been <u>very helpful</u> and <u>allowed me to focus on what needs improving</u>.
- <u>Fast, detailed</u> feedback so I could <u>identify where to improve</u>.
- Lots of feedback and <u>suggestions to improve on studying</u>.
- It was <u>clear, precise</u> and helped me <u>see where I needed to improve</u>.
- Feedback on all tests was helpful. It was made clear <u>which aspects of learning needed improvement</u>.
- [Feedback was] Very helpful, also <u>invites us to reflect upon how much more we put in, how we could improve</u>.
- Received a huge amount of feedback! Study plans and personal reflections are a great idea <u>to get students thinking about their learning and progress</u>.

To summarise, regarding research objective (i), these SELT results clearly indicate the usefulness of the feedback-based SSAPs for facilitating students' understanding and use of teacher feedback to improve learning. This finding strongly suggests that the three-step cycles were extremely effective in encouraging students to perceive feedback positively as part of an ultimately successful learning process.

Personal reflective commentary

The qualitative analysis identified five categories of description, representing different themes and issues found in the PRs. Table 5 summarizes all of the identified categories of description, and each category is then discussed.

Categories of description (n of PRs)	Sub-categories of description (n of PRs)
1. Brief and scant reflections n=129/564 (23%)	
2. Practising SRL to develop study skills n=368/564 (65%)	a) Setting goals and developing motivation n=243/368 (66%) b) Monitoring and evaluating own behaviour n=204/368 (55%) c) Monitoring and assessing own learning needs and actions n=286/368 (78%) d) Discovering and evaluating own study methods n=324/368 (88%)
3. Adoption of deeper study methods and learning strategies n=296/564 (52%)	
4. Influence of students' perceptions of time on learning approaches n=18/564 (3%,)	
5. Developing transferable study skills n=23/564 (4%)	

Table 5: Summary of categories of description

1. Brief and scant reflections

As mentioned previously (Table 3), 20 per cent (n=32/160) in J1B and 24 per cent (n=97/404) in J1A of the PRs contained nothing or little by way of reflection. Typical qualities of these PRs were brevity and avoidance. They were often short (less than 200 words) and if longer, were typically characterised by detached or superficial commentary:

- I have found learning *kanji* very difficult and my marks in the *kanji* section will reflect this. I gave up on it at some point. I apologise to you.

Among such brief and scant PRs (23 per cent, n=129/564), 28 PRs contained nothing, as a minority of students left the PR page completely blank during the test. It is possible that these students were just not interested in participating in the SSAP exercises. However, one reason for such brief and scant PRs could be a lack of time during the test. Therefore, this time factor could be explored by allowing students to write their PRs outside class and submit them by a due date, to see if any differences occur in the nature and/or quality of students' reflections.

2. Practising SRL to develop study skills

The majority of the PRs (65 per cent, n=368/564) provide strong indications that regulating aspects of learning were being operated and practised. Students' reflections demonstrated students' monitoring and evaluation of their own study methods, progress and behaviour, while showing sustained motivation, guided by the goals they set for themselves. The following categories emerged from the PR commentary, pinpointing four different aspects of self-regulation in learning (Table 5).

(a) Setting goals and developing motivation (66 per cent, n=243/368)

Some students described that they set specific goals for the subsequent assessment, typically with intent, confidence and motivation to follow through with the SSAP. Furthermore, many described their experience of success through their self-set goals, whilst learning the requisites to improve upon their test scores. As these students strove for their personal best, the experience of achieving at a higher level, according to their current goals and abilities, further engaged and motivated them to achieve more successes, as the following commentary shows:

- I have achieved a number of goals that I set myself ... I will work harder at this new study plan as I feel that I can definitely improve.
- I think I had followed my study plan 1, and this plan worked well and I will follow the study plan 2 continuously to achieve my goals.

(b) Monitoring and evaluating own behaviour (55 per cent, n=204/368)

Students reflected, often critically, upon what they did or did not do to prepare for the previous test, and why. Those students who did this demonstrated a strong sense of taking responsibility for their own learning. Thus, the three-step cycles helped bring out students' sense of responsibility for their learning through developing their SRL. The comments below exemplify this process:

- Before I studied for this test, <u>I had been fairly lax in my efforts ... because I was overconfident</u> ... I listened to the voice tools on MyUni for the first time ... This helped me more than writing ... This test [with SSAP] forced me to develop new technique which I can use in the future!
- I should have paid more attention to *kanji* and done more comparison with Chinese [characters]. ... <u>I didn't do it simply because I thought it was easy</u>.
- <u>Since submitting the study action plan 2, I have tried really hard to use many different methods</u> ... and become a lot more organized with the notes I take and other bits and pieces I am using during my study time.

(c) Monitoring and assessing own learning needs and actions (78 per cent, n=286/368)

Many students described their realisation of their learning needs and what concrete action/s they had taken in response. In doing so, they were willing to acknowledge and articulate their own weaknesses and failures openly:

- ... the words <u>I left to the last minute to learn I cannot remember now</u> ... doing a small amount of revision every day should ensure that I really am absorbing and learning the language.
- There was a definite improvement in my learning when I began using *kanji* flashcards ... <u>I felt they [*kanji*] were my weak point</u>, so I focused on them more than I did on vocabulary or grammar.
- When I started my Japanese revision, <u>I don't [sic] know how to start it</u> ... Follow [sic] through my study plan, <u>I find [sic] out ... 'vocabulary' area is the most important part I need to improve</u> ...

(d) Discovering and evaluating own study methods (88 per cent, n=324/368)

A pleasingly large number of students described with surprising openness and sincerity how they experimented with new study methods listed on the SSAP form and even created their own;

- After receiving feedback ... I decided to challenge myself more ... by trying to do dictation without pausing the voice recordings. It was very difficult at first because I would panic ... but I feel I became better as I did more practice.
- After a lot of different methods I have realized that cue cards help me learn best. I seem to have a very visual memory so if a picture can be drawn to match the vocabulary in which I'm trying to learn, it helps greatly.

As these excerpts demonstrate, addressing research objective (ii), the three-step cycles were extremely effective in developing students' study skills through SRL. Moreover, core to this finding is that students developed a sense of responsibility for their own learning processes that will underpin their SRL in the long term.

3. Adoption of deeper study methods and learning strategies

The second finding that emerged from the PRs (52 per cent, n=296/564) suggests that this systematic development of study skills promoted students' use of deep approaches to learning, in addition to or instead of surface (or rote) learning strategies. The following comments signal such a shift:

- To be honest, it did take me a while to realise that <u>simply learning by rote was just not enough</u>. Japanese ... cannot be simply learnt by just loading information into the head. It has to be used and practised, to be learnt.
- I've found that the best way to remember vocabulary is <u>not to write them out many times</u> ... Recently, I've begun to look for simple Japanese texts on the internet ... it takes me a while to recognize the characters, but I can definitely notice an improvement in how quickly I can read ...

- At first, I studied Japanese in my way. I read and wrote down new words, repeated. However, this method was not useful … I even wanted to drop this course …Then, Sensei [=teacher] … taught me how to study Japanese [using SSAP]. I tried to use some other methods to study … In the third exam, I got a better mark.

These excerpts indicate that students previously using surface learning strategies were influenced to shift to deeper processing strategies through the SSAP exercises, and, in some cases, this may have contributed to student retention as suggested by the final excerpt. This concurs with the established view that surface and deep learning are amenable to the influence of learning environments (Wilson et al. 1997; Wilson & Fowler 2005). Furthermore, as the following excerpts exemplify, the project found evidence that students discovered the importance of previewing to gain background knowledge before class, and the usefulness of integrating new information into what they already knew:

- Before going to the lecture, I read the lecture note in advance and memorize the new vocabularies. Sometimes I failed to do these then I felt behind when I was sitting in the lecture … I think I will do more preview before the lectures.
- I still made flash cards and this time, instead of trying to learn each of the *kanji* individually, placing them in actual words really helped to learn them.

In these ways, addressing research objective (iii), it is clear that the SSAPs encouraged students to experiment with and practise new deeper learning methods, and increased their enthusiasm for doing so.

4. Influence of students' perceptions of time on learning approaches

One particularly interesting issue emerged from a minority of the PRs (3 per cent, n=18/564) produced mainly by science, engineering, and medicine and surgery students. These reflections were characterised by perceptions of not being in control of time, and that was the reason for not being able to experiment and practise new, deeper learning methods. Here, there was little description of adoption of deeper methods, but a continuing use of surface methods. In their reflections of behaviour, this student cohort commonly described what deeper study methods and strategies they would have experimented with, had they had 'more time':

- The main problem I had, following through with my Study Action Plan, was time. Other university subjects got in the way of my Japanese study. As a result, I didn't have much time to use the Voice Tools, and reviewing … (B. Engineering)

- Due to other commitment, such as medical studies, I failed to <u>study Japanese before each lesson</u> [deep method] ... If I have <u>more time</u>, I would want to study more and <u>be prepared for each lesson so that I could participate during class and understand</u> ... (B. Medicine & Surgery)

This finding is supported by Case and Gunstone (2003), who found that, for those students who are not using a deep (conceptual) approach, a highly time-pressured learning environment militated against the adoption of a deep approach. Similarly, Kember and Leung (1998) also found perception of heavy workloads to be associated with surface approaches to learning.

One implication of this finding is that, if we are serious about valuing study skills training and deeper approaches to learning, then students' perceptions of time pressure and heavy workloads need to be alleviated. One way to encourage the process could be through helping students understand that a deep learning approach will ultimately help them become more efficient in their use of available time, and that deeper learning strategies are not course-specific but are transferable across all courses. How to promote such understanding, however, demands further research.

5. Developing transferable study skills

Another interesting finding that emerged from a minority of PR comments (4 per cent, n=23/564) suggests that some students' SSAP experiences helped them develop and identify transferable generic study skills and habits. This is reflected in the following commentary:

- I got a low mark in the first test ... I followed my study plan. In my second test, I got a higher mark and found the new method very useful ... <u>I might try using this method in my other subjects</u>.
- From the feedback, I found my mistakes and disadvantages exactly... [the SSAP] made me confident and taught me how to study independently. I think <u>it is also good for my other courses</u>.
- I am happy to [have] chosen this course because it requires lots of [SSAP] exercises, I have to work hard to keep up [with my SSAP] and I haven't concentrated on any other study that hard for a long time. So, <u>it is good for me for my further studies</u>.
- The study plan is a very helpful method to help to learn. Also, <u>I think the study plan can be used in other language learning</u>.

These excerpts indicate that some students recognised the transferability of what they did and realized that their SSAP or 'learning how to learn' exercises were not just Japanese course-specific, but generic study skills development tools.

Conclusion

There are major challenges in enhancing student course engagement and motivation, as well as learning outcomes, in today's larger and more diverse teaching and learning environments, especially in the teaching of foreign, Asian languages. To tackle such challenges and to contribute to globalizing higher education pedagogy and research, this project focused on students' perceptions of learning and of their learning process; the project examined the effectiveness of feedback-based SSAPs as learning skills development tools for enhancing students' proactive use of feedback, and for developing their study skills through SRL in a first-year Japanese course.

The project found that the SSAPs facilitated students' engagement with feedback and study skills development, enabling students to clearly see and understand what feedback really means and what they could practically do to improve their skills for the next assessment. Furthermore, the cycles of the feedback-based SSAP enhanced students' SRL, while facilitating their adoption of a deep approach to learning. The SSAPs encouraged students, including those who might initially have perceived teacher feedback negatively, to be proactive in using feedback and to benefit from their study skills development. In summary, this research project clearly demonstrates the benefits of using a feedback-based SSAP for developing study skills in a language learning context, and shows how SRL and deeper approaches to learning can both be promoted through such SSAP exercises.

These findings are limited here to a first-year Japanese language-learning context, and to students' written reflections. Future research could examine interview data to further investigate the developmental processes through which students reflect upon their study experiences, and the ways in which they develop their study skills. It might be also worthwhile to employ a follow-up questionnaire/survey to examine quantitatively the effect of feedback-based SSAPs on student learning. A particularly important outcome of this project is the light it sheds on the potential pragmatic value of feedback-based SSAPs beyond Japanese language courses and in other academic disciplines, particularly in first-year courses. Further research options could explore the possible application and impact of feedback-based SSAPs on student learning in a variety of other learning contexts, especially where student cohorts are characterised by complex and diverse learning backgrounds.

Notes

1. An earlier version of this paper appears as Enomoto, K 2010, 'Promoting self-regulated learning: a feedback-based study skills action plan for students from diverse cultural, linguistic and disciplinary backgrounds', in *Crises and opportunities: proceedings of the 18th Biennial Conference of the ASAA*, 2010, eds E Morrel & MD Barr, Canberra, ACT, Asian Studies Association of Australia, viewed 11 November 2011 at <http://asaa.asn.au/ASAA2010/index.php>. The author wishes to thank Kazuko Glass, Hiroko Hayashi, Midori Kagawa-Fox, Maki Sugimoto and Miwako Takasawa, for providing teacher feedback in Japanese 1A (2010) and Japanese 1B (2009). Their support was invaluable for the implementation of the feedback-based SSAPs.
2. Source: Access Adelaide <http://www.adelaide.edu.au/access/>. See Table 1.
3. Whilst extensive discussions for and against the deep/surface model are beyond the scope of this paper, it is important to note here that this notion has been critiqued and its limitations pointed out (Webb, 1997; Entwistle, 1997 in response to Webb). Here, the deep (more conceptual)/surface (less conceptual) metaphor is used for the purpose of describing the types of study methods and learning strategies which students adopted and experienced through their SSAP exercises, not as a convenient labelling of students.
4. No other background details of these students are given here to preserve anonymity.
5. J1B is a continuation of J1A; students who have completed Japanese 1A with a pass or above can enrol in J1B. Because the SSAP was piloted in J1B in 2009, participants in J1B (2009) and J1A (2010) did not overlap.
6. Source: Access Adelaide <http://www.adelaide.edu.au/access/>.
7. Test 1, Test 2 (both formative assessments) and Test 3 (summative assessment) each consisted of three sections: 1) *Kanji*, 2) Vocabulary and 3) Grammar. Minna no Nihongo (structural syllabus based) textbooks (Volume I; Tokyo, 3A Corporation) are used in J1A and J1B.
8. In J1A and J1B, students meet for four contact hours per week for 12 weeks during one semester.
9. The SELT is an evaluation tool used at the University of Adelaide, designed by the Centre for Learning and Professional Development (CLPD). See <http://www.adelaide.edu.au/clpd/selt/>.
10. As the survey was to be administered on the same day by a staff administrator, those who were absent did not participate; invalid/machine-unreadable answers were not counted.
11. A total of 19 statement questions and 3 open-ended questions were in the survey.
12. Designed by the CLPD; this standard SELT, unlike the extended standard SELT, does not include Questions 16, 18 and 22. Therefore, in relation to these three questions, neither control-group nor university-wide data were available for comparisons in this project.
13. Only participants who wrote both PR 1 and PR 2 were included. [n=80x2PRs+202x2PRs=564PRs] See Table 3.
14. Interviews represent the most common data source for phenomenographic analysis. However, Säljö (1996) cautions that phenomenographic research assumes what people say in interviews to be a direct reflection of the way they experience the world, by arguing that what happens in an interview is primarily a social event.
15. Source: <https://www.adelaide.edu.au/clpd/selt/aggregates>
16. This non-parametric test, unlike its parametric counterpart (t-test), does not assume normal distribution of data; the use of the non-parametric test was more appropriate in this study because the distributions of the obtained data did not present normal distribution, but a tendency to be truncated at the high end of the scale.

References

Åkerlind, G 2005, 'Variation and commonality in phenomenographic research methods', *Higher Education Research & Development*, vol. 24 no. 4, pp. 321–334.

Biggs, JB 1989, 'Approaches to the enhancement of tertiary teaching', *Higher Education Research and Development*, vol. 8, pp. 7–25.

Biggs, JB 1999, 'What the student does: teaching for enhanced learning', *Higher Education Research and Development*, vol. 18 no. 1, pp. 57–75.

Butler, DL & Winne, PH 1995, 'Feedback and self-regulated learning: a theoretical synthesis', *Review of Educational Research*, vol. 65, pp. 245–281.

Case, J & Gunstone, R 2003, 'Approaches to learning in a second year Chemical Engineering course', *International Journal of Science Education*, vol. 25, pp. 1–19.

Cheek, GD & Campbell, C 1994, 'Help them use what they learn', *Adult Learning*, vol. 5 no. 4, pp. 27–28.

Connell, J 2003, 'Orientation for adult learners in problem-based learning', *Australian Journal of Adult Learning*, vol. 43 no. 1, pp. 85–100.

Crisp, B 2007, 'Is it worth the effort? How feedback influences students' subsequent submission of assessable work', *Assessment & Evaluation in Higher Education*, vol. 32 no. 5, pp. 571–581.

Crosling, G, Heagney, M & Thomas, L 2009, 'Improving student retention in higher education', *Australian Universities' Review*, vol. 51 no. 2, pp. 9–18.

Department of Education, Employment and Workplace Relations (DEEWR) 2008, *Good practice principles for English Language proficiency for internationalsStudents in Australian universities — Final report*, viewed 28 September 2011, <http://www.deewr.gov.au/HigherEducation/Publications/Documents/Final_Report-Good_Practice_Principles.pdf>.

Duncan, N 2007, '"Feed forward": improving students' use of tutors' comments', *Assessment & Evaluation in Higher Education*, vol. 32 no. 2, pp. 271–283.

Enomoto, K 2011, 'Fostering high quality learning through a scaffolded curriculum', in C Nygaard, N Courtney & C Holtham (eds), *Beyond transmission: innovations in university teaching*, Libri Publishing, Faringdon, Oxon, pp. 167–184.

Entwistle, N 1991, 'Approaches to learning and perceptions of the learning environment', *Higher Education*, vol. 22, pp. 20–204.

Entwistle, N 1997, 'Reconstituting approaches to learning: a response to Webb', *Higher Education*, vol. 33, pp. 213–218.

Entwistle, N 2009, *Teaching for understanding at university: deep approaches and distinctive ways of thinking*, Palgrave Macmillan, Basingstoke, Hants.

Furnborough, C & Truman, M 2009, 'Adult beginner distance language learner perceptions and use of assignment feedback', *Distance Education*, vol. 30 no. 3, pp. 399–418.

Gustafsson, C & Fagerberg, I 2004, 'Reflection, the way to professional development?', *Journal of Clinical Nursing*, vol. 13, pp. 271–280.

Haggis, T 2003, 'Constructing images of ourselves? A critical investigation into 'approaches to learning' research in higher education', *British Educational Research Journal*, vol. 29 no. 1, pp. 89–104.

Hounsell, D, McCune, V, Hounsell, J & Litjens, J 2008, 'The quality of guidance and feedback to students', *Higher Education Research & Development*, vol. 27 no.1, pp. 55–67.

Johnson, M 2008, 'An investigation into pedagogical challenges facing international tertiary-level students in New Zealand', *Higher Education Research & Development*, vol. 27 no. 3, pp. 231–243.

Kember, D & Leung, D 1998, 'Infuences upon students' perceptions of workload', *Educational Psychology*, vol. 22, pp. 293–307.

Krause, K & Coates, H 2008, 'Students' engagement in first-year university', *Assessment and Education in Higher Education*, vol. 33 no. 5, pp. 493–505.

Krause, K, Hartley, R, James, R & McInnis, C 2005, *The first year experience in Australian universities: findings from a decade of national studies*. DEST, Canberra, ACT.

Lambert, WE 1991, 'Pros, cons, and limits to quantitative approaches in foreign language acquisition research', in K de Bot, RB Ginsberg & C Kramsch (eds), *Foreign language research in cross-cultural perspective*, John Benjamins, Amsterdam, pp. 53–71.

Leggett, M, Kinnear, A, Boyce, M & Bennett, I 2004, 'Student and staff perceptions of the importance of generic skills in Science', *Higher Education Research & Development*, vol. 23 no. 3, pp. 295–312.

Leveson, L 2000, 'Disparities in perceptions of generic skills: academics and employers', *Industry and Higher Education*, vol.14, pp. 157–164.

Lizzio, A, Wilson, KL & Simons, R 2002, 'University students' perceptions of the learning environment and academic outcomes: implications for theory and practice', *Studies in Higher Education*, vol. 27 no. 1, pp. 27–52.

Long, M, Ferrier, F & Heagney, M 2006, *Stay, play or give it away? Students continuing, changing or leaving university study in their first year*, ACER, Monash University Press, Clayton, Vic.

Malcolm, J & Zukas, M 2001, 'Bridging pedagogic gaps: conceptual discontinuities in higher education', *Teaching in Higher Education*, vol. 6, pp. 33–42.

McInnis, C, James, R & Hartley, R 2000, *Trends in the first year experience in*

Australian universities, AGPS, Canberra, ACT.

Nicol, DJ & MacFarlane-Dick, D 2006, 'Formative assessment and self-regulated learning: a model and seven principles of food feedback practice', *Studies in Higher Education*, vol. 31 no. 2, pp. 199–218.

Niemi, PM 1997, 'Medical students' professional identity: self-reflection during the preclinical years', *Medical Education*, vol. 31 no. 6, pp. 408–415.

Pintrich, PR 2000, 'The role of goal orientation in self-regulated learning', in M Boekaerts, PR Pintrich & M Zeidner (eds), *Handbook of self-regulation*, Academic Press, San Diego, pp. 451–502.

Pintrich, PR, & Zusho, A 2002, 'The development of academic self-regulation: the role of cognitive and motivational factors', in A Wigfield & JS Eccles (eds), *Development of Achievement Motivation*, Academic Press, San Diego, CA, pp. 249–284.

Race, P 2001, *The lecturer's tool kit: a practical guide to learning, teaching & assessment* (2nd ed.), Kogan Page, London.

Roberts, M 2009, 'Assessment and diversity: a collaborative project between academic staff and learning support staff', viewed 4 April 2010, <http://www.isana.org.au/academic/assessment-and-diversity-a-collaborative-project-between-academic-staff-and-learning-support-staff.html>.

Säljö, R 1996, 'Minding action — conceiving of the world versus participating in cultural practices', in G Dall'Alba & B Hasselgren (eds), *Reflections on phenomenography — towards a methodology?*, Acta Universtatis Gothoburgensis, Gothenberg, Sweden, pp. 19–33.

Schunk, DH & Zimmerman, BJ 1994, *Self-regulation of learning and performance: issues and educational applications*, Laurence Erlbaum, NJ.

Selby, S 2007, 'A pilot study investigating the use of action planning statements in tutoring clinical skills to second year medical students', *The Journal of the Education Research Group of Adelaide (ERGO)*, vol. 1 no. 1, pp. 7–14.

Sumison, J & Goodfellow, J 2004, 'Identifying generic skills through curriculum mapping: a critical evaluation', *Higher Education Research and Development*, vol. 23 no. 3, pp. 329–346.

Trigwell, K & Prosser, M 1991a, 'Improving the quality of student learning: the influence of learning context and student approaches to learning on learning outcomes', *Higher Education*, vol. 22, pp. 251–266.

Trigwell, K & Prosser, M 1991b, 'Relating approaches to study and quality of learning outcomes at the course level', *British Journal of Educational Psychology*, vol. 61, pp. 265–275.

Warner R 2010, 'Giving feedback on assignment writing to international students — the integration of voice and writing tools', in WM Chan, KN Chin, M

Nagami & T Suthiwan (eds), *Media in foreign language teaching and learning*, Centre for Language Studies, National University of Singapore, Singapore, pp. 355–381.

Webb, G 1997, 'Deconstructing deep and surface: towards a critique of phenomenography', *Higher Education*, vol. 33, pp. 195–212.

Wilson, KL & Fowler, J 2005, 'Assessing the impact of learning environments on students' approaches to learning', *Assessment and Evaluation in Higher Education*, vol. 30 no. 1, pp. 85–99.

Wilson, KL, Lizzio, A & Ramsden, P 1997, 'The development, validation and application of the Course Experience Questionnaire', *Studies in Higher Education*, vol. 22, pp. 33–53.

Wingate, U 2006, 'Doing away with "study skills"', *Teaching in Higher Education*, vol. 11 no.4, pp. 457–469.

Zimmerman, BJ & Schunk, DH 2001, *Self-regulated learning and academic achievement: theoretical perspectives*, Laurence Erlbaum, NJ.

Appendix A: Example of Feedback Form

Your overall Achievement Level	
1 (0-39.5) - **2** (40-51.5) - **3** (52-59.5) - **4** (60-67.5) - **5** (68-80)	
Rating Scale: 1= Not Satisfactory, 2= Pass, 3=Credit (Good), 4=DN (Excellent), 5=HD (Outstanding)	
Part 1 Kanji (Units 6, 7, 9 & 10)	**Areas to be improved for the Final Exam**
Overall knowledge	More time and practice into kanji writing and reading needed
Kanji writing	Mixing or substituting Japanese kanji characters with Chinese characters
Accuracy	Size, proportion, shape & number of strokes, stroke endings (stop, tick, thinning manner)
Kanji Reading	Weakness in くんよみ (readings of Japanese origin) 紙、起、見、友、下
	Weakness in おんよみ (readings of Chinese origin) 写、真、主、人、達
Part 2 Vocabulary (L6-L12)	**Areas to be improved for the Final Exam**
Overall knowledge	More time and practice into learning vocabulary needed
Accuracy(J⇒E)	Knowledge : translation in English
Accuracy(E⇒J)	English spelling, neatness & legibility
	Knowledge: hiragana words, katakana words Script writing: Neatness & legibility
Usage and Meaning	Ability to group words into different categories, synonyms & antonyms Knowledge of adjectives & nouns
Part 3 Grammar (L6-L11)	**Areas to be improved for the Final Exam**
Knowledge, Accuracy & Use	**Particles** : tool noun で、place noun で、place noun に、location words に、indirect object (e.g. person)に/から、direct object (e.g. things) を 、も+negative verb、adjective +noun、quantifiers (counters)、adverbs、が+verbs、が+adjectives、other particle usages (N＋の＋N/ーかい/ーや、ー (など))
	[Interrogatives+か] sentences (e.g. どのくらい、どうして) Verb forms & tenses, Adjective forms, Knowledge of adverbs
	Knowledge of counters, Sentence construction & word order Vocabulary knowledge & word choice when constructing a sentence/s Conjunctions (＿。そして、＿。＿。それから、＿。＿が、＿。＿から、＿。)
General	Legibility, neatness, accuracy of characters in writing answers Punctuations
	Following test instructions correctly
Other comments if applicable:	

Appendix B: Example of SSAP form

Vocabulary Study Ideas – Tick ☑ all the study methods <u>you choose to adopt</u> for the Review Test (2).

- ☐ I will practice new words in each lesson by writing them several times over.
- ☐ I will pay particular attention to katakana words on the vocabulary lists.
- ☐ I will pay attention to new words containing double consonants っ/ッ、long vowels and words containing や/ヤ、ゆ/ユ、よ/ヨ.
- ☐ I will create and use flash cards for my vocabulary practice.
- ☐ I will create my own vocabulary lists for new words in each lesson in my own way.
- ☐ I will 'group' all the vocabulary I have learned so far by listing 'names of drinks/fruits/sports', 'names of stationary items', 'names of tools', 'verbs', 'na-/i-adjectives', adverbs, 'colours', 'family members', or 'objects/items to be written in katakana', etc.
- ☐ I will create a list of nouns/verbs according to which nouns can be used with which verb, e.g. for the verb たべます (to eat); ○パンをたべます。×テレビをたべます。
- ☐ I will create my own vocabulary tests to test myself.
- ☐ I will make use of the Index List of Vocabulary in the Minna no Nihongo Textbook for my vocabulary study.
- ☐ I will download the Voice Tools (containing vocabulary lists) onto my iPod/MP3, etc. to practise and remember new vocabulary through "my ears", when I am on a bus, walking, etc.
- ☐ I will preview the vocabulary list every week before my tutorial class so that I can get the most out of the tutorial practice.
- ☐ I will review the vocabulary list every week after my tutorial class so that I can consolidate my vocabulary knowledge before my workshop class.
- ☐ I will meet and work with a classmate/s to practise vocabulary and to test each other on a regular basis.
- ☐ I will practice and review all vocabulary lists on a regular basis, rather than leaving all of them to remember just before the tests.
- ☐ Any other vocabulary study methods you will devise/use: _____

Study Contract

This is my Study Action Plan (2) I will adopt for the Review Test (2). I will follow through with this Study Action Plan to achieve the best I can.

Family name: _____ Given names: _____ ID: _____

Your signature: _____ Date of submission: / /

Appendix C: Example of PR form

Part I: How far did you follow through with your Study Plan 1, when you were studying for Review Test 1? Indicate your self-assessment % on the scale below with a tick ☑.
Kanji   0%_____ 25%_____ 50%_____ 75%_____ 100%
Vocabulary 0%_____ 25%_____ 50%_____ 75%_____ 100%
Grammar   0%_____ 25%_____ 50%_____ 75%_____ 100%

Part II: Write your "personal reflective commentary" in 200-250 words in English.

Write your own "personal reflections" on how you have been learning Japanese independently outside the class, involving reflective analyses of your own study methods you had chosen to adopt in your Study Action Plan 1. Your personal reflective commentary may include:

1) any study methods that you devised which have worked/failed and why they worked/failed,
2) any difficulties that you may have had and/or overcame in your Japanese study,
3) what you are happy to have done or you regret not having done so far in your study,
4) self-assessment on your progress and performance in relation to what you have done or have not done in your study,
5) how and what areas in particular you are going to study for the Review Test(2).

Marking criteria: 1) length & 2) your ability to reflect upon how you are learning. This is not an English (language) assignment. So, focus on your 'self-reflections and content' - No marks will be deducted for grammar mistakes.

6

The challenge of motivation: Teaching Japanese *kanji* characters to students from diverse language backgrounds[1]

Naomi Aoki

Introduction

Globalisation has increased the number of international students in many countries and the process is still going on. The number of enrolments by international students in Australian educational institutions is also increasing year by year and the majority of enrolments in Australia are in higher education (Gillard 2009). From 2002 to 2009, the top five sources of these enrolments each year have been from Asian countries and the top country has been China (Australian Education International, 2002, 2003, 2004, 2005, 2006, 2007, 2008, 2009). These huge inflows of diverse students have affected Japanese language programs in Australian universities, which have experienced greatly increased enrolments of international students, particularly Chinese-background students from China, Taiwan, Hong Kong and Singapore. As a result, academic staff in Australia are now extremely challenged by their responsibility for satisfying the learning experiences not only of local students but also often of large numbers of international students.

However, for most of the programs established to teach Japanese as a foreign language in Australian higher education, program structures, courses and curricula have been designed to meet the needs of Australian society and Australian students who have English as their first language. Now, in many Japanese courses there are not only Australian students but also international students from countries where high Japanese competence is needed for study, work and cultural exchange — and where this need is more pressing than in Australia. In fact, Korea, China, Indonesia, Australia and Taiwan are the five countries that have the largest number of students learning Japanese as a foreign language, and these countries have quite different practices in Japanese language education according to their own social needs (Japan

Foundation 2011).² For example, the majority of Japanese learners in Korea are secondary school students who are expected to know their neighbouring country by learning its language and culture. The majority of learners in China study Japanese in tertiary education or in college-preparatory courses. Many learners of Japanese in these two countries go to Japan for tertiary education as undergraduate and postgraduate students. Thus, Japanese language education in Korea and China aims to equip learners with high communication skills both in spoken and written Japanese for the purpose of studying at a university.

Australia, however, has a tendency to stress speaking skills as the most important communication skill. In fact, only a small number of Japanese language learners in Australia go to Japanese universities to use the full range of language skills and study in degree courses (Japan Student Services Organization 2009). Also, besides the social needs of learners' home countries, their language backgrounds significantly influence their learning, especially in reading and writing (Katashima 1999, p. 91). A large body of findings shows that prior knowledge plays an important role in learning since learning proceeds primarily from prior knowledge (Roschelle 1995; McNamara & Kintsch 1996; Strangman & Hall 2009, p. 2). Thus, it is vital for educators to know students' background knowledge as well as understanding their motivation for learning.

Japanese is a character-based language, using three kinds of characters: *hiragana*, *katakana* and *kanji*. In 2010 the Japanese government increased the number of *jouyoukanji*, which refers to modern Japanese *kanji* for daily use, to 2,136 characters by adding 196 new characters to the list of characters that had previously been made in 1981 (Yomiuri Shinbun 2010; Agency of Cultural Affairs 2010).³ Each Japanese *kanji* character has multiple readings and there are a large number of compounds to be used as words. *Kanji* is a key element in Japanese literacy education and native speakers of Japanese in Japan spend 12 years of their school education learning the proper use of all *jouyoukanji* characters. Learners of Japanese as a foreign language need to spend considerable time and effort if they wish to learn the *jouyoukanji* to obtain reading and writing competence to a high level.

Japanese *kanji* characters were originally the characters used in the *Han* dynasty of China and the meanings and forms of many *kanji* characters are the same as those of the *Han* characters. There are, however, key differences between the *Han* characters and *kanji* in areas such as pronunciation, usage in sentences and some forms and meanings. In fact, about 30 per cent of the forms of the *jouyoukanji* characters are different from those of the Chinese characters currently used in Taiwan and Hong Kong, and the difference is slightly larger again for simplified Chinese characters now used in China (Kojima 2003, p. 6). In China, an ordinary literate Chinese person knows and uses somewhere between 3,000 and 4,000 Chinese characters (Norman

1988, p. 73). In Korea, 1,800 Chinese characters are taught as the basic Chinese characters in secondary schools (Cho 1994, p. 62). There are also common points and differences between these Chinese characters taught in Korea and Japanese *kanji*. A growing literature on teaching *kanji* in Japanese as a foreign or second language indicates that there are different problems in learning between students with knowledge of Chinese characters and students without (Okita 1995; Fujiyama 2002, p. 41; Koyama 2007). Due to the huge increase of international Chinese and Korean students in Australia, it is now crucial for Japanese language teachers to become aware of the specific issues that these new students are confronting.

In the Japanese program at The University of Adelaide, about 500 characters are introduced in seven elementary level courses from the first year to the third year. Compared to Japan and other countries, this speed of teaching is very slow. In Japan, international students as well as Japanese students who enter universities are expected to know all the *jouyoukanji* characters to meet the literacy standard for tertiary education. Thus, Japanese college-preparatory courses for Japanese language learners from overseas teach their students about 2,000 *kanji* in a year to pass Level 1 of the Japanese Language Proficiency Test accredited by the Japanese government. Furthermore, many Japanese programs in European countries require their students to master from 1,000 to 1,500 *kanji* by the end of the second academic year (Kawaguchi 2009, p. 123). Considering that many Chinese and Korean students pass the test after this year of preparation and enter Japanese universities, and that the number of Australian degree students in Japan is so small, *kanji* seems to constitute a major obstacle for Australian students.

A further complexity for teaching is evident in that, in the current Japanese courses conducted in Australian universities, there are local students and international students who have not studied Chinese characters at all before, alongside international students who have studied Chinese characters but not Japanese *kanji* characters in their home countries. The presence of these mixed groups of students with completely different language backgrounds in the elementary level class now presents a significant challenge for Japanese language education. There has been a pressing need to investigate the extent to which the current practice of teaching *kanji*, that is, through conventional teaching methods and materials, is meeting the needs of all students.

Such an investigation necessarily involves reflection and re-evaluation of students' profiles as learners. Situational analysis is one of the essential processes for informing curriculum design and evaluation: information about students, including such aspects as their experience of learning the target topic, prior knowledge, interest, motivation, learning styles and strategies, provides key insights for pedagogic analysis (Print 1987, p. 51; Rowntree 1981, p. 19). Information about each student's experience in studying Japanese, such as the length of study and the proficiency level, is obtainable from students at the time of enrolment or at the beginning of a course. Apart from the role that intellectual capacity and language aptitude play in second and foreign language learning, interest and motivation are also major factors in the successful study and acquisition of language. These affective factors are considered goal-directed and they have been defined as the combination of effort plus desire to achieve the goal of learning, together with favourable attitudes toward learning the target language (Gardner 1985, p. 10). Nevertheless, despite the significance of these factors, there is little information about international students' interest, motivation and learning styles for Japanese-language study in Australia.

In fact, scholarly investigation of the topic of learning motivation, interest and attitude in foreign-language (FL) contexts has been quite limited. Substantial work has been conducted on social-psychological explanations of second-language (SL) learning, the most influential work in this field being that of Gardner and Lambert and their associates in Canada in the 1950s and continuing to more recent times (Crookes & Schmidt 1991, p. 471). Gardner and Lambert (1972, p. 3) made the distinction between integrative motivation and instrumental motivation to explain why individuals set certain goals in learning a language. They identify integrative motivation with positive attitudes toward target language users and the potential for integrating into this group. Instrumental motivation refers to more functional reasons for learning a language, such as to perform well in required examinations or to get employment. This form of motivation is widely thought to be less likely to lead to success in long-term learning than integrative motivation. Gardner's socio-educational model stresses the idea that language learning involves learning aspects of behaviour typical of another cultural group, and that learners' attitudes toward the target language community will at least partially determine their success in language learning (Gardner 1979; Gardner 1985, p. 39; Gardner 1988; Gardner & Lambert 1959, p. 267).

FL learners often do not have enough contact with the target language community to form coherent and well-founded attitudes about them (Chen et al. 2005, p. 610). In this respect, they are quite different from SL learners who are immersed in the target language culture. Thus, there are many cases in which the research results obtained from SL learning contexts are not directly applicable to FL learning situations (Dornyei 1990, p. 45). Furthermore, Toohey (1999, p. 6) points out that international students in English speaking countries often struggle with study that requires using English as a SL, as well as with an unfamiliar academic culture that expects them to think and learn independently. In Australia, despite increases in numbers and the complete change of student demographic in recent years, there has been little research conducted about the socio-educational role of attitude and motivation in relation to the education of Japanese as a FL. Moreover, there has been little recognition that because international students often struggle with their study in other courses in English as a SL, this affects their motivation for learning Japanese. Therefore, it has become urgent to gather and update information about these diverse students' interests, motivation and learning attitudes for the purpose of improving the effectiveness and relevance of Japanese courses in Australia.

Research objectives

This research aimed to investigate whether there were significant differences in interest and motivation in the use of learning strategies, and in achievement in the study of *kanji* at an elementary level among students with different language backgrounds. The research paid special attention to a comparison between the local students who were native speakers of English and international Chinese students who had studied Chinese scripts in their home countries. The outcome of the research was intended to be used to examine whether the current curriculum designed for Australian students in an Australian university was meeting the needs of international students as well. The project leader hoped that the research outcome obtained would benefit educators who are involved in teaching a diverse group of students, local students and international students from Asian countries, to investigate their students' learning motivation and attitudes in the future.

Methods

The study was undertaken in 2010 in a Japanese 2B course, the second year level Japanese course of The University of Adelaide. Sixty-six students, 39 local students and 27 international students participated. The language backgrounds of the local students can be categorised into the following three groups (see Table 1): English only (36 per cent of the all enrolments in the course); bilingual English-Chinese spoken language (15 per cent); and bilingual English-a language other than Chinese, such as Vietnamese and Khmer (8 per cent). The first language backgrounds of the international students can also be grouped into three: Chinese (35 per cent), Korean (3 per cent), and Malay (3 per cent). These international students had English competency sufficiently high to meet the University's entrance requirement for English, but their levels varied from a near-native level to a level that just meets the minimum requirement. Amongst the 23 Chinese international students, 22 students spoke Mandarin and one student spoke Cantonese as a native speaker. Table 1 shows the participants' language backgrounds.

The participants studied *kanji* in two ways. The first way was to learn 64 *kanji* characters as the compulsory characters that were subsequently to be assessed by

Participants	Language backgrounds	Enrolments (n=66)	%
Local students 59%	English only	24	36%
	English and Chinese spoken language	10	15%
	English and a language other than Chinese	5	8%
International students 41%	Chinese (Mandarin/Cantonese) + English as a second language (ESL)	23	35%
	Korean + ESL	2	3%
	Malay + ESL	2	3%

Table 1: Participants' language backgrounds

tests. To teach these characters, two different methods were used over six weeks: 1) traditional lectures were given in the first three weeks; 2) a learner-centred approach that allowed students to study with materials of their own choice at their own pace was implemented as an experiment in the final three weeks. The participants' achievement was then measured by *kanji* tests that consisted of two tests for reading and another two tests for writing. The second learning style was self-directed study, in which each student selected their own way to learn more *kanji* characters by a method of their own choice. This self-directed study aimed to provide those students who wanted to extend their language mastery with an opportunity to advance their skills and to attain higher reading proficiency. The students were assigned to search for appropriate reading materials that were interesting for them and to study extracurricular *kanji* using the retrieved materials. Students were informed at the beginning of the course that no tests would be given to assess *kanji* knowledge gained by this self-study.

As a preparation for this research, computer workshops were held first so that all participants could be equipped with computer skills in Japanese. The participants learned how to word-process Japanese scripts using MS Office software, how to use the functions and tools of Japanese Input Mode Editors, Japanese search engines, and online dictionaries and translation tools. Some websites that include learning tools of *kanji* were also introduced. After these workshops, the participants were assigned to focus their study on *kanji* by reading Japanese authentic materials of their own choice. Consultations were given to those participants who needed help in making a study plan, finding materials and managing self-directed study. All participants were asked to monitor their learning throughout the course by writing in a diary what actions they took daily for their learning.

In order to find out specifically what degrees of interest and motivation students had, and what strategies they used for learning *kanji*, an anonymous written survey was conducted at the end of the course. A questionnaire was developed by drawing upon some published learning motivation/strategy scales (Oxford 1990; O'Malley & Chamot 1990; Okita 1995) but this study conceived at least half of the items newly (see Appendix). The questionnaire focussed on the following three areas: learning motivation, learning strategies, and self-evaluation of self-directed study. The participants answered the questions based on their monitoring of their own study. The questionnaire consisted of multiple-choice questions, multiple-answer questions, yes-no questions and open questions for comments. Participant responses were categorised into four groups by the participants' language backgrounds: English, Chinese, Korean and Malay. Although the numbers of participants in the last two groups were small, these participants were formed into different groups from the English and Chinese since their language backgrounds are unique and quite different from the other groups in terms of the study of Chinese characters in their home countries. Data collected comprised the responses to the questions in the three areas (motivation, strategies and evaluation of self-study) together with the results of the four tests. These data were cross-compared to analyse the needs of the participants in the four different language groups. The research analysis paid special attention was paid to the local students and the international Chinese students among the four groups since the sizes of the Korean group and the Malaysian group were quite small.

Results

The study investigated learning motivations by focussing on two aspects. The first was the participants' prior knowledge of the compulsory *kanji* characters for the course. This was investigated in the following three areas: (1) basic knowledge of Chinese characters, that is, the shapes and meanings (2) ways of reading the characters in Japanese words, and (3) ways of writing the characters. The second aspect was the participants' interest in learning *kanji*. The study asked questions to investigate if the participants in the different groups had different degrees of interest in studying how to read and how to write.

In relation to basic information about Chinese characters, the Korean students had the most knowledge, the second group was the Chinese students, the third was the local students and the last was the Malaysian students (see Table 2). The Korean students reported that they knew the forms and meanings of about 80 per cent of the compulsory *kanji* characters, while the Malaysian students knew 40 per cent. However, as far as prior knowledge of reading is concerned, the Malaysian students had the most knowledge, the second group was the Korean students, the third was the Chinese and the last was the local students. The Chinese students knew how to read about 46 per cent of the compulsory *kanji* characters in Japanese ways, while the local students knew about 36 per cent. Then, as far as prior knowledge of writing is concerned, the Chinese students had the largest amount of knowledge, the second group was the Korean students, the third was the local students, and the last was

Q1. I already knew the forms and meanings of the compulsory *kanji*. (1=None, 2, 3, 4, 5=All)	E (2.4, 0.9) C (3.6, 0.97) K (4.0, 0) M (2.0, 0)
Q2. I already knew how to read the compulsory *kanji*. (1=None, 2, 3, 4, 5=All)	E (1.8, 0.74,) C (2.3,1.24) K (3.1, 0) M (4.0,0)
Q3. I already knew how to write the compulsory *kanji*. (1=None, 2, 3, 4, 5=All)	E (2.1, 0.93) C (3.9,1.19) K (2.5,0.5) M (1.0,0)
Q4. I was interested in learning how to read the compulsory *kanji*. (1=Not At All, 2, 3, 4, 5=Very Much)	E (4.0, 0.94) C (4.2, 0.76) K (5.0, 0) M (3.5, 0.5)
Q5. I was interested in learning how to write the compulsory *kanji*. (1=Not At All, 2, 3, 4, 5=Very Much)	E (3.9, 1.03) C (3.5, 1.41) K (4.5, 0.5) M (4.0, 0)

Questions (a scale of options to choose from)
Language groups: E = English, C = Chinese, K = Korean, M = Malay
Statistics figures (Mean, SD)

Table 2: Motivation to learn the compulsory kanji

the Malaysian students. The Chinese students reported that they knew how to write about 78 per cent of the compulsory *kanji* characters, while the Malaysian students knew only about 20 per cent.

In relation to the second goal of the investigation, that is the degree of interest in studying how to read *kanji*, the Korean students expressed the deepest interest (5 out of the range of 5), the second group was the Chinese students (4.2), the third was the local students (4) and the last was the Malaysian students (3.5). All participants showed less interest in studying how to write *kanji*, compared to studying how to read them. The Korean students showed the deepest interest in studying how to write (4.5 of 5), followed by the Malaysian students (4), the third group was the local students (3.9), and the last was the Chinese students (3.5). Table 2 shows the questions and responses (means and standard deviations) of each group.

The students received options for materials to use for learning the compulsory *kanji* characters (that is, the textbook, dictionaries, video clips and a web page that includes a tool to show the stroke orders for writing *kanji*). They were encouraged to use a variety of strategies that have been recommended widely to learners of a foreign or second language. The questionnaire results showed that first, the majority of students used the textbook as the primary learning material. Then, with respect to the video clips for studying how to read *kanji* in words, the Chinese students accessed these most often among the four groups, the second was the Malaysian students, the third was the local students, and the last was the Korean students. The clips, which were made to introduce stroke orders, were used most frequently by the Korean students, followed by the Malaysian students, and then the local students.

The Chinese students were the least users of the clips to study writing. About 56 per cent of the participants also used the web page to study stroke orders, the most common users being the Korean students and the least being the Malaysian students.

As far as strategies are concerned, all students used a variety of strategies of their own choice (see Table 3). The majority of the students spent considerable time studying *kanji* outside class. The Korean students spent more time than the students in other groups and the Chinese students spent the least. All students reviewed *kanji* outside class on a regular basis. Comparing the revision of reading and that of writing, all students reviewed reading more frequently than writing. The Chinese students reviewed reading most frequently among the groups, the second was the Malaysian students, and the third was the local. The local students, on the other hand, reviewed writing most frequently; the Chinese students tied with the Malaysian students for

Q6. I used videos to study how to read *kanji*. (1=Never, 2, 3, 4, 5=3 or more times)	E (2.9, 0.95) C (3.2, 1.13) K (2.0, 0) M (3.0, 0)
Q7. I used videos to study how to write *kanji*. (1=Never, 2, 3, 4, 5=3 or more times)	E (2.7, 1.11) C (2.3, 1.2) K (3.5, 1.5) M (3.0,0)
Q8. I used the recommended web page to study stroke orders. (No=1 –Yes=2)	E (1.3, 0.45) C (1.3, 0.44) K (1.5, 0.5) M (1.0, 0)
Q9. Outside class, I spent time to learn the compulsory *kanji*. (1=Not At All, 2, 3, 4, 5=Very Much)	E (3.2, 0.73) C (2.7, 1.05) K (3.5, 1.5) M (3.0, 0)
Q10. I reviewed readings of *kanji* regularly. (1=No, 2, 3, 4, 5=Yes)	E (2.6, 1.53) C (4.5, 0.5) K (2.5, 0.5) M (3.2, 0.83)
Q11. I reviewed writing of *kanji* regularly. (1=No, 2, 3, 4, 5=Yes)	E (2.9, 0.61) C (2.5, 1.14) K (2.0, 0) M (2.5, 0.5)
Q12. I used flash cards. (1=Never, 2, 3, 4, 5=All kanji)	E (2.7, 0.82) C (1.7, 1.05) K (2.5, 1.5) M (3.0, 0)
Q13. I used *kanji* for communication. (0=Never, 2, 3, 4, 6=6 or more)	E (2.2, 1.26) C (2.8, 1.5) K (1.5, 0.5) M (3.0, 1)
Q14. I can study *kanji* by myself without class lectures. (1=No, 2, 3, 4, 5=Yes)	E (4.2, 0.94) C (4.5, 0.88) K (5.0, 0) M (3.0, 1)

Table 3: Strategies to study the compulsory kanji characters

second place. The Malaysian students used flash cards most often among the groups, and the Chinese students used them the least. Then, in terms of applying the *kanji* characters they studied for real communication using email and the Internet, the Malaysian students used them most frequently, the second group was the Chinese students, the third was the local students and the last was Korean students.

After the students experienced both the traditional lectures and a learner-centred approach to study the compulsory *kanji* characters, the majority of them expressed the opinion that they could now study *kanji* without any formal lectures. The Korean students responded to this question most strongly by a rating of 5 of 5, the second was the Chinese students by rating 4.5, the third was the local students, 4.2, and the last was the Malaysian students, 3.0. Table 3 shows the questions and responses (means and standard deviations) of each group.

With regard to the self-directed study for extracurricular *kanji*, the study asked three questions to investigate the students' motivation in advancing their learning (see Table 4). The most motivated students were the Koreans by rating 5 of 5, the second group was the Chinese students by rating 4, the third was the local students by rating 3.2, and the last was the Malaysian students who rated 3. The Korean students expressed the deepest interest in becoming able to select appropriate *kanji* when they word-process Japanese scripts by rating 5 of 5, the second was the Chinese students by rating 4.2, the third was the local students by rating 4.1, and the last

Q15. I am motivated to study how to read extra-curricular *kanji*. (1=Not At All, 2, 3, 4, 5=Very Much)	E (3.2, 0.60) C (4.0, 0.78) K (5.0, 0) M (3.0, 0)
Q16. I want to be able to select appropriate *kanji* when I word-process Japanese. (1=No, 2, 3, 4, 5=Yes)	E (4.1, 0.89) C (4.2, 0.98) K (5.0, 0) M (3.0, 0)
Q17. I am interested in learning how to hand-write *kanji*. (1=No, 2, 3, 4, 5=Yes)	E (3.8, 1.27) C (4.1, 1.19) K (4.0, 0) M (3.0, 0)
Q18. I made a good plan for extra-curricular study of *kanji*. (1=No, 2, 3, 4, 5=Yes)	E (3.0, 0.83) C (3.3, 0.75) K (3.5, 0.5) M (2.5, 0.5)
Q19. I am satisfied with the amount of *kanji* that I learned for extra-curricular study. (1=No, 2, 3, 4, 5=Yes)	E (2.9, 0.73) C (3.7, 0.95) K (2.5, 0.5) M (2.5, 0.5)
Q20. I am confident in studying *kanji* as an independent learner. (1=No, 2, 3, 4, 5=Yes)	E (3.2, 0.91) C (4.4, 0.88) K (3.5, 1.5) M (3.0, 0)

Table 4: Self-directed study for extracurricular kanji

Test	Kanji Reading Test 1	Kanji Reading Test 2	Kanji Writing Test 1	Kanji Writing Test 2
Full mark	5	5	5	5
English	3.85	3.93	3.30	3.10
Chinese	4.50	4.15	4.40	4.81
Korean	4.75	4.25	4.50	3.63
Malaysian	4.38	4.75	4.75	5.00

Table 5: The average test scores of each language group

was the Malaysian students who rated 3. Compared to the interest in learning how to read, all of the groups expressed less interest in learning how to hand-write *kanji*. The Chinese students showed the deepest interest in this by rating 4.1 of 5, the second group was the Korean students by rating 4, the third was the local students by rating 3.8, and the last was the Malaysian students by rating 3.

With respect to their own plan for extracurricular study of *kanji*, many students reported that they had difficulties and evaluated their plans by rating from 3.5 to 2.5 of 5. The Korean students gave the best score of 3.5, the Chinese students second by giving 3.3, the third group was the local students by giving 3, and the last was the Malaysian students by giving 2.5. The Chinese students expressed the most satisfaction with the amount of extracurricular *kanji* characters that they studied by rating 3.7 of 5, the second group was the local students by rating 2.9, followed by the Korean and Malaysian students rating 2.5 respectively. With regard to the question about their confidence in studying *kanji* as an independent learner, the Chinese students gave clearly the highest rating of 4.4 of 5, the second highest was 3.5 by the Korean students, the third was 3.2 by the local students and the last was 3 by the Malaysian students. Table 4 shows the questions and responses (means and standard deviations) of each group.

Finally, in relation to the *kanji* tests, the average scores of the international students were higher than those of the local students for all the four tests (see Table 5). All three groups of international students received an average of 4 or above for the reading and writing tests, except for the Korean students whose average score for the writing test 2 was 3.63. There were no distinct differences in the achievement of the international students in reading and writing. On the other hand, the local students' scores for writing tests were lower than those for the reading tests. Table 5 shows the test results.

Discussion and implications

Not surprisingly, there was significant difference in the amount of prior knowledge of *kanji* between the local students and the international students. The Chinese students reported that they already knew how to write the majority of the compulsory *kanji* characters before they started the course and the amount was much higher than that of students in the other three groups. On the other hand, the amount of the Chinese students' prior knowledge of reading *kanji* was similar to that of the other three groups. The Chinese students showed a high degree of interest in the study of reading *kanji*, but showed a significantly low degree of interest in studying writing. They spent much less time for studying writing than for studying reading, and they spent the least amount of time for reviewing the stroke orders of *kanji* among the four groups. Thus, the data indicates that the Chinese students were interested and motivated to study reading *kanji*, of which they had only a little prior knowledge, and that they were less interested and motivated to study writing *kanji* of which they had had much more experience.

Prior knowledge has been widely considered to play a positive role in students' learning. However, the above data show that there can be cases where prior knowledge is negatively correlated with interest and motivation. Noticeably, although they expressed lower motivation, the average marks of the Chinese students for *kanji* tests were high. Thus, this study assumed that many Chinese students performed well in the tests with a minimum of effort. However, some Chinese students received low marks even though they had much prior knowledge. This negative correlation, which was contradictory to findings of previous studies, indicates that further research is needed to find what socio-educational factors are associated with the Chinese students' motivation. It is particularly important to investigate whether their study in other courses in English as their SL affects their choice to learn Japanese, and, if this is the case, to what extent both their integrative motivation and their instrumental motivation are affected by their English language levels as well as their time management skills. In terms of the other students, the local students had the smallest amount of prior knowledge among the four groups as both the Korean and Malaysian students had greater levels of prior knowledge, but all these students had a high degree of interest and motivation in the study of all three aspects of *kanji*.

There was also significant difference between the local students and the Chinese students in the area of learning styles. In terms of selection of learning materials and tools, 50 per cent or more students in all the groups used computer-aided-language-learning (CALL) materials such as video clips and online tools as supplementary aids. Note that the Chinese students accessed the video clips to learn how to read *kanji* words most frequently of all the four groups. Some Chinese students accessed each clip five to ten times, while the class average number of accesses to each clip was 1.7 times. The Chinese students' tendency to favour the CALL materials to learn reading *kanji* words may be positively associated with an integrative interest and motivation in the study of reading *kanji*, or in the use of technology, or both of these reasons together.

The majority of students in the course shared some learning strategies, but there were differences in the use of some strategies depending upon language background. The use of flash cards has been recommended to Japanese language learners for a long time as one of the most effective learning strategies for the study of characters and vocabulary. However, it was found that the Chinese students did not appreciate this method as much as the local students. Some local Australian students reported that after the Japanese word-processing skills were introduced in the computer workshops, they found online flashcard software that enables users to make their own flashcards. They then created their own online flashcards to learn Japanese words and *kanji*, and kept using them by updating them regularly. The international students, however, showed little interest in such use of flashcards. Instead, the Chinese and Malaysian students reported that they tried to use *kanji* words for real written communication, that is, through email and blogs. Thus, it seems that the Chinese students avoided unnecessary simple practice for memorising *kanji* but they used more advanced techniques for practice. This finding indicates that there could be other learning strategies that any particular group of students tends to prefer or avoid. Further research could be very useful in the area of study styles of students with different backgrounds so that teachers can implement appropriate strategies in their teaching.

In relation to the self-directed study to advance *kanji* learning, the Chinese students expressed a high degree of motivation in learning extra-curricular *kanji* by rating 4 of 5 on the scale. Interestingly, they showed the highest degree of interest among the four groups in learning how to handwrite *kanji*. It appears that these data were inconsistent with the finding that the Chinese students were not motivated in the study of writing *kanji*. However, it may be the case that the Chinese students were not interested in studying writing the compulsory lower elementary-level characters, but that they may have been more motivated to study how to write *kanji* at a higher level. This point needs clarification since further investigation may contribute to improving the teaching of these diverse students with clearly different motivations. Further research is also needed to investigate if the Chinese students' interest in self-directed study to learn how to write extra-curricular *kanji* correlates with integrated/instrumental motivation, or if they are influenced by their Chinese culture that highly values the handwriting of characters.

Students in all the groups showed interest in being able to master Japanese word-processing skills. These data seem associated with the students' desire to be able to update their skills for using technologies for study and communication via the Internet. The majority of the students also expressed the desire to be able to work using Japanese-language in the future. It appears here in the study of *kanji* that both the local students and the international students had strong instrumental motivation that is related to their future career paths. Many students reported that they met difficulties in making a plan for self-directed study, finding resources and managing time, despite the fact that information retrieval skills in Japanese together with the basic word-processing skills plus skills for dealing with unfamiliar *kanji* characters and words by using technologies, were all taught in the computer workshops. This finding has shown that all students at the lower elementary level need more scaffolded teaching and careful support in the self-study of *kanji*. Yet, despite the difficulties of the self-study, 50 per cent or more students in all the groups were satisfied with the amount of *kanji* that they learned by self-study. The Chinese students especially began to feel confidence in learning *kanji* as independent learners at a higher level than the local students.

The above findings of this study have certain general implications for further research to conceptualise motivation of both local and international students in FL learning. Motivational and affective factors, especially integrative motivation as well as aspects of instrumental motivation, should now be compared among students with diverse backgrounds. At the lower elementary level, it was evident that some Chinese international students are more motivated in learning *kanji* to communicate in writing in broader ways than the tasks given in the course, which is a clear sign of integrative motivation. In contrast, other Chinese students and many local students are studying *kanji* as a linguistic item to pass the required tests, and thus demonstrate a more instrumental motivation. Also, in future research on teaching Japanese as a FL, more attention should be given to the differences which are drawn from language backgrounds as well as from individual situations at different language proficiency levels, in order to respond positively to the needs of such diverse student groups in this globalised contexts. From a pedagogical perspective, it is now vital to implement a learner-centred approach to teaching *kanji* in formal instructional situations in class, as well as to assist students embarking on autonomous learning of *kanji* because this research has indicated that international students have clearly different prior knowledge, motivation and learning strategies from those of local students.

Conclusion

This research aimed to investigate whether there are significant differences in students' needs depending on their language backgrounds in terms of studying *kanji* characters in a foreign language learning context. The study showed marked differences in prior knowledge, interest, motivation and study styles between international students and local Australian students. First, the international Chinese students had significantly higher prior knowledge of stroke orders of *kanji* than the local students, and this prior knowledge did not influence interest and motivation in a positive manner in the students' study of writing *kanji* at this lower elementary level. This result indicates that prior knowledge may not always produce a positive motivation in the case of international students. Moreover, there were significant differences in the use of some learning strategies between the Chinese students and the local students. For example, local students favoured the use of flashcards but this was not a Chinese students' preferred strategy. However, the practice of using *kanji* in real communication through mail and blogs was more appreciated by the Chinese students than by the local students. These findings clearly suggest that some learning strategies may be more appropriate for a particular group of students than for other groups, depending on their backgrounds. Finally, the study found that the Chinese students were more interested in independently advancing their learning of *kanji* than the local students. It may be the case that the Chinese students have a higher degree of integrative motivation than the local students, for example, the desire to use the Japanese language for communicating with native speakers of Japanese. Further research is now needed to investigate the specific nature and degrees of both integrative and instrumental motivation between international students and local students, and to compare them to inform pedagogy and teaching.

These findings and discussion have pedagogical and theoretical implications for FL learning and for teaching students from diverse backgrounds. It is crucial for researchers and teachers to recognise students' different needs, which have derived from these students' diverse socio-educational backgrounds, in order to enhance students' learning. Implementing a learner-centred approach helps all students to learn what they want and need to learn at their own pace, and thus more computer-aided-language-learning materials should be made available to enrich opportunities for learning and generate appropriately targeted learning activities. Furthermore, in order to fulfil the needs of those students who are motivated to advance their already competent levels of command, it is essential that teachers design and implement autonomous learning for enhancing students' competence and improving their written communication. For all these reasons, successful teaching of Japanese and other Asian foreign languages now demands that teachers rise to the challenge of exploring and engaging with students' diverse learning capacities and motivations, if they are to meet their students' integrative and instrumental needs in today's globalised university programs.

Notes

1. A shorter version of this paper appeared as Aoki, N 2010, 'Teaching *kanji* to students from diverse language backgrounds in Australia', in *Crises and opportunities: proceedings of the 18th biennial conference of the ASAA, 2010*, eds E Morrell & MD Barr, Asian Studies Association of Australia, Canberra, ACT, viewed 2 November 2010 at <http://asaa.asn.au/ASAA2010/index.php>.
2. According to the surveys on Japanese-language education abroad which were conducted by the Japan Foundation, the top five countries in numbers of students of the Japanese language were as shown in the table below. These figures include learners of Japanese-language in primary education, secondary education, tertiary education and language schools.

	2003	2006	2009
1	Korea (894,131)	Korea (910,957)	Korea (964,354)
2	China (387,924)	China (684,366)	China (827,171)
3	Australia (381, 954)	Australia (366,165)	Indonesia (716,353)
4	U.S.A. (140.200)	Indonesia (272,719)	Australia (275,710)
5	Taiwan (128,641)	Taiwan (191,367)	Taiwan (246,641)
6	Indonesia (85,221)	U.S.A. (117,969)	U.S.A. (141,244)
7	Thailand (54,884)	Thailand (71,083)	Singapore (78,802)
8	New Zealand (28,317)	Hong Kong (32,959)	Viet Nam (44,272)
9	Hong Kong (18,284)	Viet Nam (29,982)	Hong Kong (28,224)
10	Viet Nam (18,029)	New Zealand (29,904)	Canada (27,488)

3. In 2010, the Culture Discussion Committee of the *Agency for Cultural Affairs* in the Ministry of Education, Culture, Sports, Science and Technology, Japan, reviewed the use of *joyo-kanji* after 29 years and made a recommendation that the number of *joyo-kanji* should be increased to 2,136 characters. The recommendation was endorsed by the Cabinet and the change was announced in the Cabinet Notice of 30 November 2010 (Yomiuri Shinbun 24/11/2010; Agency for Cultural Affairs 30/11/2010).

References

Agency for Cultural Affairs 2010, *Jouyoukanji hyou, Heisei 22 nen naikaku kokuji dai-2-go* (List of the jouyoukanji, Cabinet notice, no. 22, 2010), Ministry of Education, Culture, Sports, Science and Technology, Japan, viewed 30 November 2010, <jouyoukanjihyou_h22[1].pdf,http://www.bunka.go.jp/kokugo_nihongo/kokujikunrei_h221130.html>.

Australian Education International 2002, 2003, 2004, 2005, 2006, 2007, 2008, 2009, *International student data*, Australian government, viewed 08 June 2010, <http://aei.gov.au/research/International-Student-Data/Pages/default.aspx>.

Chen, E, Warden, CA, & Chang, HT 2005, 'Motivators that do not motivate: the case of Chinese EFL learners and the influence of culture on motivation', *TESOL Quarterly*, vol. 39 no. 4, pp. 609–633.

Cho, HC 1994, '*Kanji* teaching to *kanji* area students: focusing on Korean students studying Japanese', *Japanese-Language Education around the Globe*, vol. 4, pp. 61–75.

Crookes, G & Schmidt, RW 1991, 'Motivation: reopening the research agenda', *Language Learning*, vol. 41 no. 4, pp. 469–512.

Dornyei, Z 1990, 'Conceptualizing motivation in foreign-language learning', *Language Learning*, vol. 40 no. 1, pp. 45–78.

Fujiyama, T 2002, '*Kanji* education toward Chinese students: what do we teach?', *Journal of International Student Centre, University of Nagasaki*, vol. 10, pp. 41–51.

Gardner, RC 1979, 'Social psychological aspects of second language acquisition', in H Giles & R St. Clair (eds), *Language and social psychology*, Basil Blackwell, Oxford, pp. 193–220.

Gardner, RC 1985, *Social psychology and second language learning: the role of attitudes and motivation*, Edward Arnold, London.

Gardner, RC 1988, 'The socio-educational model of second-language learning: assumptions, findings, and issues', *Language Learning*, vol. 38 no. 1, pp. 101–126.

Gardner, RC & Lambert, WE 1959, 'Motivational variables in second language acquisition', *Canadian Journal of Psychology*, vol. 13, pp. 266–272.

Gardner, RC & Lambert, WE 1972, *Attitudes and motivation in second-language learning*, Newbury House, Rowley, MA.

Gillard, J 2009, *Record growth in international students in 2008*, Ministers Media Centre, Media release, Hon Julia Gillard MP, 26 February 2009, Department of Education, Employment and Workplace Relations, Australian Government, viewed 08 June 2010, <http://www.deewr.gov.au/ministers/gillard/media/releases/pages/article_090226_151822.aspx>.

Katashima, Y 1999, 'A study of course design for a Japanese language program as a foreign language', *Journal of Nagasaki Wesleyan University*, vol. 22, pp. 91–98.

Kawaguchi, S 2009, 'Teaching and learning *kanji* in Europe: some efforts to develop learner's autonomy', *Journal of Seigakuin University*, vol. 22 no. 2, pp. 121–137.

Kojima, K 2003, 'Common points and differences of *kanji* characters in Japan, China, Taiwan and Hong Kong', *Studies in Comparative Culture*, vol. 62, pp. 63–74.

Koyama, R 2007, 'Japanese language ability of Chinese students: the actual state and the remark of teaching', *Journal of the Faculty of Humanities, College of Saitama-Gakuen*, vol. 7, pp. 237–242.

Japan Foundation 2007, *Survey report on Japanese-language education abroad 2006:*

present condition of overseas Japanese-language education (summary), viewed 21 November 2010, <http://www.jpf.go.jp/e/japanese/survey/result/survey06.html>.

Japan Foundation 2010, *Survey on Japanese-language education abroad 2009*, viewed 21 November 2010, <http://www.jpf.go.jp/e/japanese/survey/result/survey06.html>.

Japan Foundation 2011, *Present condition of overseas Japanese-language education, survey report on Japanese-language education abroad 2009*, viewed 19 September 2011, <http://www.jpf.go/e/japanese/survey/result/index.html>.

Japan Student Services Organization 2009, 'Number of international students by region of origin', *International Students in Japan 2009*, viewed 10 April 2010, <http://www.jasso.go.jp/statistics/intl_student/data09_e.html>.

McNamara, DS, & Kintsch, W 1996, 'Learning from texts: effects of prior knowledge and text coherence', *Discourse Processes*, vol. 22, pp. 247–288.

Norman, J 1988, *Chinese*, Cambridge University Press, Cambridge.

Okita, Y 1995, '*Kanji* learning strategies and student beliefs on *kanji* learning', *Current Report on Japanese-Language Education around the Globe*, vol. 5, pp. 105–124.

O'Malley, JM & Chamot, AU 1990, *Learning strategies in second language acquisition*, Cambridge University Press, Cambridge.

Oxford, RL 1990, *Language learning strategies: what every teacher should know*, Newbury House, New York.

Print, M 1987, *Curriculum development and design*, Allen & Unwin, Sydney.

Roschelle, J 1995, 'Learning in interactive environments: prior knowledge and new experience', *Public institutions for personal learning: establishing a research agenda*, The American Association of Museums, viewed 29 November 2010, <http://www. exploratorium.edu/IFI/resources/museumeducation/priorknolwedge.html>.

Rowntree, D 1981, *Developing courses for students*, McGraw-Hill, London.

Strangman, N & Hall, T 2009, '*Background knowledge*', *Teaching methods: prior knowledge and misconceptions in learning*, National Center on Accessing the General Curriculum, USA, viewed 29 November 2010, <http://aim.cast.org/learn/historyarchive/backgroundpapers/background_knowledge>.

Toohey, S 1999, *Designing courses for higher education*, SRHE and Open University Press, Philadelphia, Pennsylvania.

Yomiuri Shinbun 2010, 'Jouyou*kanji* 29nen-buri minaoshi, 30nichi ni naikaku kokuji' (Jouyou*kanji* reviewed after 29 years, Cabinet notice on the 30th), *Yomiuri Online*, viewed 24 November 2010, <http://www.yomiuri.co.jp/national/culture/news/20101124-OYT1T00241.htm?from=main7>.

Appendix

Questionnaire on *kanji* study

What is your language background?
I am a local student and speak
(   ) English only
(   ) English and Chinese
(   ) English and a language other than Chinese
I am an international student and a native speaker of
(   ) Chinese
(   ) Korean
(   ) a language other than Chinese and Korean

Part I This section asks about your study of *kanji* characters which have been introduced in the Minna no Nihongo *kanji* textbook, Unit 11-16.

I   **Motivation to learn *kanji* introduced in the *kanji* textbook**

1. The amount of *kanji* (64 characters) introduced in the textbook was

        Too little   Appropriate   Too much

        1---------------2---------------3---------------4---------------5

2. I already knew the **meaning** of the 64 *kanji* when the course started.

        None   50%   All

        1---------------2---------------3---------------4---------------5

3. I already knew how to **read** the 64 *kanji* in the Japanese way when the course started.

        None   50%   All

        1---------------2---------------3---------------4---------------5

4. I already knew how to **write** the 64 *kanji* when the course started.

        None   50%   All

        1---------------2---------------3---------------4---------------5

5. I was interested in learning how to **read** the 64 *kanji* introduced in the *kanji* book.

        Not at all   Very much

        1---------------2---------------3---------------4---------------5

6. I was interested in learning how to **write** the 64 *kanji* introduced in the *kanji* book.

        Not at all   Very much

        1---------------2---------------3---------------4---------------5

II   Strategies that I used to learn the 64 *kanji* introduced in the textbook

7. In order to learn how to **read** the *kanji* in Unit 14-16, I used the video clips.

        Never   Once/Unit   3 times or more/Unit
        1---------------2---------------3---------------4---------------5

8. In order to learn how to **write** the *kanji* in Unit 14 & 15, I used the video clips.

        Never   Once/Unit   3 times or more/Unit
        1---------------2---------------3---------------4---------------5

9. In order to learn how to **write** the *kanji* in Unit 16, I used the web site recommended in class.   No   Yes

        1----------------------------------2

10. Outside class, I spent time to learn the 64 kanji.

        Not at all   Very much
        1---------------2---------------3---------------4---------------5

11. I made and used flash cards for practice.

        Never   For all kanji
        1---------------2---------------3---------------4---------------5

12. I reviewed the **meaning** of the *kanji* on a weekly-basis.

        Never   Sometimes   Yes
        1---------------2---------------3---------------4---------------5

13. I reviewed how to **read** the *kanji* on a weekly-basis.

        Never   Sometimes   Yes
        1---------------2---------------3---------------4---------------5

14. I reviewed how to **write** the *kanji* on a weekly-basis.

        Never   Sometimes   Yes
        1---------------2---------------3---------------4---------------5

15. I monitored my *kanji* learning process on a weekly-basis.

        Never   Sometimes   Yes
        1---------------2---------------3---------------4---------------5

16. I studied the 64 *kanji* with my friend(s).

        Never   More than 6 times
        0-----------1----------2----------3---------4----------5---------6

17. I used the main textbook to practice reading the 64 kanji.

        Never   More than 6 times

        0------------1----------2----------3---------4----------5----------6

18. I tried to use the *kanji* by writing compositions, mail, diaries, and so on.

        Never   More than 6 times

        0------------1----------2----------3---------4----------5----------6

III   Pedagogical preferences to study *kanji* introduced in the *kanji* textbook

19. The best method for me to learn the **meanings** of *kanji* is: (Choose only ONE method.)

    (   ) Minna no Nihongo textbooks

    (   ) Dictionaries (print, electronic, online)

    (   ) Lectures given to all students in class

    (   ) Video clips to be able to use individually

    (   ) Other:_____

20. The best method for me to learn how to **read** *kanji* is: (Choose only ONE method.)

    (   ) Minna no Nihongo textbooks

    (   ) Dictionaries (print, electronic, online)

    (   ) Lectures given to all students in class

    (   ) Video clips to be able to use individually

    (   ) Other:_____

21. The best method for me to learn how to **write** *kanji* is: (Choose only ONE method.)

    (   ) Minna no Nihongo textbooks

    (   ) Dictionaries (print, electronic, online)

    (   ) Lectures given to all students in class

    (   ) Video clips to be able to use individually

    (   ) Web site(s) which show(s) stroke orders

    (   ) Other:_____

22. I can study the *kanji* in the *kanji* book by myself, by using the book and dictionaries.

        No   Yes

        1---------------2---------------3---------------4--------------5

23. The video clips that we saw individually were useful for me to learn kanji.

                No   Yes

            1---------------2---------------3---------------4---------------5

24. Comments on the use of video clips:

25. The exercise materials such as Excel files to practice *kanji* & vocabulary were useful.

                No   Yes

            1---------------2---------------3---------------4---------------5

26. Comments on the use of exercise materials:

Part II This section asks about your self-directed study to learn extra kanji.

I   Motivation to learn extra *kanji*

27. I am motivated to study how to **read** extra *kanji* by myself for my own study.

                No   Yes

            1---------------2---------------3---------------4---------------5

28. Japanese sources that I am interested in reading now and in the future are:

    (Choose as many as appropriate.)

    (   ) Books   (   ) *Manga* comics   (   ) Magazines

    (   ) Newspapers (   ) Web pages   (   ) Movie/video subtitles

    (   ) Other:_____

29. I want to be able to select appropriate *kanji* when I word-process Japanese documents.

                No   Yes

            1---------------2---------------3---------------4---------------5

30. I am interested in learning how to **hand-write** extra kanji.

                No   Yes

            1---------------2---------------3---------------4---------------5

31. I study extra *kanji* to be able to use them for the following written communication:

    (Choose as many as appropriate.)

    (   ) Mail   (   ) Letters & cards   (   ) Home-pages / Blogs

    (   ) Chat   (   ) Other:_____

32. I want to study extra *kanji* to be able to work by using Japanese in the future.

                No   Yes

            1---------------2---------------3---------------4---------------5

II Strategies that I used to study extra *kanji* for my individual study:

(Choose as many as appropriate.)

( ) I made a list of *kanji* that I tried to learn.

( ) I made flash cards and used them.

( ) I studied *kanji* as words, rather than isolated *kanji* characters.

( ) I read aloud *kanji* words while I studied them.

( ) I wrote each *kanji* multiple times to memorise them.

( ) I monitored my individual *kanji* study on a weekly-basis.

( ) I tried to use the extra *kanji* I studied, for communication with others.

III Materials and tools I used to learn extra kanji: (Choose as many as appropriate.)

( ) Book   ( ) Magazine   ( ) Web page(s) to read

( ) Dictionaries   ( ) Japanese IME   ( ) MS Word

( ) MS Excel   ( ) Moji/Rikaichan/Furiganizer

( ) Web sites(s) for stroke orders   ( ) Web site(s) for radicals

( ) Other:_____

IV Evaluation of my individual study of kanji

33. I made a good plan for my *kanji* study.

        No   Yes

        1---------------2---------------3---------------4---------------5

34. I am satisfied with the amount of *kanji* I learned by myself.

        No   Yes

        1---------------2---------------3---------------4---------------5

35. I am confident in studying *kanji* as an independent learner.

        No   Yes

        1---------------2---------------3---------------4---------------5

7

Personal growth through intercultural communication: Engaging native speakers and reflective learning in Japanese language curriculum

Akiko Tomita

Introduction

The communicative language teaching (CLT) approach has been used in foreign language classes to meet many learners' primary goals, as the development of speaking ability is the one of the key areas of achievement for those learning a language. With this approach teachers emphasise authentic interaction, conversation and language use as much as they can, as distinct from just focussing on learning about the language (Lightbown & Spada 1993). In the past, traditional foreign language teaching had focused primarily on knowledge of the language as a code, whereas the CLT approach is based on performance rather than linguistic knowledge. Student-to-student interaction in pairs and small groups working on student-centred activities are common practice in this approach. Nevertheless, it is usually the case that students are unable to use the language in realistic interaction as their oral communication skills are at relatively low levels. To address this issue, and for students to be able to use the language authentically, foreign language courses in Australian universities promote study abroad programs as one of the best ways to study the target language in the target community. Language students are encouraged to visit the country of their target language and immerse themselves in the language and culture. However, the unfortunate fact is that only limited numbers of students can take advantage of such opportunities. Thus, we as teachers are challenged to create activities and resources in order to provide our students with realistic opportunities to experience the target language and culture within Australia.

Depending on a teacher's ability and capacity within their environment and circumstances, there are many ways of producing the necessary resources. One of the most common of these is through technology and computers. Using such devices, students of Japanese in Australia are able, for instance, to communicate with native speakers (NSs) in Japan. Teachers may also encourage students to be involved in local Japanese community events and to find language partners for language practice. Moreover, teachers may invite native speakers into their classes. At Monash University, for example, an 'immersion program' was created in which NS experts in the fields of Japanese education and Japanese food were invited into the classroom (Imura 2004a). Furthermore, Griffith University carried out a 'Community Involvement Project' in which Japanese language students were matched with locally based NSs as language partners for a minimum of 10 hours outside of class (Imura 2006). As a result of this interaction with NSs in the above interventions, students reported enjoyable and motivating language practice with corresponding improvement of communication skills and cultural understanding, giving good grounds for recommending these kinds of teaching interventions. However, despite such examples, the CLT approach itself does not necessarily involve students in authentic, real-life exchange, nor make it necessary for them to engage in self-motivated intercultural exploration. Furthermore, universities and educators have often attempted to implement it as if it were in a monolingual target language environment.

Thus, some scholars argue for the importance of extending beyond CLT, and believe that a targeted 'intercultural' approach to language teaching and learning can increase the efficiency of foreign language acquisition. Above all, this approach can reward students not only with enjoyable and motivating language practice and improvement of their communication skills and cultural understanding, but it can also prepare language learners by adding value to life communication outside their own cultural environment and developing in them a sense of themselves as mediators between languages and cultures (Buttjes & Byram 1991: Zarate et al. 2004). The development of intercultural language teaching and learning has prompted a theoretical shift in the understanding of the basic nature and purpose of language education. At the University of South Australia, for example, an 'Interculturality Project' and an 'Intercultural Communication Project' have been developed as a part of foreign language curricula. For these projects, which implement an intercultural approach to instruction, students view and analyse authentic Japanese dramas and movies, and engage with native speakers out of class as part of their standard language curriculum.

This issue of authentic intercultural exchange arose for me in my work with final year Japanese language students Centre for Asian Studies at an Australian university. In initial diagnostic discussions many students had expressed that they seemed to have spent their time at university learning the Japanese language but were about to graduate without having yet had to use it in a practical manner, and they found this highly disappointing. They recognised that they had gained knowledge of grammar, vocabulary, *kanji* characters, reading, writing, speaking and listening in the formal classroom situation. However, they did not feel that they had used Japanese enough and were not able to integrate their Japanese into real life scenarios, even though they might have studied as many as three years of Japanese at the University. As I became the Coordinator of a new third year course, *Japanese 3B: Practical Japanese*, in 2009, I attempted to design a course for students to have experience as if they were in Japan, and to feel that studying Japanese at the University was worthwhile. The main goal of the newly designed course was to establish the students as mediators between language and culture, and as effective communicators in the Japanese language. As such mediation promotes lifelong learning, these skills are not only used within the classroom setting but also have ongoing ramifications for students' future prospects and personal growth.

Context of teaching

The Centre for Asian Studies in the School of Social Sciences in this research-intensive, Australian university, offers Japanese language and Japanese social science courses, as well as equivalents in Chinese language and social science. Students who enrol in Japanese language courses are from a diverse range of degree structures and if Japanese is not a core component of their degree, students are encouraged to undertake the Language Diploma in Japanese Language. This Diploma requires 24 units, including seven 3-unit Japanese language courses and one Japanese cultural studies course, which amounts to the same as a major in Japanese language. In this context, due to recent restructuring of undergraduate degree programs at University level, a previously 6-unit Japanese third year course was divided into two, and a new course, *Japanese 3B: Practical Japanese*, was initiated as a complementary course to the mainstream, third year Japanese language course.

Thus, *Japanese 3B: Practical Japanese* is the only Japanese language course in which students can have the opportunity to experience something different from the mainstream Japanese language courses that employ a traditional textbook-based teaching and learning method, using the textbooks Minna No Nihongo 2 and the Shin Nihongo No Chukyu series.

Theoretical approaches to intercultural learning and teaching
Intercultural language teaching and learning

Because I took an intercultural approach to teaching this new course, I drew on the notion of the 'third space' conceptualised by the post-structuralist scholar,

Homi Bhabha (1994), who has inspired researchers in second and foreign language education. This concept essentially explores how identity is created through negotiation across differences of languages and cultures. Bhabha defines his 'third space' as:

> [a] liminal space, in-between the designations of identity ... an interstitial passage between fixed identifications [that] opens up the possibility of a cultural hybridity that entertains difference without an assumed or implied hierarchy. (Bhabha 1994, p. 4)

Kramsch (1993) takes this idea to support her notion of a 'third place', which is the space of negotiation between one's native culture and the target culture for additional language learners. Aiming to develop students' 'third place', intercultural experience is essential to the process of intercultural teaching and learning in language education. This introduces students to complex challenges demanding new understanding of their own and other cultures. The process of learning to understand one's *own* and *other* cultural viewpoints challenges learners' sense of self, their cultural identity, and their worldview. As a result, they may experience a lasting change in self-concept, attitudes, and behaviour, which ideally results in greater openness toward individuals of other cultures and an increased desire to interact with them. As Bateman (2002, p. 320) suggests, '[T]his increased self-awareness, with the accompanying changes in attitude and behaviour toward others, is perhaps the most compelling reason for culture learning'. In addition to this, the study of language has the potential to expose learners to other ways of viewing the world and develops flexibility and independence from a single linguistic and conceptual system through which to view the world (Byram 1989a; Kramsch 1993; Liddicoat 2005). In these ways, the importance and the benefit of an intercultural approach become clear, and with the acceleration of globalisation over the past two decades, the development of intercultural language teaching and learning in language education has become imperative.

Pedagogy of intercultural language teaching and learning

There is no single set of pedagogic practices that comprise intercultural language teaching and learning, though there have been different successful initiatives. Recently Liddicoat (2008) promoted the following pedagogic model. He proposes that locally situated practice is best individually developed by the teacher, based on a starting point of five principles: 1) active construction; 2) making connections; 3) interaction; 4) reflection, and 5) responsibility. This procedure is conceptualised as a cycle of four interrelated processes of noticing, comparing, reflecting and interacting (see Figure 1). Liddicoat (2008, pp. 280–4) defines these processes, summarised as follows:

1. Noticing: Noticing cultural similarities and differences is a fundamental element in intercultural learning.
2. Comparing: Comparison encompasses both making comparisons between the learner's background culture and the target culture, and also between their own knowledge of the target language and culture and the new input they are noticing.
3. Reflecting: Reflection involves the learner in making personal sense of experiences and knowledge, and engaging the learner in reflecting on what their experience of linguistic and cultural diversity means for them with regard to:
   a. how they react to diversity
   b. how they think about diversity
   c. how they feel about diversity
   d. how they will find ways of engaging constructively with diversity.
4. Interacting: Interaction occurs by the learner acting on the basis of their learning and experience of diversity with the aim of creating personal meanings about their experiences.

Developing students' practice from the above principles involves constructing learning opportunities in language learning programs that engage learners directly

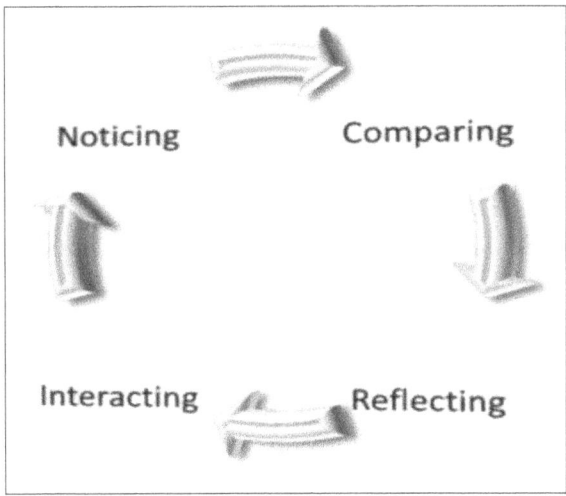

Figure 1: Interacting processes of intercultural pedagogy (Liddicoat 2008, pp. 284)

and actively with the target culture. Thus, Liddicoat's 'interacting processes of intercultural pedagogy' (2008, pp. 280–4) have the potential to be used in a wide range of manners depending on the educators' location and specific goals for practice.

Pedagogy of connection

Such processes of interaction have been explored in English language teaching through the concept of a 'pedagogy of connection' (Cadman 2005). Based on hooks (1994, p. 15) definition of 'engagement' as 'connection between ideas learned in university settings and those learned in life practices', Cadman (2005) argues for a language pedagogy that connects people, understandings, knowledge and feelings in the diverse way that an English as an Additional Language (EAL) teaching context makes possible. I believe that this is also particularly applicable to foreign and second language teaching contexts. Cadman expresses the view that 'possibly the most immediate influence on students' learning is their affective experience of the classroom itself' (2005, p. 355), and she demonstrates the importance of the role of connection with the teacher in the learning process and of how to connect students with one another.

In contrast to those who privilege a pragmatic grammatical curriculum, Cadman (2005, p. 364) argues that 'a critical, connecting pedagogy does not replace linguistic goals with social or political ones; in fact, it has often increased students' agency in the up-take and control of the genre they want'. Elsewhere, she also emphasises that

> striving for social justice is only possible through the human interactions that enable it. In EAL/EIL learning and teaching, the core elements of ethical 'connecting' — equity, joy, compassion and mutual respect — are integrally interwoven in the interpersonal relations that inspire any socially just outcomes. (2008, p. 11)

In my view, feeling is the most powerful element for the connections between humans, and related to these affective experiences, personal growth results from engagement with the emotional elements in language, beyond merely instrumental communicative effectiveness. In other words, authentic intercultural exchange is the key to making real connections between humans. Thus, connection should be attributed a large role in language learning, first in the connection between teacher and students, and then also between students and NSs as I hoped to generate and observe in my own pedagogic location.

Student motivation in relation to affective factors

Regular conversational interactions with NSs have been reported to be very beneficial to language learners in terms of both non-linguistic and linguistic aspects and learning skills (see, for example, Eisenchlas & Hortiguera 1999–2000; Imura 2004a, 2006; Ingram 1978a, 1978b, 1980; Kurts & Luna 1983; Stoller et al. 1995). In particular, it has been noted that interaction with native speakers has affective benefits. Stoller et al. (1995) demonstrate how the psychological and emotional support that NSs can provide to language learners facilitates their learning. In their study, as learners found that their NS partners were casual, friendly, encouraging and non-judgemental of their performances and accepted them as whole human beings, students' self-esteem improved (Stoller et al. 1995). Furthermore, it has been noted that this special bond with NSs in the learning environment creates room for the learners to converse voluntarily (Kurtz & Luna 1983; Long 1997). Ingram (1978b, 1980) and Eisenchlas and Hortiguera (1999–2000) noticed that students were more willing to converse and participate than before, because of the possibility of changing their perceptions and attitudes through regular interaction with native speakers.

Imura's (2006) 'Community Involvement Project' clearly demonstrates the effectiveness of such interaction in terms of developing oral communication skills and increasing L2 confidence. In this tertiary setting, students studying the Japanese language at an intermediate level were matched with a NS partner and met for 10 hours outside of the class across one semester for the purpose of the project. Imura's study concludes:

> that cognitive and affective changes which take place during the interaction with NSs outside the classroom not only have a substantial and significant impact on the development of oral communication skills, but also that these internal changes are transferable to the classroom context. (Imura 2006, p. 251)

The teaching intervention

As a result of these positive outcomes from interactions with NSs, I decided to design an intervention that would foster authentic intercultural communication in my own context. With the impact of internationalisation and globalisation on universities, both educators and learners are increasingly required to take part in intercultural communication. There have been increasing numbers of international students attending universities, so educators need to be aware of the existence of diverse student communities in their own classrooms. They also need to develop an awareness of the opportunities that exist to incorporate these students into programs as mediators of cultural learning.

In order to facilitate authentic intercultural interactions, I saw the potential for involving Japanese exchange students in classroom scenarios as helpers and mentors.

The cooperation offered by the University's International Students Office in this project seemed a perfect opportunity to allow me to draw on the cultural knowledge of these NSs and create the possibility for intercultural learning to take place. In my project, the majority of the Japanese NSs involved were aged from 20 to 25 years old. Since that was the most common age of my enrolled students in *Practical Japanese*, I was hoping that they would be able to connect with the Japanese NSs through their common experience, and enjoy and learn in this new environment.

Thus, the teaching goals for this intervention were:

1. increased proficiency in the use of the Japanese language
2. the development of independent learning
3. the broader goal of offering human beings real-life opportunities to 'connect' across the differences and diversity of culture and language.

Learners

Participants in this teaching program consisted of 18 students who were enrolled in the third year subject, *Japanese 3B: Practical Japanese*, in the second semester of 2009. There were 10 female students and eight male students in the course. Five students were from China, one from Singapore and 12 were local Australian-raised students. This group was a typical example of students with differing learning backgrounds studying together. Six students had studied Japanese for 2.5 years (five semesters) at the same University, and nine students had studied Japanese for 1.5 years (three semesters) and were continuing study from high school Japanese. One student had had six months study abroad experience in Japan after 0.5 years (one semester) of tertiary study continuing from high school Japanese.

Native speaker volunteers

In order to engage the interest of native speakers, I had communication with the Liaison Officer at the International Students' Office at the University and sought their cooperation in offering international and study abroad students from Japan the opportunity to interact with our enrolled students of Japanese. By chance, the Liaison Officer was an ex-student who had previously enjoyed my courses in 2007, especially a course segment I designed that included Japanese guest sessions for each semester. The two sessions she had experienced were only 50 minutes each, but she emphasised how much she enjoyed the interactions with NSs in the language program and how beneficial she felt they were. She had made some Japanese friends through the sessions and was herself inspired to go to Japan with a study abroad programme in 2008. She successfully completed her study abroad program in Japan after one year and when she came back to Australia became a Liaison Officer. Because of her positive experience she contacted me expressing a desire to make a connection between our enrolled students of Japanese and her Japanese international students.

As a result, I met several NSs individually before the start of the semester to explain the course curriculum and my expectation of their roles, and I also arranged two other group meetings to discuss aspects of the course and their roles within it.

Course curriculum

I adopted an approach involving Liddicoat's (2008) model of 'interacting processes of intercultural pedagogy' (see above) as the basis of the course curriculum. Students were encouraged to go through the four processes: noticing and comparing, reflecting, and interacting with cultural issues in and out of the class as often as possible.

The NSs participated in weekly one hour sessions focusing on selections of Japanese text topics including: keigo (honorific expression) practice; keigo quiz; reading articles regarding keigo; Japanese whaling; Japanese education and schooling, and; new government policy in Japan. Each session was followed by discussion.

Also, the enrolled students were given presentations by the Japanese volunteers on various aspects of cultural knowledge chosen by the speakers. These included a self-introduction, the Osaka dialect, Japanese language among young people, trilingual and tricultural identity, and Japanese greetings/courtesy. After each presentation, they then engaged in discussion with the NS presenters. For the discussions, I encouraged students to ask questions of the NSs, suggesting that they should explain their own culture then exchange their opinion and draw conclusions.

Students in the course were also required to get out-of-class assistance from the Japanese students in aspects of their course work. These included writing the following in Japanese: opinions on the relationship between human beings and animals; a cover page and CV, and; a presentation regarding a possible future job, with reflections on conducting a job interview in spoken Japanese. In this final project the NSs were authentic conversation partners and acted as authentic resources who could give responses to any questions the students might have. Throughout the course, instead of being given references such as text books or dictionaries, students were encouraged to refer to the NSs, enabling them not only to get appropriate answers but also to understand the reasons why their original answer may have been wrong and how to fix it. As the students had access to many different NSs, they in effect had access to many different resources that they could consult.

How the new initiative would be assessed

For the assessed tasks, students were required to produce their first draft then communicate with NSs to ask how they could improve upon it. I asked the NSs to try not just to give direct answers but also to offer explanations as to why their recommended changes were more appropriate. As a new course method, the improvement of students' work from their preliminary draft stages to the final draft after communication with NSs was a part of the assessment. A requirement was included for students to write a personal reflection on what they had learnt and how they would commit themselves to furthering their own learning.

Research project
Research objective

It has been established that a large number of language learners' only exposure to the target language is in the classroom. Their often unavoidable lack of opportunities to use the target language with NSs outside the classroom can often be self-imposed, even for those in the potentially interaction-rich language-as-a-second-language environment. This means that language learners are often dependent on teachers and do not seek out opportunities to interact with NSs without their teachers' arrangement.

In my teaching context, since my new course initiative emphasised creative interaction with NSs both in and out of the class, I sought to discover the effects of this process on students' willingness to interact with NSs. Also, I wished to see specifically how this experience affected students' attitudes to lifelong learning. My intention was to give the students opportunities to experience situations as if they were in Japan and seeking help from Japanese people. In fact, as individual learners, they needed to find their own solutions to their problems. I did not match students with NSs as pairs but left it as the students' responsibility to seek and negotiate help with the Japanese guests. Interaction with the NSs out of class beyond their course work was also encouraged so the enrolled students could have personal experiences with NSs in real-life situations. How they made arrangements with native speakers or how often they would meet and what they would discuss was totally up to the students.

Methods

In order to find out whether or not the new course initiative met its goals and how it affected the students, I designed a questionnaire and used it for data collection to elicit the students' points of view (see Appendix). For this purpose I modified questionnaires from Imura (2006), Bateman (2002) and Robinson-Stuart and Nocon (1996), and distributed them to all 18 students at the end of the semester when the course had finished. In the first section, the questionnaire asks how the students felt

NSs helped them to improve their Japanese language and intercultural competence regarding each of a series of items. There are 14 aspects in this section. For each of the items, there is a scale of 1–7. Then the questionnaire asks the students to write as much as they can about their feelings and opinions regarding each item. In the second section, there are 10 open-ended questions. These questions ask how the students think the Japanese NSs influenced their linguistic knowledge and perceptions as well as their understanding of Japanese culture and society. The questionnaire also asked students for their opinions about the best and worst aspects of the involvement of the international students from Japan (see Appendix).

Results and discussion

In total there were 14 responses to the questionnaire.

Quantitative

The quantitative results obtained showed that most students that responded marked 7, 6 and 5, the three highest levels of satisfactory, for all aspects of section 1. Students did not mark any category if they were absent from particular sessions or they did not get help from NSs for particular aspects; this means that students rated all aspects as

Aspects	Responses circling							
	7	6	5	4	3	2	1	mean
1) Reading 'Keigo' and discussion	3	7	4	0	0	0	0	5.9
2) 'Keigo' quiz	2	6	4	1	0	0	0	5.7
3) Assignment 1: Writing in Japanese (Whaling/animals)	4	7	2	0	0	0	0	6.2
4) Discussion (whaling)	2	3	4	1	0	0	0	5.6
5) Speech by Tom san (Self-introduction)	3	3	3	1	1	0	0	5.5
6) Speech by Hiroshisan (Osaka/Osaka dialect)	4	6	3	0	0	0	0	6.1
7) Speech by Tomomi san (Japanese language among young people)	2	7	3	0	0	0	0	5.9
8) Yufeng Dou san (Three languages and cultures)	1	3	5	0	0	1	0	5.2
9) Speech by Hiroki san (Japanese Greetings/Courtesy etc)	3	5	4	0	0	0	0	5.9
10) Writing in Japanese – what you have learned from the speeches	3	2	5	1	1	0	0	5.4
11) Assignment 2: Writing the Cover page & CV	3	5	3	0	1	0	0	5.8
12) Presentation in Japanese (Future job)	4	5	4	0	0	0	0	6
13) Job interview	4	6	1	1	1	0	0	5.8
14) Writing up the reflection in Japanese	3	4	4	1	0	0	0	5.8

Table 1: Responses to Section 1 of questionnaire for Japanese 3B: Practical Japanese Students (n=14)

over 5.2. From this result it is clear that students felt that all aspects that Japanese NSs were involved in were helpful, appropriate and enjoyable for the course.

Students felt that the most interesting topic and helpful aspect of NS interaction was 'Assignment 1: Writing in Japanese (Whaling/animals)', followed by 'Speech by Hiroshi san (Osaka/Osaka dialect)' and 'Presentation in Japanese (Future job)'. Other aspects followed in this order: 'Reading 'Keigo' and discussion'; 'Speech by Tomomi san (Japanese language among young people)'; 'Assignment 2: Writing the Cover page & CV'; 'Job interview';' 'Writing up the reflection in Japanese'; ''Keigo' quiz'; 'Discussion (whaling)'; 'Speech by Tom san (Self-introduction)'; 'Writing in Japanese — what you have learned from the speeches', and; 'Yufeng Dou san (Three languages and cultures)'.

The next section demonstrates the students' opinions on how they felt about their experiences of interacting with the NSs through doing the above tasks, as expressed in their open, qualitative comments.

Qualitative

Overall, students' comments displayed a high level of engagement and satisfaction with the learning experience they had been part of. They expressed their enjoyment and their gratitude to the NSs for their participation. Here I present the students' responses and discuss how the new course methods appeared to have worked from the students' point of view in relation to the issues that emerged as most significant for them.

Awareness of learner's own culture and language, and those of others

'Keigo' is an honorific form in Japanese and it is one of the difficult aspects for Japanese language learners. Liddicoat et al. (2003, p. 18) assert that 'learning the grammatical differences between plain, polite and honorific form in Japanese and trying to use them according to Australian norms cannot lead to successful communication'. In the first meeting with the Japanese NSs, the students read information regarding 'Keigo' followed by discussion with the volunteers. Gradually, they began to feel comfortable communicating with the volunteers and began to make friends with them. They felt that the volunteers' correction and explanation helped improve their understanding of Keigo and that through demonstration and practice they better retained their understanding of Keigo forms. As one student says:

> This was particularly useful as Keigo does not have a linguistic equivalent in English. It is extremely difficult at times to understand how to address a particular person or group. Having the Japanese helpers present allowed them to not only correct mistakes in our honorific language but to also explain

their feelings on why a particular person would be addressed in one way over another. With each correction and explanation you're able to gain more of an understanding of Japanese social customs direct from a native Japanese speaker. (Student I)

The comment above shows that the student has an awareness of cultural and linguistic differences, and compares his own culture and language with Japanese, specifically regarding Keigo. He relates to Keigo in that he cannot learn it without an understanding of Japanese social customs, as '*Keigo does not have a linguistic equivalent in English*'. He appreciates the depth of knowledge gained from native speakers and values the experience of dialogue. Another student commented:

[The NSs] were helpful as they obviously speak the language and understand how to use Keigo. However, I think one issue is that we learn Japanese in such a structured manner so that to us there can only be one possible answer, but the Japanese students couldn't give us just one answer, as, like English, realistically there are several possible ways you can speak to different people and still be polite. So this exercise highlighted the issue of learning a language through study rather than through practical application. (Student A)

Here Student A also describes her appreciation of the depth of knowledge available from the NSs and recognises the shortfalls in the traditional program. She tries to understand Keigo and compares it to English norms as she says, '*like English*'. She then draws attention to the difference between studying language forms and trying to apply them in real life interactions

The following comment is a general one, rather than focusing on specific aspects as seen in the above example. The following student displays a widening of cultural perspective through increased awareness of regional differences, and appreciates these as diversity:

The Japanese students all came from different parts of Japan, so they offered a different understanding on Japanese culture. This made me aware of the diversity in Japanese culture and what aspect some people see as more important than others. (Student E)

By being exposed to a number of different Japanese perspectives, this student has not only cultivated more awareness about Japanese culture but also has been given a foil to compare to their own. In this way Student E also shows an increased awareness of the relationship between their own language and its culture by examining that of Japan:

This course has made me think of what I would be able to contribute to a similar course on practical English-language skills in Japan. As English-speaking countries all have different cultures and expectations, I feel there would be more cultural clashes in this situation than the ones we encountered. I also feel that this would be more confusing for the Japanese speakers, as even in Australia there is a large variation in culture. In retrospect, I feel that in Australia anything is viable as long as you can support it, which makes it a very diverse and dynamic culture. For example, in a job interview, you can present yourself either as a formal or casual person, and both can be seen as appealing to the employer with relation to what kind of job you are applying for. However, I feel that in Japan, an informal interview style would be seen as disrespectful or lazy in comparison to a more formal style. (Student E)

Student E is here able to appreciate the breadth of culture in the English-speaking world as a result of gaining an increased understanding of Japan which in many ways is a mono-cultural society. He is able to recognise attitudes and behaviours that are appropriate in his own and in Japanese society and has begun to appreciate why these differences exist.

Authenticity of communication

The following comments show that once students had made the personal connections with NSs, they started to recognise their common ground and the similar experiences they share.

> They aren't as studious as our language studies lead us to believe, like any uni student they like to muck around too. (Student A)
>
> Probably the biggest thing was that Japanese struggle with their own language just as we struggle with English. (Student C)

This was particularly noticeable in relation to the topic of whaling. Following the assignment on this issue there was an opportunity to discuss whaling in the classroom setting. The following students' comments show an appreciation of the authentic relationship they built up with the NSs, who are almost like 'living dictionaries' for them. In this session, students were surprised that most of the NSs had never even seen whale meat, despite the view that the Australian media promotes. They also discovered that some NSs did not know about the large body of Australian media that reports the issue.

> Understanding whaling from a Japanese perspective was highly rewarding. This is a great area of tension between Australia and Japan, so being able to discuss it with people who have an entirely different and possibly opposite perspective really helped me to understand the issue and empathise with the Japanese rather than simply absorbing the perspective of the Australian media. (Student A)

Here student A was extending her own self-reflection and understanding her own cultural positioning through interaction with these native speakers. The authentic relationship allowed her to empathise with a divergent view across both cultural and political boundaries.

> This provided a good opportunity not only to communicate in Japanese with a native speaker in a controlled situation but it also allowed me the rare opportunity to discuss Japanese politics. I would say many Australians dislike Japan's whaling and people often say "why do they even do it?" This discussion allowed that question to be answered and facilitated a new level of intercultural understanding by highlighting cultural differences and how one should approach discussing such topics where differences exists [sic] and opinions are heated. (Student I)

This student's connection with the NSs is seen to have led to new intercultural understanding across borders of cultural difference. The empathy displayed here is achieved despite these young people's strong personal investment in their historical and national identities. Thus, we can observe intercultural sensitivity emerging. The student here does not fail to recognise that genuine communication can occur even where differences of opinion exist. It is also apparent that he is very grateful for the opportunity to be able to discuss sensitive issues in the safe environment of the classroom.

Tomomi, a student from Tokyo, gave a 20-minute speech on the language she spoke on campus and the vernacular that young people commonly use. For most of the students, the vocabulary Tomomi introduced was new as it is not part of standard language and not in the textbooks that students use for the mainstream Japanese language courses. Her speech was particularly interesting, especially for the young students, and presented a practical insight into spoken Japanese:

> This was really interesting and amusing. We learn Japanese in such a structured fashion that it was great to hear how people our age actually talk. (Student A)

The above comment was from a student who had never been to Japan. Here she is able to recognise that the phenomenon of young people breaking away from their parents' values by developing their own language is not unique to her own culture and in fact occurs in Japan too. She also notes the contrast between the pedagogical approach that she is engaged with and that of the mainstream. The following comment is from a student who had experienced studying abroad in Japan. From both these comments it is clear that Tomomi's speech touched on what was relevant to these students in a personal way and the value they place on the authentic nature of the information:

> This speech was a favourite of mine because of how relevant it was to me as well as for the same reasons as in Speech by Hiroshi san — Osaka and Osaka

> dialect. Particularly interesting was the discussion of what certain slang means/how the word was formed and that was all first hand commentary which made it all the more useful. I know that as a result of that talk I will now be far more confident in how 'hip' I am. (Student I)

After Tomomi's speech, all the NSs made comments on their own experience. I, as an ex-Japanese university student from long ago, made some remarks on how different talk between young people is now and when I was a student. Following this presentation, the NS students were included in discussion. Both groups were clearly all very excited about this topic and there was a lot of laughter.

There were many other comments that showed that students became aware of the differences between their teachers' formalised mode of speech and the use of language by native speakers. They also recognised that they gained a great deal more through their interaction with NSs compared to mainstream language courses. They made the explicit distinction between conventional language learning and real communication between people:

> I learnt lots of grammar and new words. But the most important thing is that I learnt how to communicate with Japanese people. During the communication, they teach me lots of knowledge about modern Japanese. (Student N)

> Native speakers, also know the inside knowledge of what is use in Japan, and hence you learn how to converse normally, rather than formally which is what you learnt in the books. Also you learn terms which only the younger people use, which will help you converse in Japan as well. (Student F)

> The students would speak to us in more colloquial language than our Japanese teachers, and use phrases we might not yet be familiar with. As they were not aware of what language we knew, it was interesting to attempt conversations with them as they would use phrases and words we haven't yet learned, and then need to explain these terms to us. Thus, we learnt more language than what our language courses planned for, simply due to conversation. Not all the Japanese students would speak the same clarity and emphasis of a teacher, which meant that we had to concentrate on what they were saying. This was beneficial as it gave an insight into what interacting with Japanese speakers in every-day life would be like if we were to be in Japan. (Student E)

Students' comments show that they appreciate NSs interaction as authentic communication. NS interactions are different from those with the teacher, or the textbook, and students are also aware of individual differences. The native speakers are unaware of the students' level of knowledge so they must negotiate communication and understanding. The above students clearly appreciate this negotiation with practical intercultural interactions. They also appreciate the valuable practical information they have gained though the connection with young people. Student E in particular appreciates this as an insight into how they may experience life in Japan, with a living community.

One international student from China commented on the relationship between the logic of thinking and language structure. She expressed that the deeper understanding they gained into how Japanese think and speak helped them as language learners to use Japanese appropriately:

> For me, I think it is more of the way they think. Once I understand more about how their logic works, the more I realise why Japanese language is structured in the way it is. Afterwards, it is easier to use the tones and grammar correctly once I became more used to the way Japanese speak. (Student M)

This student values the practical experience with the NSs as she feels that the authentic relation gave her an understanding of how to use Japanese tones and grammar as a result of the way language is connected to thinking. Her comment is very interesting as it shows how she considers that understanding how NSs think helps her language and communication skills.

Other comments demonstrate that students clearly felt that their language skills in speaking, writing and comprehension had increased. More significantly, at an emotional level, they felt that the opportunity to learn about the life and culture of young Japanese people had increased their passion for learning Japanese and their interest in visiting Japan:

> I am glad that the Japanese exchange students agreed to assist us in learning practical Japanese. Involving the exchange students from Japan has undoubtedly improved our ability to speak and write and comprehend the Japanese language. Not only have we improved our language, but many of us have become friends beyond the classroom, where we have had the opportunity to learn about life as a young Japanese person, life in Australia as a foreign exchange student. (Student K)

Student K here feels that the close connections had led to his increased cultural awareness. He values not only learning about life as a young Japanese person, but also about life in Australia as a foreign exchange student. For him, his connection with the native speakers has been at a personal level and he expresses his pleasure and satisfaction in the empathy he experienced in coming to understand what it is like to be a Japanese exchange student. In the following comment, student H expresses the same satisfaction, but her focus is on the culture and social structure impacting on Japanese youth:

> Through meeting the Japanese students I feel I have a better perception of Japanese culture in general, and particularly what it is like to be a younger

person in Japan. Through meeting these students I found it much easier to understand certain elements of Japanese culture that I learnt within other courses, such as the differing levels of respect. (Student H)

This comment shows that student H feels that learning about Japanese culture is different to *understanding* the culture, and through the NSs' interaction, she is able to understand much more exactly certain cultural issues such as the differing levels of respect. Similarly, student F shows that through this experience she feels herself to have a much deeper involvement in the Japanese culture:

They help explain things we don't understand, and they tell us the reason why it happens, so you know how to do it, and you know why. Also they can show you, and you feel like you are a part of the culture. (Student F)

This student considers the interaction with NSs has actually allowed her to engage at a deeper level with Japanese culture. She is not just connected with NSs at a personal level but also at a cultural level. Another student also reached across what she had seen as a cultural divide, as a result of her interactions with the NS exchange students:

I think that due to these sessions I feel there is less of a culture gap then [sic] I perhaps previously envisioned. (Student H)

The above examples clearly show the valuable information and insights into the Japanese language that students gained through interaction with the NSs, which due to the authenticity of their interactions were unavailable to them through traditional course structures.

Affective experiences and emotional responses

(a) Negative interpretations

It was noticeable that in many cases the students felt free in their written comments to express clearly emotional attitudes to the learning experiences they had been part of. Interestingly, there were only three negative comments in these questionnaire responses. One shows a student's desire for deeper connection with NSs, and a marked irritation with the Japanese politeness she experienced:

The Japanese student who helped me was helpful and offered me practical advice, however, I wish that he would've been less polite and less afraid of offending my feelings so that I could really develop my Japanese and recognise my errors clearly. (Student A)

This is an example of a relationship not being successfully developed with a NS. This NS did not feel comfortable criticising the student, which means she feels her learning was impeded. She recognises the interactive pattern she was engaged in but was unable to negotiate it to her satisfaction. Another student, from China, is able to see beyond the limitations of the age groups, and comments:

> In fact, it is only the young generation that we had come into contact with. I hope someday, we get older generations so that we would know more about the Japanese culture. (Student M)

This student would have valued the perspective of an older generation of volunteers in learning about Japanese culture, and it is interesting that local, Australian-raised students were generally more appreciative of the opportunity for bonding with similar age group students and did not mention this. It is possible that student M from China shows a willingness to learn from older people that could be connected to her culture's rich respect for their elders. Another Chinese student makes the following comment:

> Because most of Japanese helpers are students, they still need to study or work. I am not sure whether it is convenient for them to come to the Japanese class to help us. (Student N)

Here the student is not concerned about herself as a learner but about the volunteers. This could also be another Chinese cultural difference, showing concern about others in this way. The personal relationships and discussions that the students developed with the NSs may have also contributed to the concern this student has.

(b) Positive experiences

However, the overwhelming majority of responses were positive in nature. It was apparent from students' reflections that the personal connections they developed with the NSs increased their motivation for the learning of the language. For students, having NSs who became good friends in the class was incredibly enjoyable and made the class atmosphere a different and much more positive environment for learning. It became clear that the students wanted to impress the NSs in class too, and in their reflections they recognise the effect of having the native speakers join them:

> I really enjoyed having the Japanese students help us in this course. Some students were more enthusiastic than others in helping us in the course, but even the contribution of a few made a great difference to the atmosphere of the class. Their contribution made the students feel like someone besides the teacher was involved in their learning and made students more committed to doing well in the class in an effort not to embarrass themselves or let the Japanese volunteers who had helped them down. More importantly, many of the Japanese students became our friends, and friendships have forged outside of class, which defines this course as special apart from all others. (Student E)

Student E here presents a very perceptive insight into the promoted learning processes. He sees how students in the class committed more to their own learning because the relationship with the NSs meant that they did not want to embarrass themselves in front of the NSs whom they respected. Their special bond with the NSs created a much greater willingness to converse and participate than before. Student E particularly appreciates his special connections and friendship with the NSs as being extremely beneficial to his learning.

In terms of the affective engagement that this approach generated, the following three comments show how strongly students feel that the interaction with NSs was beneficial and encouraging. The intercultural relationships made them more willing to ask and to try to understand more about the culture of the NS visitors:

> It was incredibly beneficial. Not only did they help us develop our skills beyond the structure of the textbooks but we also made new friends. Having Japanese friends means that we can gauge more about the culture as well as develop more passion for learning Japanese. (Student A)

> They were very helpful and willing to assist us whenever we had any questions and I found that extremely encouraging in the learning process. It made me more willing to ask and understand about the Japanese culture. (Student B)

> It is a very important step in Japanese learning. We made many Japanese friends and have helped each other in learning languages. It actually brought us closer to the real Japanese culture and increased our interest in knowing more about the Japanese society. (Student M)

Students A, B and M are clearly stimulated by the NSs' friendship and willingness to assist students; as they say, they developed more 'passion' for learning Japanese language, and about Japanese culture and society. I believe that the interaction with the NSs built their openness toward Japanese culture, which in turn increased their desire to interact with them more. This is one of the core theoretical goals for intercultural language teaching and learning, and the friendship and close relationship with NSs proved itself a powerful educational motivator:

> The experience of having a number of Japanese students in the class with us was what made the course for me. Although what I took most from their presence was not so much their help with the work but their friendship. To make Japanese friends my age opened up a huge number of opportunities to learn about Japan and Japanese, ask about things relevant to young people but not necessary appropriate to discuss with a teacher. I was introduced to music, movies, TV shows, video-games, comics etc that the helpers where [sic] interested in and that I would enjoy. In the end this experience resulted in a powerful motivator for Japanese learning. (Student C)

For Student C, what he feels was relevant to himself is the most powerful motivator for him, which is not related to the language or to the culture but is to his life.

A written assignment regarding whaling from a Japanese perspective was expanded into a discussion of relationships between human beings and animals. Firstly, the students received an article written in Japanese and illustrating whaling from a Japanese point of view. There were related questions for reading comprehension and students were asked in their written assignment to express their opinion on the issue of whaling and on the relationship between humans and animals, in written Japanese. After they had written their draft, they were required as part of the exercise to consult the Japanese volunteers, who would then proofread their work and offer their recommendations, corrections and explanations. After this, the students would then complete the final draft followed by written reflections on the assignment in English. These written reflections display clearly how the students appreciated the instrumental benefits of the NSs knowledge.

> Tom-San edited the draft of my written piece on whaling and dissected each sentence with corrections where necessary. This was extremely helpful as it gave me insight into where I had made mistakes and explained where I had confused some language points. I found this particularly helpful as he would explain what I had said in relation to what I say trying to say, and gave an alternative grammar point or word I could use. (Student E)

In the above comment the student expresses his genuine appreciation of the NSs' help, due to the additional information afforded beyond merely being given an answer. The student is aware of the additional explanation provided to him, giving him a deeper understanding and increased awareness of linguistic possibilities. Also in the following comment, Student I praises the efforts of the NSs and in doing so gives some insight into the value he places on the relationship with the NSs and the valuable knowledge available to him as a language learner:

> In terms of the Japanese helpers assistance — again, it was invaluable. Corrections from native speakers are always extremely useful particularly when they're willing to give their time generously and heavily annotate drafts explaining why a particular word might convey an unintended nuance and why a particular word might be more suitable. That is, I think one of the reasons interaction with native speakers must be encouraged in the classroom. Textbooks have their place but discussion with native Japanese speakers in person addressing your specific questions is really helpful. (Student I)

Student I is here showing the great value he feels for the extra learning potential provided by the nuanced input of the NSs, He displays particular insight in recognising the benefits of this new methodology, and clearly mentions the limitations of the traditional one. He additionally shows his willingness to have more interactions.

Student D also sees the benefits conferred by the NSs as positively instrumental:

> My Japanese language skills need vast improvement if I want to speak Japanese fluently. This course is a good measurement in student's progression with their language skills. (Student D)

It is clear that this student gained a measurement of his language skills in the class by the authenticity of the interaction. Thus, relationships with NSs can give students awareness of their own level of proficiency and motivation, and again it is significant that this student does not fail to notice this, and wants to point it out. The following student also remarks on the instrumental benefit of the relationship she formed with the NSs in relation to the confidence it gave her to exercise her linguistic skills:

> I think that if I had missed out on such sessions my ability to speak Japanese would not be as good, as having Japanese students in class improved most students confidence when speaking Japanese. (Student H)

A further, and particularly interesting, aspect that emerged from the reflective writing relates to the image of Japanese people that the students had before their opportunities to interact with NSs. After establishing personal connections with the NS young people, these students' dismissed their previously held stereotypes of Japanese people:

> I would think that Japanese are always timid and quiet if I had not come to these sessions. (Student M)

> I have now realised that Japanese youth are just like Australian youth. Before I believed that they were incredibly polite, modest, and studious. Even though they do possess these qualities, much more apparent is their similar sense of humour and fun-loving attitude, which has enabled us all to bond strong friendships. (Student A)

This personal level of observation made these students change their own perceived stereotypes of Japanese culture. Because they had had chance to talk and exchange ideas with NS students, whose age and common experience mirrored theirs, their participation in the course strengthened their cultural awareness, established strong bonds of friendship, and contributed to their personal growth in ways that will extend way beyond the instrumental learning of the Japanese language.

Furthermore, just as Cadman (2005) has argued (see above), as the previous two students became more open and aware of cultural issues so too did they, and others, come to new linguistic realisations and resulting improvements. This is one of the key goals of language education and of this teaching intervention in particular. The following student describes how her perception of the Japanese language has changed:

> They don't just teach us what we learn in the textbook. We learn how to use Japanese realistically with these students. My perception of the language has changed dramatically as I now realise how little we learn and how informal Japanese can be. (Student A)

Student A clearly recognises the value of the information she gained from the NSs in that it is knowledge unavailable in textbooks and traditional course methodologies but incredibly useful in everyday interactions. The following student also has had their awareness of the usage of the Japanese language expanded beyond classroom-based preconceptions, enabling them to engage in deeper and more personally meaningful interactions when communicating in Japanese:

> By introducing me to the casual conversation style of university peers they expanded my perception of conversation and conversational intimacy. Within this style of speaking comes a whole new category of slang and 'less-polite'/'less-formal' vocabulary. (Student C)

This casual style of conversation that is only used between friends demonstrates the strong bonds which were formed between students. These friendships not only have personal growth ramifications but have also resulted in increased cultural awareness and a drive for further learning about Japan, as well as for the language itself. After the course many students went on to pursue their interest in Japan. Out of the 18 students, two students were accepted in to Honours programs in Social Science specific to Japanese culture and society, three students took part in study abroad programs to Japan, six students continued studying Japanese at the next level, and one student commenced a relevant Masters of Linguistics. These numbers indicate the continuing interest in Japanese that these students carry with them, and which are far greater in number than students from mainstream courses who have little authentic classroom experience with NSs.

Thus, not only did this pedagogic innovation produce continuing interest in Japanese but for immediate effects it was apparent from all the reflections that the integration of the NS input into the curriculum produced heightened positive affective responses from the students. Overwhelmingly they felt that the involvement of the NSs was a positive motivator for their own learning and an invaluable authentic resource.

Implications for future teaching and research

The outcomes of this intercultural teaching project initiative are extremely fruitful for future teaching and research directions.

Implications for teaching

Involving NS interaction in and out of the class was an extremely worthwhile experience for all students in the course. Previous studies have suggested that students' interaction with NS partners outside the classroom reduces their anxiety and also contributes to changing students' feelings, beliefs and attitudes associated with using and learning the language. The results of this study conducted in a specifically Australian context not only support these previous studies but also demonstrate that integrating the building of personal connections with NSs into the curriculum makes a much more productive learning environment and motivates students to put more effort into classroom activities. It also demonstrates that not only does the linguistic aspect of the learning of another language affect the feelings, beliefs and attitudes of students but also that, just as importantly, the learning of that language's culture and social mores impacts the students greatly. Most significantly, such a pedagogic intervention not only affects a student's academic life but also their personal life and internal wellbeing, which will have an impact on their future as self-motivated learners and their openness to other cultures and ideas.

These findings have important practical implications for how teachers can effectively provide language development with real world emphasis on authentic communication for foreign language learners. Teachers can be key facilitators to make the connection between learners and NSs, and so address the issue that foreign language learners in practice rarely seek interaction with NSs in the community unless the language teacher makes the arrangements and integrates the interaction into their language curriculum (see Pellegrino 1998; Yorozu 2001; Thomson & Iida 2002). In this case, for these students the experience of interaction with their own age group of NSs in and out of class was enjoyable because they felt that they were using the language in order to communicate meaningfully with Japanese people.

At the beginning of this course, I was not sure whether this teaching invention would achieve its pedagogic goals. I expected that there might be some distractions or problems, such as students relying on NSs too much for help with assignments, or students asking NSs for correction of their assignment without also seeking an explanation. Another possibility was that perhaps the students might enjoy the NSs' company too much, so that instead of coming to class they might meet elsewhere, and skip classes. Regarding the NSs, there was the risk that, as volunteers, they could quit anytime — I anticipated that I may lose some of them in the course of the program. There was also the risk that if I picked sensitive topics, some of them may feel offended or uncomfortable. Fortunately, none of these misgivings eventuated. The NSs were especially helpful and generous with their time, and their interactions with the students meshed appropriately with the classroom setting to create the hoped-for positive learning environment.

This suggests several recommendations for future teaching. The first of these is that the students and NSs should be introduced to one another as early as possible in the program. This is to allow as much time as possible for relationships to form that are integral to the effectiveness of this teaching method. Secondly, course convenors should strongly reinforce to NSs and students that they will gain the best outcomes if Japanese is used as often as possible when in the class. It was often the case during this course that when conversation became animated between NS and student, they would default to English. A suggestion made by one of these enrolled students that would be of great benefit to others is to provide students with vocabulary lists during NS talks, which would clarify unfamiliar terminology and allow NSs to present with less concern for the knowledge levels of their audience. A final point, also raised by a student, is to incorporate NSs of differing ages and backgrounds into the course when possible. Although the positive relationships that the NSs had with the enrolled students can in part be attributed to their shared experience as young people and students, it is reasonable to assume that being presented with differing points of view and knowledge bases would enrich the learning experience for all.

Implications for future research

For this research study, I used student questionnaires as quantitative data, and their reflective comments as qualitative data. In future, in addition to these, I would suggest analysing test results and comparing them to those of mainstream courses, as another method of measuring students' improvement or achievement.

Another interesting angle to take would be to increase the length of the study by interviewing students after the completion of the course for as long as is practical and possible. This data might well be able to shed more light on the study's broader goal of examining personal growth, an attribute that becomes more evident over time. Such a strategy would also help to make apparent the long-term effects of the intervention on the students in relation to the teaching goals.

A final suggestion is to collect data from the NSs, possibly in the form of questionnaires, as given to the students. In doing this, it may be possible to gain more insight into the relationships between students and NSs, as well as the motivations and goals of the volunteering Japanese students.

Conclusion

Originally this study was conceived due to feedback from Japanese language students who related their dissatisfaction at not being given the opportunity to use Japanese in real-life situations in their programs of study. NSs were invited in order to bring the students closer to useful real-life interactions and to explore the possibilities of rectifying what students believed to be most lacking from mainstream Japanese language education.

The first two teaching objectives for this study aim to increase linguistic proficiency and foster independent learning within students. The third was a much broader but no less important aim, to enable students to create connections across cultural and linguistic divides, in other words, developing students as effective intercultural communicators, able to negotiate communication through differences in language and culture. In this chapter, I have described the teaching intervention that resulted, and presented many examples of students directly attributing the participation of NSs to increases in their linguistic competence and knowledge. However, without the relationships that students formed with the NS volunteers, the students' access to this knowledge and all other exchanges of information would not have been as free. Thus, in order to effectively learn from the NSs, the students first had to negotiate intercultural communication, which was a key goal. As has already been seen, the relationships forged between the NSs and students also served as a powerful motivator for self-directed learning. Thus, the relationships that were one teaching goal can be seen be as the facilitator of another, which was fostering self-learning.

The study has highlighted the use of two important theoretical concepts. The first one is the application of intercultural pedagogy, and the second is the pedagogy of connection. Interestingly, in this context the intercultural pedagogy turned naturally into a connection pedagogy. The result of increasing intercultural awareness and understanding provided the means by which students were able to seek their own and the other's cultural point of view through their initially structured interaction with NSs. Their learning was transformed by making good personal connections as they became willing, and then enthusiastic, to know about each other in a very curious, interpersonal and comfortable manner. This study shows that this bonding created a new human dimension of effective language learning.

In the classroom, I felt that my students were full of enjoyment and motivation, and the NSs also became full of pleasure and willingness to assist the enrolled students. They wanted to talk with each other and put more questions to me both as a teacher and as a person, compared to the questioning I had experienced in mainstream courses. They stayed in the classroom even after we had finished the classes and kept talking. From my position as the teacher, I believe that without the NS volunteers, the students would not have had the positive learning experiences that they were able to experience, nor would they have generated the friendships and international connections that they did.

The friendships and new connections that students formed may have also affected their continuing language development and growth of cultural awareness. Some students have even wanted to explore this interest so far as to visit Japan and experience full authentic interactions, which they envisaged as easier due to the friendships made in class. Some were also inclined to challenge themselves by pursuing further academic study in Japanese language and culture. Both of these outcomes have given these students more experiences academically and personally in the fields of culture and language. These outcomes strongly suggest personal growth of the students.

Perhaps most importantly for this study, the students improved their intercultural communication skills and their openness towards another culture, which ultimately contributes to broadening their worldview and life understanding. Through this experience students have developed skills that will aid them to interact between cultures without guidance and to become effective independent learners. Thus, this project added a lifelong, human dimension to the learning experience, and made a remarkable difference to the learners in relation to both linguistic and non-linguistic outcomes. A final recommendation is for regular interaction with NSs amongst higher level language students, and it should be made available to these FL learners whenever possible. Although the academic and linguistic goals were clearly achieved, the most compelling result from this study is that students have not merely improved their linguistic command and increased their intercultural performance but have learned skills beyond the confines of academic learning, and advanced skills that traditional textbook and CLT teaching methodologies cannot provide.

References

Bateman, BE 2002, 'Promoting openness toward culture learning: ethnographic interviews for students of Spanish', *Modern Language Journal*, vol. 86 no. 3, pp. 318–331.

Bhabha, HK 1994, *The location of culture*, Routledge, London.

Buttjes, D & Byram, M 1991, *Mediating language and cultures: towards an intercultural theory of Foreign Language education*, Multilingual Matters, Clevedon, MA.

Byram, M 1989a, *Cultural studies in Foreign Language education*, Multilingual

Matters, Clevedon, MA.

Byram, M 1989b, 'A school visit to France: ethnographic explorations.' *British Journal of Language Teaching*, vol. 27 no. 2, pp. 99–103.

Byram, M, & Feng, A 2005, 'Teaching and researching intercultural competence', in E Hinkel, Lawrence Erlbaum (eds), *Handbook of research in Second Language teaching and learning*, Mahwah, NJ, pp. 911–930.

Cadman, K 2005, 'Towards a 'pedagogy of connection' in research education: a 'REAL' story', *Journal of English for Academic Purposes (Special Edition on Advanced Academic Literacies)*, vol. 4 no. 4, pp. 353–367.

Cadman, K 2008, 'From correcting to connecting: a personal story of changing priorities in EAL teaching', *TESOL in Context*, vol. 17 no. 2, pp. 29–37.

Cadman, K & O'Regan K 2006, 'Speaking for ourselves: teachers challenging issues of identity in English language teaching', in K Cadman & K O'Regan (eds), *Tales out of school: English language teaching and identity, TESOL in Context*, Special Edition no. 1, pp. 10–19.

Coleman, JA 1997, 'Residence abroad within language study', *Language Teaching*, vol. 30 no. 1, pp. 1–20.

Coleman, JA 1998, 'Language learning and study abroad: the European perspective', *Frontiers: The Interdisciplinary Journal of Study Abroad*, vol. 4 no. 1, pp. 167–205.

Corbett, J 2003, *An intercultural approach to English Language Teaching*, Multilingual Matters, Clevedon, MA.

Crozet, C & Liddicoat AJ 1999, 'The challenge of intercultural language teachings: engaging with culture in the classroom', in J LoBianco, AJ Liddicoat & C Crozet (eds), *Striving for the third place: intercultural competence through language education*, Language Australia, Canberra, ACT, pp. 113–126.

Eisenchlas, S & Hortiguera H 1999–2000, 'Beyond the classroom: the target language community as a resource for teaching and learning', *Babel*, vol. 32 no. 3, pp. 16–20 & 38.

hooks, b 1994, *Teaching to transgress: education as the practice of freedom*, Routledge, New York.

Imura, T 2004a, 'Let learners talk with native speakers outside the classroom in your home country: community Involvement project', *Japanese Language Education around the Globe*, vol. 14, pp. 125–148.

Imura, T 2004b, 'The effect of anxiety on oral communication skills', in B Bartlett, F Bryer & R Dick (eds), *Education: weaving research into practice*, 2nd Annual International Conference on Cognition, Language, and Special Education, Griffith University Press, Brisbane, vol. 2 no. 3, pp. 174–186.

Imura, T 2006, *Community involvement as a means of developing oral communication skills and L2 confidence: the case of tertiary students in an intermediate Japanese course*, Unpublished doctoral dissertation, The University of Queensland.

Ingram, DE 1978a, *An applied linguistic study of advanced language learning*, unpublished doctoral dissertation, University of Essex, UK.

Ingram, DE 1978b, 'Learning through use: a projected community-based course for tertiary students of French', in DE Ingram & TJ Quinn (eds), *Language learning in Australian society*, 1976 Congress of the Applied Linguistics Association of Australia, Australia International Press, pp. 117–125.

Ingram, DE 1980, 'To see, to speak: participate: community involvement in language teaching', *Unicorn*, vol. 6 no. 3, pp. 276–283.

Knutson, EM 2006, 'Cross-cultural awareness for second/foreign language learners', *Canadian Modern Language Review*, vol. 62 no. 4, pp. 591–610.

Kramsch, C 1993, *Context and culture in language education*, Oxford University Press, Oxford.

Kurts, DL & Luna, AM 1983, 'Utilizing community resources: the conversation lab', *Foreign Language Annals*, vol. 16 no. 6, pp. 433–436.

Liddicoat, AJ 2005, 'Culture for language learning in Australian language-in-education policy', *Australian Review of Applied Linguistics*, vol. 27 no. 2, pp. 1–28.

Liddicoat, AJ 2008, 'Pedagogical practice for integrating the intercultural in language teaching and learning', *Japanese Studies*, vol. 28 no. 3, pp. 277–290.

Liddicoat, AJ 2011, 'Language teaching and learning from an intercultural perspective' in E Hinkel (ed.), *Handbook of research in Second Language teaching and learning, Volume II*, Routledge, New York.

Liddicoat, AJ & Papademetre L etc. 2003, *Report on intercultural language learning*, Department of Education, Science and Training, Canberra, ACT.

Lightbown, PM & Spada N 1993, *How languages are learned*, Oxford University Press, Oxford.

Long, DR 1997, 'The experiential course: an alternative to study abroad for non-traditional students', *Foreign Language Annals*, vol. 30 no. 3, pp. 301–310.

Pellegrino, VA 1998, 'Student perspectives on language learning in a study abroad context', *Frontiers: the Interdisciplinary Journal of Study Abroad*, vol. 4, pp. 91–120.

Roberts, C, Byram, M, Barro, A, Jordan, S, & Street B 2001, *Language learners as ethnographers*, Multilingual Matters, Clevedon, MA.

Robinson-Stuart, G & Nocon H 1996, 'Second culture acquisition: ethnography in the foreign language classroom', *Modern Language Journal*, vol. 80 no. 4, pp. 431–449.

Sobolewski, P 2009, 'Use of ethnographic interviews as a resource for developing intercultural understanding', *Babel*, vol. 43 no. 2, pp. 28–33.

Stoller, FL et al. 1995, 'Examining the value of conversation partner programs', *Applied Language Learning*, vol. 6 nos. 1 & 2, pp. 1–12.

Thomson, DK & Lida S 2002, 'Nihongo kyouikiu ni okeru seisa no gakushuu: oosutoraria no gakushuusha no ishikichousa yori [*Gendered language in Japanese: learner perceptions in Australia*]', *Japanese Language Education around the Globe*, vol. 12, p 1–20.

Turner, R 2004, 'English as academic purpose', *Journal of English for Academic Purposes*, vol. 3 no. 2, pp. 95–109.

Yorozu, M 2001, 'Interaction with native speakers of Japanese: what learners say', *Japanese Studies*, vol. 21 no. 2, pp. 199–213.

Zarat, G & Gohard-Radenkovic A 2004, *Mediation didactique et didactique des language*, Council of Europe Publishing, Kapfenberg.

Appendix

Questionnaire for Japanese 3B: Practical Japanese students

This questionnaire was devised by Akiko Tomita, a lecturer at the Centre for Asian Studies at the University of Adelaide. The aim of this questionnaire is to collect data on the assignment reflection **on personal growth as an intercultural Communicator with the involvement of international students from Japan** by Japanese 3B: Practical Japanese students.

There are no right or wrong answers; please answer giving your own opinions. If you feel that a particular question is too personal, then skip it and go to the next one. I assure you that your responses will be completely confidential and that they will not be used for any purpose other than this research.

Information about yourself

Your name:_____

Your age:_____

Your degree:_____

What language(s) do you speak?

    First language_____

    Second language_____

    Third language_____

    More language(s)_____

If you are an International student, where is your home country and when/which year did you come to Australia to study?

Section1

This question asks how you felt the Japanese students have helped improve your Japanese language/intercultural competence. For each of the items, a scale of 7 is provided. Please circle '1' if you think it was not useful and circle '7' if it was very useful. If you were not involved in any communication with the Japanese helpers for your assignment or you were absent circle '4'. Then write as much as you can about your feelings/opinions regarding each item.

    1) Reading "keigo 敬語" and discussion   1234567
        Comment:
    2) "keigo 敬語" quiz   1234567
        Comment:
    3) Assignment 1: Writing in Japanese (whaling/animals)   1234567
        Comment:

4) Discussion (whaling)   1234567
   Comment:
5) Speech by Tom san (Self introduction)   1234567
   Comment:
6) Speech by Hiroshi san (Osaka/Osaka direct)   1234567
   Comment:
7) Speech by Tomomi san
   (Japanese language among young people)   1234567
   Comment:
8) Yufeng Dou san (Three languages and cultures)   1234567
   Comment:
9) Speech by Hiroki san (Japanese Greetings/Courtesy etc)   1234567
   Comment:
10) Writing in Japanese what you have learnt from the speeches   1234567
    Comment:
11) Assignment 2: Writing the Cover page & CV   1234567
    Comment:
12) Presentation in Japanese (Future job)   1234567
    Comment:
13) Job interview   1234567
    Comment:
14) Writing up the reflection in Japanese   1234567
    Comment:

Section 2

1) Please explain what you feel or think about involving international students from Japan in the Japanese 3B: Practical Japanese course.
2) Please explain why and how international students from Japan influenced your linguistic knowledge and perception.
3) Please explain why and how international students from Japan influenced your understanding of Japanese Culture.
4) Have any of your thoughts/beliefs about your own culture or society been changed or challenged due to a wider understanding of Japanese Culture through these sessions?
5) What did you learn the most in the class room situations with international students from Japan?
6) Did you learn anything you believe you would not have been able to learn or would not have experienced had you not come to these sessions?
7) In 2008 we invited Japanese people who were not just university students but also graduates, people on working holidays, high school students and permanent residents. Compared to the 2008 sessions what were the positives and negatives of using only university students from Japan? Which of the two types of sessions did you prefer and why?
8) Did you learn anything about Japanese culture that you were particularly surprised or shocked by?
9) What was the worst aspect regarding the involvement of the international students from Japan?
10) Do you have any suggestions in order to improve Japanese 3B: Practical Japanese regarding involvement of international students from Japan?

Would you mind if I contacted you with any further questions? Please circle.

Yes/No

Thank you very much for your feedback and cooperation.

ご協力ありがとうございました。

Akiko Tomita

Part IV

Capitalising on Asian social and cultural studies in contexts of diversity

8

Increasing cultural flexibility: A psychological perspective on the purpose of intercultural education
Delia Lin

Introduction

Farjad was an academic from the Middle East doing his PhD at a typical Australian research university.[1] He was enrolled in the University's *Integrated Bridging Program* (IBP), which offers training in language, communication and research skills for international research students in the first semester of their candidature and works with them to bridge the possible differences in academic expectations across cultures. Farjad was an enthusiastic participant and had made good progress, but half way through the program he started to withdraw himself from learning and became quiet. Asked to respond to a self-reflection on 'resistance' to learning, Farjad drew a dot on a piece of paper, as Figure 1 shows, and said to the IBP Coordinator, 'This is where you want me to be'. He then drew a circle about 10 centimetres away from the dot and said, 'But this is where I was and who I was'. He then commented, 'The

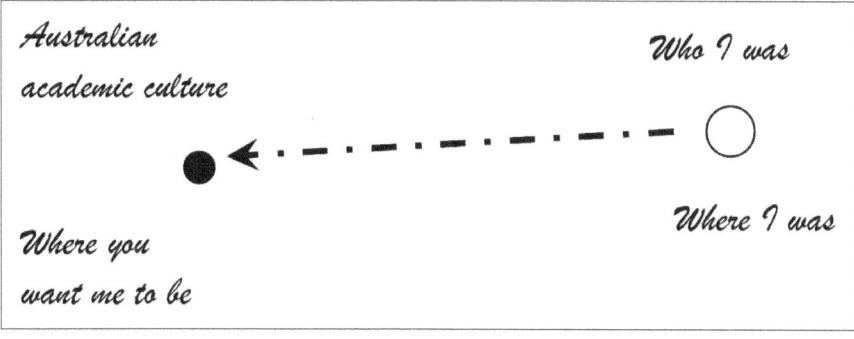

Figure 1: Diagram drawn by Farjad

closer I am to where you want me to be, the further I am away from where and who I was. I feel torn apart and I don't feel I want to go further down this path'.

This story demonstrates an emotional dilemma we often face when negotiating cultural borders in intercultural education. As Roberto Salvadori (1997, p. 186) stresses in his discussion of difficulties of interculturalism, while we may well be inclined to be in solidarity with others, we are at the same time attached to our own culture and are likely to 'harbour a certain amount of misanthropy and a desire to distance ourselves from others'. He argues that intercultural education will only be valid when both parties to the relationship — teacher and student — transform each other. Salvadori further points out that this process of change, or transformation, is not a painless one — it may involve 'a feeling of confusion and even the loss or weakening of an identity that seemed to be priceless and irreplaceable' (Salvadori 1997, p. 187).

Salvadori (1997) argues that interculturalism only serves as a pathway to the final objective of 'transculturalism', where changes happen in both cultures. The scope of transculturalism shows that 'learning the other' is not the target goal of intercultural education, but rather 'changing together', and that in this respect, the teacher and the learner are on the same footing. Furthermore, the process of changing is by no means straightforward. As we have seen from the above example, changing is a psychological process that involves doubting, vulnerability, insecurity, confusion and frustration. No change is effective, healthy or sustainable unless it comes from within, in other words, unless it comes through a connection with 'self' and a constructive dialogue between 'self' and 'the other'.

In this chapter, I will interrogate some well-established psychological principles of cognitive behavioural therapy in order to work towards a better understanding of appropriate goals for intercultural education. In doing this I will first point out that the commonly accepted conception of intercultural competence is problematic in that it potentially thwarts rather than supports an equal and dialogic relationship between the teacher and the learner. I then offer an alternative thinking about the purpose of intercultural education — to increase cultural flexibility — and discuss the implications of this for the respective paradigmatic shift on pedagogy.

Tension between intercultural competence and a dialogic approach to intercultural education

Scholars have argued for the importance of a dialogic intercultural pedagogy for success of intercultural education. This is evident in the key words such as 'connection', 'interaction' and 'reflection' chosen in pedagogies they advocate.

For example, Liddicoat et al. (2003) propose a set of principles for developing Intercultural Language Learning that include active construction, making connection, interaction, reflection and responsibility. As Liddicoat (2008, p. 282) points out, these principles all amount to a constructivist theory of learning, which focuses on learners generating knowledge and meaning from their own experiences. He explains that, for intercultural communication, each of these principles requires development into practice, which can be conceptualised as a series of four interrelated processes of noticing, comparing, reflecting and interacting (Liddicoat 2008, p. 282). Cadman (2005, p. 357) goes further along the line of dialogue between the teacher and the learner. She proposes a 'pedagogy of connection' that asks the teacher to walk into the classroom not as a *believer* in what she teaches, but offering scope for interrogation and dialogue, respecting and capitalising on students' own epistemological diversity. Such a pedagogy admits an unmediated 'human' dimension into the classroom relationships, in which the teacher allows her own vulnerabilities, confusions and insecurities into the decision-making. Through joint effort with students and sharing responsibilities, a *rhetoric of connection* is generated (Cadman 2005, p. 360).

The emphasis on equal dialogue and interaction between teacher and learner echoes the pedagogy that Freire (1972, p. 13) calls 'dialogical encounter'. For Freire, authentic education is not carried on by the teacher for the learner or by the teacher *about* the learner, but by the teacher *with* the learner, mediated by a world that impresses and challenges both parties, giving rise to 'views and opinions impregnated with anxieties, doubts, hopes or hopelessness' (Freire 1972, p. 66). Freire (1972) lists a few requirements for dialogue such as love, humility, faith in humankind and critical thinking. Indeed, a truly dialogic pedagogy requires a 'heart' for building an equal and understanding relationship, a 'heart' that has no desire to create an ideal 'good man' but a 'heart' that looks at 'the concrete, existential, present situation of real men' (Freire 1972, p. 66).

It is along the line of a *prior* requirement for a dialogic pedagogy that I see the weakness of the commonly adopted competency model of conceptualising intercultural education. This is because the presumptions underpinning the competency model fail to free the teacher from treating herself as a strong, authoritative representative of 'truth', which, in turn, stops a teacher from humbling herself to engage in true, meaningful dialogic encounters with the learner.

Intercultural, sometimes referred to as cross-cultural, competence has been at the core of discussion of intercultural education. Since American social psychologist George Gardner (1962) posed the question of what it takes for a person from one culture to communicate with persons of another culture, different models of intercultural competence have been proposed. Gardner (1962, p. 248) introduces the concept of 'universal communicators', that is, individuals equipped with an unusual capacity for intercultural communication, who attain a recognisable repertoire of personality traits: integrity, stability, extroversion, socialisation in universal values, special intuitive and even telepathic abilities. Another much-quoted model is the one proposed by Gertzen (1990). Asking what makes a successful expatriate, Gertzen (1990, p. 346) challenges existing one-dimensional approaches and proposes a three-dimensional model of intercultural competence that includes an affective dimension, a cognitive dimension, and a communicative, behavioral dimension.

Although intercultural competence is a much-contested concept with multiple definitions and its assessment is problematic, cultivating and improving intercultural communication competence has been commonly assumed to be the purpose of intercultural education. Scholars who call for an interactional, reflexive and dialogical pedagogy also assume the goal of improving students' intercultural competence (for example, Nagata 2004). However, I would like to draw attention to some presumptions of a competency mode of thinking in order to suggest that a competency model may pose a potential obstacle to achieving an open and effective, dialogic pedagogy. Briefly, these are:

1. A competency model pre-assumes a less competent being, the learner, and a more competent being, the teacher. The presumably more competent ones are given the authority and power over the presumably less competent ones in order to alter them.
2. A competency model pre-assumes a 'universal' or 'correct' standard to measure success of communication. But questions remain: who sets the standard and how is success measured?
3. A competency model pre-assumes the validity of the saying 'when in Rome do as the Romans do'. This places an emphasis on accepting and adapted to the other, as if the more a learner moves away from her own background or cultural root, and becomes more like 'the other', the more 'successful' she is as an intercultural communicator.

These three presumptions show that a competency model intrinsically entails authority over truth, and dominance over the 'mapping' of knowledge. It sees the learner as one that needs to be instilled with the perceived 'good' personality traits, skills and knowledge to be more like 'the other'. As such, it can hardly support the principles of intercultural language learning put forward by Liddicoat et al. (2003) and the intercultural pedagogy associated with them. It also obstructs the implementation of a 'pedagogy of connection' (Cadman 2005, p. 357), as in such a pedagogy, a hierarchical teacher-learner relationship and authority over truth and knowledge are not encouraged. The stronger a teacher feels about the necessity to improve the learner's intercultural competence, the less likely she is to adopt a dialogical intercultural pedagogy in an effective, non-threatening way.

Cultural flexibility: An alternative

How a teacher answers basic questions such as the purpose of teaching and what her role is determines the language she uses, and the rhetoric and discourses she creates in the classroom. If she thinks the purpose of her teaching is to improve students' competency level, she would be more likely to see herself as an 'expert' communicator, use a language that is authoritative and expect students to perform to a pre-designed and pre-set standard. She would also be more likely to overlook the emergence of an awareness of participants' full humanity (her own as well as students') that entails frustration, doubts and insecurity, as she would tend to see these emotional struggles as being negative and signs of lacking 'competency'. If, however, she abandons the theoretical conceptualisation of competency, and sees the assumptions, beliefs, feelings, behaviour patterns, communication styles, language uses and subjectivities that students and herself bring to the classroom as coming from a certain cultural context, she is much more likely to be willing to engage in mutual exploration, analysis and dialogues with her students. This is to say, a pedagogy cannot be properly learned or effectively implemented if we do not take a step back to conceptualise the purpose of the education that supports that certain pedagogy.

As I have argued earlier, the commonly accepted concept of intercultural competence potentially thwarts rather than supports a dialogic approach to intercultural education. If, however, we are to think in the domain of *trans*culturalism, that is, if we are to see 'changing together' as the goal of intercultural education, we need a framework that is able to guide our pedagogy towards one that facilitates change in a healthy and sustainable way. Such a framework should be (1) focused on an analytic goal rather than seeking to achieve universal attributes that make up a 'successful' or more 'competent' communicator, and (2) capable of constructively dealing with the psychological dilemma one inevitably faces when negotiating cultural borders, instead of seeing the dilemma as being negative or undesirable.

I propose an alternative framework that conceptualises a specifically transcultural goal of education. Instead of seeking to improve the learner's intercultural competence, transcultural education aims at increasing cultural flexibility, as flexibility is what makes change possible, effective and constructive.

Intercultural learning and teaching and psychological flexibility

A dialogic approach to intercultural teaching places an emphasis on a 'feeling' teacher and learner. For example, in their discussion of principles for developing intercultural language learning, Liddicoat et al. (2003) hold that for learners, intercultural learning is more than a process of absorption of facts. Rather, it is a continuous process to develop thinking, feeling and changing intercultural beings. In her discussion of a 'pedagogy of connection', Cadman (2005) emphasises that 'a *connecting* classroom comes alive through the presence of a teacher as a feeling being as well as a thinking one' (Cadman 2005, p. 357, emphasis in original). It can be understood that a culturally flexible person is one who is psychologically flexible in intercultural contexts. In other words, cultural flexibility can be understood as psychological flexibility in intercultural communication. I would therefore like to further explore the concept of cultural flexibility through the concept of psychological flexibility in third wave cognitive-behavioural therapy — Acceptance and Commitment Therapy (ACT).

The cognitive-behavioural therapy tradition began in the 1950s and blossomed in the 1960s (Hayes et al. 2004). First generation behaviour therapy was largely based on a straightforward stimulus-response association. If therapists perceived individuals to have poor social skills, they gave clear, direct verbal instructions of components of 'good social skills' so that the individuals could change their behaviour. However, the first generation of behaviour therapy failed to provide an adequate account of human language and cognition. The cognitive therapy movement in the 1970s attempted to do so, which gave rise to the second generation of behaviour therapy, known as cognitive-behavioural therapy (CBT). Through questionnaires and interviews, clinicians learned to identify cognitive errors in individual groups and develop direct means to correct these problems and reduce symptoms. CBT has enjoyed great success over the past 30 years or so. However, it is now challenged by a third generation of cognitive-behavioural therapy known as Acceptance and Commitment Therapy (ACT).

The third generation of cognitive-behavioural therapy emerged 15–20 years ago with the rise of constructivism and similar postmodernist theories that abandoned mechanistic assumptions of behaviour. It focused on an area that the previous two generations of therapy overlooked, that is, the context in which events happened. The new behaviour therapy conceptualises psychological events as 'a set of ongoing interactions between whole organisms and historically and situationally defined contexts' (Hayes et al. 2004, p. 7). It draws attention to the function and context of psychological phenomena rather than to their form. It therefore abandons the whole idea of directly changing individuals' behaviour. Instead, it focuses more on contextualistic assumptions and contact with experiences in the present situation. ACT differs from the previous two generations of therapy in that it does not perceive difficult thoughts and feelings as 'symptoms' nor see them as harmful, undesirable or irrational. The goal of ACT, therefore, is not to reduce symptoms or to correct behaviour. Rather, ACT aims at increasing individuals' psychological flexibility by transforming their relationship with difficult thoughts and feelings.

ACT and psychological flexibility are particularly relevant to our conceptualisation of a transcultural goal for education, as we need a framework that pays attention to the context, that can help us reject seeing difficult thoughts and feelings associated with crossing cultural borders as 'symptoms' of incompetency, and that can provide an analytic rather than 'corrective' approach to issues associated with transcultural communication. In the following section, I will take a closer look at the model of psychological flexibility in ACT to further draw its relevance to transcultural education.

The model of psychological flexibility in ACT

As mentioned earlier, the goal of Acceptance and Commitment Therapy (ACT) is to produce more psychological flexibility, defined as the ability to change or to persist with classes of functional behavioural when doing so serves valued ends (Hayes et al. 2004). Unlike previous cognitive-behavioural therapies, ACT draws attention to the context of behaviour rather than the form of behaviour itself. It resists the attempt to remove or eliminate language processes that create difficulty for human beings, as it is these same processes that are essential to human functioning. Instead, ACT seeks to bring these processes under contextual control so that the processes serve a person's values in a healthy and effective way. The idea of contextual control is based on a complex and comprehensive functional contextual program of basic research on language and cognition called 'relational frame theory' (Hayes et al. 2001). Relational frame theory research finds that human beings are extraordinarily able to learn to derive and combine stimulus relationships and to bring them under arbitrary contextual control. These derived stimulus relations, in turn, alter the functions of events that participate in relational networks — a process that is also under contextual control. Relational frame theory argues that together, these features form the foundation of human language and higher cognition.

Hayes et al. (2004) give a simple example. Think of a child who has never seen or played with a cat. After learning that C-A-T → animal, and C-A-T → "cat", the child is able to derive four additional relations: animal → C-A-T, "cat" → C.A.T., animal → "cat" and "cat" → animal. Suppose the child is later scratched by the cat, and she cries and runs away. Every time she hears people say, 'Oh, look! A cat!' she may cry and run away. What brings these situations together is not their formal properties at the time of utterance but the relations that the child derives among them.

Human beings use relational frames to think and talk about events that are not present and to make associations among things. For example, seeing a door locked, a human being may use frames of coordination, contingency and comparison, and say: 'If I do this, that will happen, and that would be good.' Hayes et al. (2004) state that this process is enormously helpful and seems to underlie the tremendous ecological success of human beings. However, it is this same process that may create human misery. For example, a socially anxious person may use the same frames and say, 'If I avoid speaking to other people, I won't get anxious and I will be fine'.

Hayes et al. (2004) list some key processes fostered by relational frames that cause negative psychological inflexibility. Firstly, for evolutionary reasons, human organisms are especially attuned to aversive stimulations and relational frames enormously increase the reach of aversive events. The human mind can be like a Radio Doom-and-Gloom playing at full volume, with difficult thoughts swirling around. This is called *the ubiquity of pain*. Secondly, verbal rules and evaluations, for example a statement like 'I am not worth it', narrow the range of behaviour available to make contact with here-and-now experience (Harris 2007). They tend to dominate over other sources of behavioural regulation in humans. This is called *cognitive fusion*. Thirdly, as a result of the domination of evaluative and judgmental language, human beings tend to be unwilling to remain in contact with particular experiences. This is the phenomenon of *experiential avoidance*.

These areas of psychological inflexibility are addressed by ACT, which aims at increasing psychological flexibility by helping individuals actively contact the costs of psychological inflexibility and then by establishing core skills to tackle the phenomena above. The psychological space within which ACT works is shown in Figure 2. It includes six core processes: (1) establishing acceptance skills (2) establishing cognitive *defusion* skills (3) distinguishing *self-as-context* from the conceptualised/evaluated self (4) contacting the present moment (5) distinguishing choice from reasoned action, clarifying personal *values* and distinguishing them from goals and actions, and (6) teaching *committed* behavioural changes and persistence skills to serve chosen values (Hayes and Strosahl 2004). The following is a brief explanation of the six processes in more practical terms.

Acceptance

Acceptance involves contacting psychological experiences directly and fully, embracing the experience of thoughts, feelings, and bodily sensations as they occur, without needless defence. It makes space for unpleasant feelings, sensations or urges, instead of trying to avoid them, control them, suppress them or push them away.

Cognitive defusion

Cognitive defusion conveys the opposite to cognitive fusion. Cognitive fusion means blending thoughts and feelings with the 'stories' or 'events' that they refer to, as, for example, we react to the word 'lemon' as if the lemon is actually present. Cognitive defusion involves separating thoughts and feelings from the relations made through these thoughts. Techniques of defusion try to undermine a person's fusion with the idea of a conceptualised self such as 'I am incompetent'. In doing this, defusion techniques focus on looking at thoughts as thoughts, feelings as feelings, and sensations as sensations. For example, instead of pushing these thoughts away, defusion techniques train individuals to step back and write down the thoughts as they are, such as 'I am having the thought that I am incompetent'. This involves acknowledging and noticing thoughts, feelings and sensations as they occur, rather than being caught up in them (that is, infused with them).

Self as context

Self as context is often called 'observing self' (Harris 2007). As ACT sees excessive fusion with a conceptualised self as a threat to psychological flexibility, it tries to elevate the sense of self as the context in which thoughts, feelings, memories, and so on happen. An observing self tries to see things as they are, without judging them or criticising them. It supports acceptance and gives acceptance 'its truest and purest form' (Harris 2007, p. 193). This is a process of developing awareness of awareness itself.

Contact with present moment

ACT promotes effective and open connection with the present moment. Individuals are trained to observe and notice what is present in the environment rather than dwell on the past or worry about the future. They are also taught to label and describe what is present, without excessive judgment or evaluation. These two elements together help to establish a sense of self as a process of ongoing awareness.

Values

Values are chosen qualities of purposive action. They are reflections of what is important in a person's heart, what a person stands for and what kind of person an individual wants to be. Values provide a general direction for a person's behaviour patterns and motivate a person to make important changes to reach a rich and meaningful experience. ACT involves a variety of exercises to help individuals connect with their hearts' deepest desires and clarify their fundamental values.

Committed action

Committed action is overt behaviour in the service of values. It refers to value-guided, effective and mindful action along a person's valued path. The goal is to

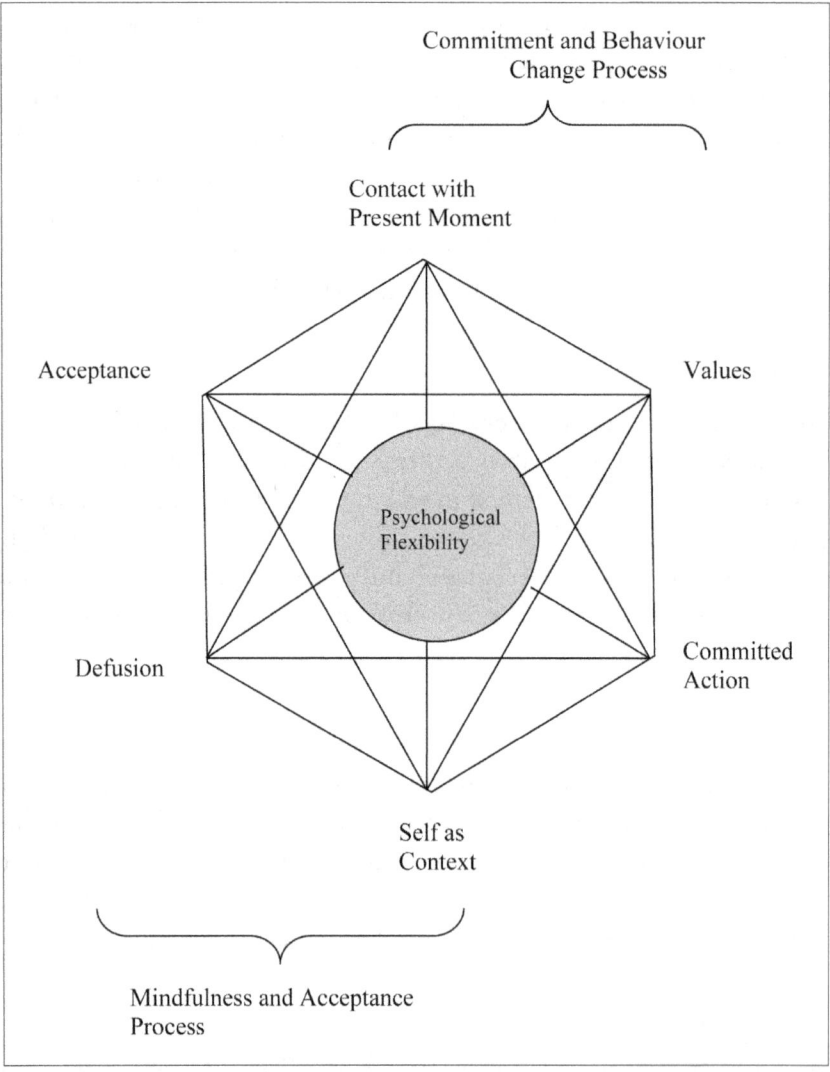

Figure 2: Facets of psychological flexibility according to the model of change underlying Acceptance and Commitment Therapy (ACT) (Hayes and Strosahl 2004, p. 7)[2]

construct behavioural patterns that begin to work for the person, not against them.

As Figure 2 shows, these six key processes of the ACT model of psychological flexibility can be seen as two large groups: 'Mindfulness and Acceptance Processes' that involve the four processes to the left, and 'Commitment and Behaviour Change Processes' that involve the four processes to the right. Furthermore, the six processes of this model of psychological flexibility relate to and interact with one another, as represented by the lines connecting all points. ACT intervention can enter into the space from any of the six processes and can move through them in any order.

From psychological inflexibility to cultural inflexibility

As outlined above, cultural flexibility can be understood as psychological flexibility in intercultural communication. Just as psychological inflexibility and flexibility co-exist in each of one of us, cultural inflexibility and flexibility co-exist too. We can easily observe that the three areas of psychological inflexibility mentioned earlier, namely the ubiquity of pain, cognitive fusion and experiential avoidance, manifest themselves in intercultural communication as cultural inflexibility.

The ubiquity of pain

Our organisms are naturally attuned to aversive stimulation (psychological inflexibility) and are enormously capable of relating bad past or remote events with a present situation. For example, a person who has had a bad experience with a person from another culture might feel the same pain whenever she encounters a person from the same culture again, even if that person has no intention to hurt her.

Cognitive fusion

We tend to form our view about a new culture through spectacles of our own culture and make sweeping judgments and evaluations of the new culture. As verbal rules and evaluations make an individual less in contact with the present situation (psychological inflexibility), stereotypical judgments similarly prevent us from directly experiencing what is here and now (cultural inflexibility).

Experiential avoidance

As a result of evaluative language, a person is unwilling to remain in contact with a particular experience (psychological inflexibility). To avoid frustration, confusion, loneliness or insecurity caused by crossing cultural boundaries, we tend to remain in our cultural comfort zones and guard a certain amount of misanthropy (cultural inflexibility). As Salvadori (1997, p. 186) puts it, sociability and non-sociability coexist in every human being and 'violence towards others is an ingredient of the human soul'.

Cultural inflexibility, as psychological inflexibility, can be seen as a result of human evolutionary process. In some situations, it protects us from danger, but in other situations it prevents us from opening ourselves to new experiences. It should not be seen as signs of weakness or incompetence; it is natural, though it may not always help us build trusting, healthy and harmonious relationships between one another.

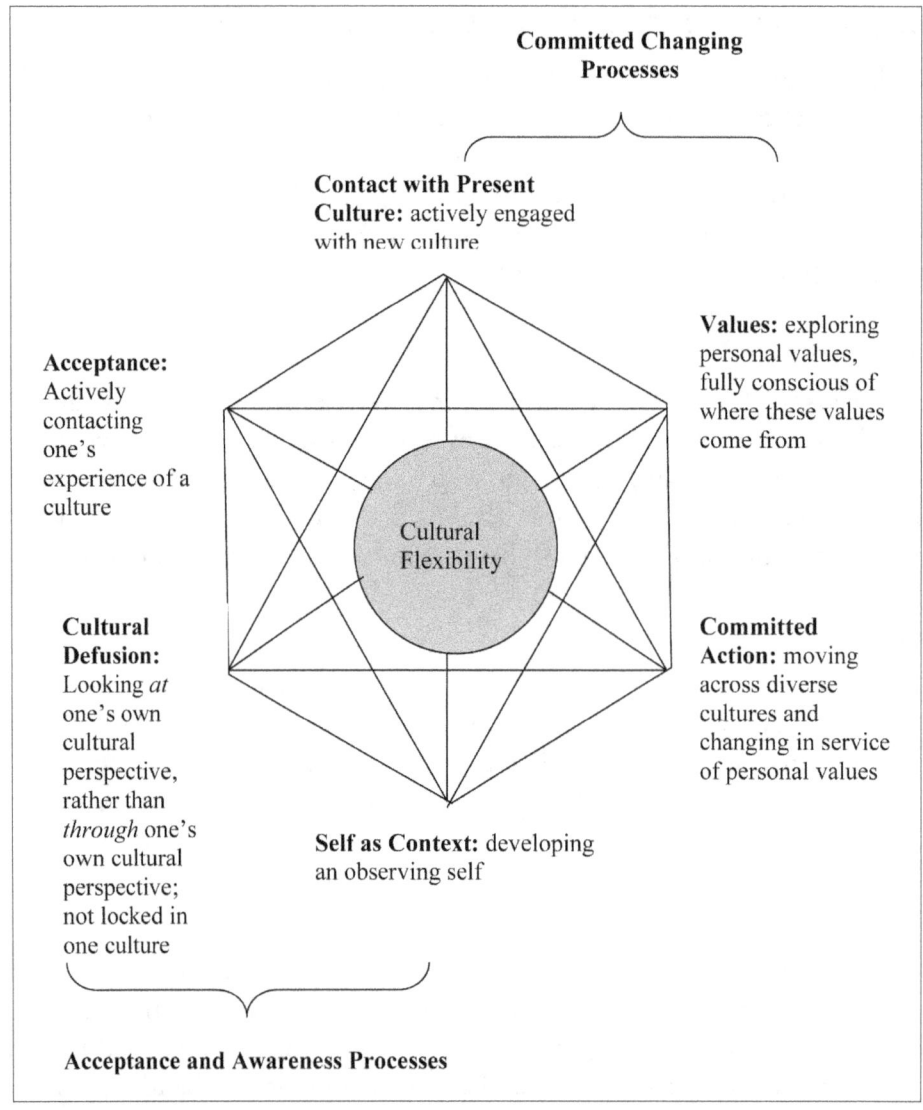

Figure 3: Proposed facets of cultural flexibility

From psychological flexibility to cultural flexibility: Towards a framework

The purpose of transcultural education is to produce greater cultural flexibility so that we can use it to create better, healthier and more sustainable relationships with others. Drawing on the concept of psychological flexibility, I define cultural flexibility as the propensity to distance oneself from the bondages of one's own culture as a conscious and informed human being, and to move across diverse cultural, social and language groups and environments for valued goals. The processes of psychological flexibility underlying ACT can shed light on the model of cultural flexibility, as shown in Figure 3.

Applying psychological flexibility to the context of transcultural education, cultural flexibility can be established with a focus on six core processes: Acceptance, Cultural defusion, Contact with present culture, Values, Committed action, and Self as context. As with psychological flexibility in ACT, for cultural flexibility these processes can be grouped into two parts: 'Acceptance and Awareness Processes' that involve the four processes to the left of Figure 3, and 'Committed Changing Processes' that involve the four to the right. Cultural flexibility is about (1) being fully aware of and embracing one's own cultural experience without needless defence, and (2) moving in and out of a culture, that is, changing in the service of values.

Acceptance

Acceptance means to open oneself fully to experience in one's own culture without defence or judgment. It involves actively contacting one's experience, thoughts and feelings directly and fully, instead of suppressing them, controlling them, hiding them, leaving them, or avoiding them, even if these thoughts and feelings are unpleasant ones. For this process, students of another language and culture are trained to make active contact with their own framework of culture and become aware of how that culture has influenced the way they feel, behave and speak, but without making judgment. What is important in this process is a direct, unaltered contact with and an honest acknowledgement of feelings that arise from the underlying assumptions, cultural beliefs and culture-affected values, which are often unconscious to the students themselves. This can be a painful process as students may be inclined to take for granted what they believe in and take a defensive attitude towards their culture. In this process, it would be important for the teacher to be open and honest about her own framework of culture and language, so that a dialogue of mutual exploration can be created.

Cultural defusion

Cultural defusion is based on an understanding that we as human beings have a tendency to stay in our cultural 'comfort zones'. As well as wanting to experience what is new, we are also attached to our own culture and tend to distance ourselves from others. Cultural defusion means to be defused from rather than infused with one's own framework of culture so that one does not remain unaware of the feelings and thoughts that may come from certain cultural perspectives. Teachers and students work together to look *at* their cultural perspective rather than looking *through* it. This process involves an analytical understanding and reflection on teachers' and students' own cultural perspectives. Teachers guide students to notice their thoughts and feelings caused by certain cultural experiences as they occur, rather than being caught up in these thoughts and feelings. The aim of cultural defusion is to be fully engaged with one's own culturally encoded experience and facilitate explicit awareness of language, cultural and cognitive processes so as to free one from bondages of a blindly cultural perspective.

Self as context

In ACT, a conceptualised self, that is, a judgment about oneself such as 'I'm incompetent', is seen as a threat to psychological flexibility. Therefore, an essential component of ACT is to develop an alternative type of self-experience, known as self-as-context, or observing self. In the same way as ACT sees fusion with conceptualised self, I here see excessive fusion with conceptualisations gained predominantly through one cultural perspective, in other words, as a threat to cultural flexibility and an impediment to positive intercultural relations. We aim to train students to develop an alternative sense of self, an observing self, that observes thought and language processes without being affected. The observing self offers a consistent perspective from which to observe and accept all changing experiences when crossing one's own culture borders, and when moving in and out of experiences and ideas about another culture.

Contact with present culture

In this process, both teachers and students actively engage themselves with a different, perhaps unfamiliar new culture. They work together to observe and notice what is present in the new environment introduced. They analyse and describe the new culture without excessive judgment. Throughout these activities, teachers are open and also encourage students to be open about what they feel about aspects of the new culture and how it has affected them intellectually and emotionally.

Values

An important component of increasing cultural flexibility is to allow a space for students to explore and discuss their own values as individuals and become aware of where these values come from and how these values may change based on new understandings of other cultures. As discussed earlier, change or transformation is at the core of transcultural communication, but a healthy change is not one that is imposed upon an agent but one that comes from within and that is in line with one's personal values and beliefs. Transcultural teaching is not about training students to be more like 'the other', but to work with them to know themselves better and to be more like the type of person they want to be, as a conscious and informed human being.

Committed action

Once cultural and psychological barriers of fusion and rejection are opened up to be dealt with and personal values are explored, teachers can work with students to take responsibility for making and keeping commitments for behavioural change. Students and teacher can share goals that need to be set to meet new needs, as well as the overt behavioural changes necessary to accomplish these goals, and the frustrations that come with the changes.

Conclusion

This chapter has argued that a commonly used competency model of conceptualising intercultural learning and teaching undermines a dialogic pedagogy due to its presumptions of single truth and hierarchical relationship between the teacher and the learner. Here I have proposed that, instead of trying to achieve a higher intercultural competency level, a transcultural model of education can aim at increasing cultural flexibility. Adopting the concept of psychological flexibility used in cognitive-behaviour therapy, I have explored the facets of and processes involved in cultural flexibility.

Theoretically this chapter offers a conceptualisation of the purpose, goals and process of transcultural education from a psychological perspective. Such a conceptualisation is based on a recognition that cultural inflexibility, as psychological inflexibility, is an integral part of our very humanity and should not be seen as being negative or evidence of incompetence. The purpose of transcultural education is to produce greater cultural flexibility in order to facilitate healthy, sustainable change or transformation in transcultural communication. Practically, this chapter draws attention to the psychological foundation of pedagogy and offers a shift in thinking about transcultural pedagogy. Seeing cultural flexibility instead of intercultural competence as the goal of teaching liberates the teacher from seeing herself as an authoritative judge and assessor of students' competency levels. Such a perspective leads the teacher to creating a classroom rhetoric that is not authoritarian, patronising nor judgmental, but one that is equal, rational and understanding. It encourages the teacher to capitalise on students' prior learning and backgrounds, and to mutually explore feelings and thoughts involved in transcultural experiences openly and honestly through engaging in dialogical encounters with students.

In his discussion of a critical pragmatic theory of classroom talk, Robert Young (1992) argues that dialogue is fundamental to the processes of schooling in democratic states and that outcomes of dialogues change human identities and relationships. In an increasingly globalising world where learners and teachers come from diverse language, cultural and social backgrounds, an effective integration of cultural flexibility into global education will help build positive, healthy and sustainable transcultural relationships when cultural borders are being negotiated, and thus enhance social harmony among people.

Notes

[1] Farjad is a pseudonym; the incident is an anecdote from Dr Kate Cadman, then the Coordinator of IBP (pers.comm).
[2] The author wishes to thank Springer Science+Business Media B.V. for their kind permission to reprint the Figure.

References

Cadman, K 2005, 'Towards a 'pedagogy of connection' in critical research education: a REAL story', *Journal of English for Academic Purposes*, vol. 4 no. 4, pp. 353–367.
Freire, P 1972, *Pedagogy of the oppressed*, Penguin Education, Auckland, NZ.
Gardner, GH 1962, 'Cross-cultural communication', *Journal of Social Psychology*, vol. 58, pp. 241–256.
Gertsen, MC 1990, 'Intercultural competence and expatriates', *The International Journal of Human Resource Management*, vol. 1 no. 3, pp. 341–362.
Harris, R 2007, *The happiness trap: stop struggling, start living*, Exisle Publishing,

Auckland, NZ.

Hayes, SC, Barnes-Holmes, D & Roche, B (eds) 2001, *Relational frame theory: a post-Skinnerian account of human language and cognition*, Plenum Press, New York.

Hayes, SC, Follette, VM & Linehan, MM (eds) 2004, *Mindfulness and acceptance: expanding the cognitive-behavioral tradition*, The Guilford Press, New York.

Hayes, SC and Strosahl, KD (eds) 2004, *A practical guide to Acceptance and Commitment Therapy*, Springer, New York.

Hayes, SC, Strosahl, KD & Wilson, KG 1999, *Acceptance and Commitment Therapy: an experiential approach to behavior change*, Guilford Press, New York.

Liddicoat, AJ 2008, 'Pedagogical practice for integrating the intercultural in language teaching and learning', *Japanese Studies*, vol. 28 no. 3, pp. 277–290.

Liddicoat, AJ, Papademetre, L, Scarino, A & Kohler, M 2003, *Report on intercultural language learning*, DEST, Canberra, ACT.

Nagata, AL 2004, 'Promoting self-reflexivity in intercultural education', *Journal of Intercultural Communication*, vol. 8, pp. 139–167.

Salvadori, RG 1997, 'The difficulties of interculturalism', *European Journal of Intercultural Studies*, vol. 8 no. 2, pp. 185–191.

Young, R 1992, *Critical theory and classroom talk*, Multilingual Matters, Clevedon, MA.

Reflections of a 'Korean' teaching about Japan in globalising Australia

Sejin Pak

Introduction

Teaching about Japanese society and culture in a Western university is probably different from teaching about any other country, whether Eastern or Western. That is because many of the students who enrol in a course on Japanese society and culture do so because they like Japan. From my experience, and as I will elaborate later, I would venture to say that the case of liking a country before studying it is more likely to be stronger in the case of Japan than other countries. This is probably the case when the course is about Japanese culture rather than Japanese politics or economy. Many students know something about Japanese culture but little about Japanese politics or economy, except that Japanese electronic products and cars have a very good reputation for quality. For university-aged students, the biggest area of contact with things Japanese is popular culture, especially *anime* (Japanese animation) and *manga* (Japanese comics). In Australia, where more Asian languages are taught at high school level than in any other Western countries (Japan Foundation, 2000, 2004), the encounter with Japanese language before starting university is also an important supporting factor. These same factors also operate in East Asian countries so a positive image of Japan is also often present there. However, there are other factors that operate in East Asian countries that diminish the positive image of Japan and these also influence students' attitudes. In other words, though not unique, Australia is a rather special environment to teach about Japan.

This essay is a reflection on my experience of teaching courses on Japanese society and culture in an Australian university for more than fifteen years. One is an introductory course called *Introduction to Japanese society and culture*, and the other is an advanced course called *Cultures and identities in contemporary Japan*. Introduction *to Japanese society and culture* covers in its first half some key topics in Japanese history, including the origins of Japanese, the Tokugawa society (the last pre-modern period), the Meiji Restoration, and imperialism and militarism. The latter half covers several key topics in contemporary Japan, including politics, education, the employment system, and the position of women. *Cultures and identities in contemporary Japan* covers diverse topics related to identities in contemporary Japan: they include Japaneseness, nationalism, the minorities, Okinawa, youth, popular culture, and spirituality, among others.

In discussing the issues relating to teaching about Japan, it is important today to understand the character of students. In terms of the disciplinary background of students, all students majoring in Japanese language or Japanese studies are required to take one of these courses, although many of them take both. However, the students majoring in Japanese language or Japanese studies typically constitute less than 20 per cent of the class, the size of which varies between 45 and 80 students year to year. Others are made of Chinese Studies majors, arts degree majors, and international studies majors, which all together constitute about 40 to 50 per cent. The rest come mostly from the Commerce majors who take these courses as electives.

In terms of national and ethnic background, the non-commerce students include Australian students of Anglo background (the largest group) and non-Anglo backgrounds (the second largest group), the largest number of the latter being from Asian backgrounds (overseas Chinese, Malay and Vietnamese). Then there are the international students of various backgrounds, the most significant group being the students from China. This latter group experienced a sudden increase in the last five years, although there has been a small but a steady number from various other countries from Asia. Finally, there have always been a steady number of exchange students (short term, visiting students) from all over the world, including the US, Europe, Asia, as well as from Japan.

The composition of students' national and ethnic backgrounds has changed significantly from there being an Australian-born and largely Anglo majority to an extremely diverse one, the most important being an increase in the number of students from Asian backgrounds, both from Australia and overseas. The Australian-born Anglo background students still constitute the largest group, but its relative size has steadily decreased. The most visible new group is the international students from China, some of whom major in Arts, but the majority are Commerce majors. The linguistic competence of international Chinese students has in general been much lower than that of the average Australian students, thus creating a problem of a dual structure in tutorial classes. The exchange students from non-English speaking countries, such as France or Germany, or even Japan, seem to cope much better than local overseas students, most of whom who do not major in Arts.

International students also differ greatly in their previous exposure to Japanese language and Japanese studies. In my experience of the exchange students at The University of Adelaide, the US students came from small universities and colleges and had no such background whereas French students came from a particular provincial university where they were Japanese majors. Asian students fell into two different groups: one group studied Japanese language while the other, as represented by the Chinese students majoring in Commerce, did not.

As this description of the student composition shows, over recent years the student background has changed from 'diverse' to 'very diverse', and, in my observation, this situation would be similar in many courses taught in Australian universities. However, its significance in a course on Japanese society and culture may be somewhat different from that in other courses, even including the courses on Chinese society and culture. The China-related courses have been growing in size due mainly to the pragmatic interest among students about China following the remarkable growth of the Chinese economy. The same factor seemed to operate in relation to the student interest in Japan about fifteen years ago when students admired the Japanese economy, but no longer. In fact, the Japanese economy stopped growing about 20 years ago, but Japan was a rich country and the students were not aware of the economic problems that Japan has since faced. As a result, their motivation was inspired by Japan's economic and technological advancement. Today, however, more students taking a course on Japan do so because they like Japan. This student background also suggests students' disposition to see Japan as unique.

The uniqueness of Japan

The issue of the uniqueness of Japan has always been a difficult one to discuss. The notion that Japan is unique is widespread in Western writings (see Dale 1986) and many of my Australian students share this view even without having read them. One of the reasons why students think this way may be that they have a rather limited exposure to the diversity of cultures around the world, most of them being bound by a dualistic view of the world: Australia versus Japan, where Australia is culturally situated in the familiar West. Japan is a land of ancient tradition, of *samurai*, *geisha*, *kimono*, and, more recently, of electronic goods, *manga* and *anime*. Most students note that Japan is a country of a unique mixture of tradition and modernity, and they actually use the expression 'unique' quite often.

From my observation of student discussions, it has become clear that most see the uniqueness of modern and contemporary Japan as coming from the uniqueness of Japanese tradition. To most students of Japan, Japan is an exotic country, a land of ancient tradition and of the descendants of the noble men (aka *samurai*). It is this exotic aspect that attracts their interests. Added to this is a positive view of the country, its culture and people, often coming from the not unreasonable understanding that Japan has been and is a very successful and rich country, economically first, but also culturally. Many, and indeed most in the case of the white-skinned, who have the experience of visiting Japan would also add that the society is so orderly, and people are so kind and polite. Moreover, this dominant view is not only found among novice students but shared by many intellectuals, academics and opinion leaders both in the West and in the non-West (Dale 1986). It is no wonder that the core body of Australian students who are interested in Japan are what may be called 'Japan lovers', who may be represented by the statement, which I have often heard: 'Everything about Japan is so unique, I love everything about Japan'.

As a teacher in Japanese studies, I welcome the high level of interest about Japan and the level of enthusiasm of these hard-core Japan lovers. However, I am mindful that such a stereotypical and rosy perspective of Japan may work as an obstacle towards a deeper understanding, and the holder of such a view may end up being disappointed in learning about the complex nature of the 'real' Japan. Therefore, I regard it my responsibility as a teacher to shake up this dominant view of Japan, but, at the same time, to do so without killing the valuable enthusiasm of the 'Japan lovers'. By contrast, such an extreme view is uncommon among the students from Asia, but a milder form of the uniqueness view is also found among them mixed with negative feelings. We shall come back to this point later. As a teacher, then, the following questions challenge me: How can one critique such a stereotypical but dominant view of Japan among the students of Japanese studies? And how, if at all, can the diversity of students' cultural backgrounds be engaged towards this goal?

Love of a foreign country comes not simply from an intellectual curiosity but from admiration of certain qualities, whether imagined or real, of that country. Those are superior qualities that we desire but do not have now. One recalls that in accounts of modern world history, countries or cultures have been placed in a hierarchy of civilisations (Hawkins 1997). It was not very long ago that most Westerners accepted the superiority of Western civilisation above all others. It was Max Weber (the German sociologist who has been regarded as one of the founding fathers of sociology as an academic discipline) who used the concept of the uniqueness of the West as one of the central theses of historical sociology (Weber 1930). Weber was a product of Western civilisation, and he admired the wonders and uniqueness of the civilisation that produced the dynamism of industrial capitalism for the first time in world history. He searched for the sources of this dynamism in the West among all places, particularly in religion, in Protestant ethics to be more specific. The purpose of telling this story to the students of Japan, especially to the Japan admirers, is to stress that they are not holding a unique view of a country, though of course Weber's was self-admiration whereas Japan lovers' is other-admiration. However, Max Weber's view was also shared by Australia's founding fathers, and, to the students' surprise, by the founding fathers of modern Japan in the late nineteenth century. I add the point that even the hegemonic superiority of the Western civilisation that was almost universally accepted was established partly at gunpoint.

Through this exercise in historical understanding the students begin to appreciate that a power hierarchy lies behind the admiration and respect of one country by another, and historically both Japan and the West admired the West, and the West acknowledged it. The concept of 'Orientalism' is typically used to describe how the image of or discourse about a non-Western country was shaped by the power relationship between the West and the non-West (Hall 1992). In the Orientalist perspective, the non-West would look both childish and child-like, whereas the West would appear as more mature and more reasonable. Historically, such a discourse was often constructed to maintain the power hierarchy in the international relations between the West and the non-West. As such, the concept of Orientalism has been a key concept to be utilised in international studies and area studies.

As Japan caught up with the West in terms of power, Japan's self-perception changed to self-respect and self admiration, again, as happened with the West. Moreover, Japan's perception of East Asia, especially that of China, also gradually changed from admiration to disdain. It is from this point on that what may be called 'uniqueness syndrome' became established in Japan. Separating itself both from the West as well as the East, Japan's identity looked unique. The uniqueness notion also played a key role in maintaining the modern political order Japan created by constructing an Emperor worship. Though this was a pre-war construction, this perspective was revived in the post-war 'economic miracle'. What is important to note here is that Japan's self-perception as unique or her discourse of uniqueness in turn had an effect on the students of Japan outside, including those in Australia. In this manner, the Australian students gain a historical understanding of the images of Japan they have. However, the students from Asia tend to look at Japan from a different perspective, thus their presence in the same class serves to challenge the rosy uniqueness view of the Australian Japan-lovers.

Another point about the uniqueness of Japan that is often mentioned by the first year students is that Japan's geographic isolation from other countries may perhaps have contributed to the notion that it is especially unique. First, Japan's geographic position is that it is a series of islands separated from the continent, a point that can be raised without having studied Japanese history. Secondly, Japan had a self-imposed policy of isolation from the beginning of the seventeenth century, a point that is studied in the first half of the introductory course. The combination of these may be called an 'indigenous development theory' of Japanese culture. This has been a popular view also in Japan, eagerly supported by the Japanese government authority from the Meiji period to the post-war period (Chamberlain 1912; McCormack 1996; Iwabuchi 1994). A related view is the theory known as *Nihonjinron*, with implicit suggestion for the uniqueness of Japanese people (Befu 1993; Iwabuchi, 1994). There has been a strong cultural nationalist tendency, desire and demand in post-war Japan to see its own culture and people as unique and to be of indigenous origin (Befu1993). In fact, this is not to deny that there has been a strong element of indigenous development in Japan, but the point to be made here is about an evident tendency to deny or minimise the external influences.

With regard to this distinction between cultural isolation and cultural contact, the students from China and Korea are likely to differ from the Australian students. The students from China and Korea know (or come to know through their study) that Japan shares Confucianism, which may be called civic religion, with their own country, in the same way most nations in Europe share Christianity. There are other shared elements such as Buddhism and Taoism, Oriental medicine, the material culture of rice production and consumption, and also the related food cultures, such as bean paste (*miso*) and soy source (*shouyu*), and even the use of chopsticks. Despite all of these, the theory of indigenous development due to isolation remains strong among the Japanese and in the Western popular imagination.

On the Western (including the Australian) side this may be due to the large volume of exposure to the Western public of Japan displaced and in isolation from the East Asian context, from China and Korea in particular. Most students studying Japanese language do not study about China and do not see any or much cultural connection between them except in the use of Chinese characters in the Japanese writing system. On the Japanese side, as mentioned earlier, the Japanese themselves also developed, from the second half of the nineteenth century, a tendency to compare themselves with the West, and see themselves through the Western mirror. After having gone through the phase of imitating and following the West, the Japanese began to assert the opposite, the superiority and uniqueness of Japan, at least in a moral and spiritual sense. Having been defeated in World War Two, the superiority element disappeared, or at least became subdued, but the uniqueness view became popular during the period of economic growth in post-war Japan. This has been the context in which the Australian students have been exposed to Japanese language and culture.

The notion of uniqueness based on Japan's separation from the rest of Asia is challenged when an understanding is developed about the historical connection of Japan to China and Korea. And the presence of the students of these countries in this class naturally stimulates this process. It would be difficult to consider the history of Britain in separation from that of continental Europe. The same is naturally true in the case of Japan's connection to the continent throughout history from the very origin of its people to the founding of the first state. The use of Chinese characters in Japanese writing is not equivalent to the borrowing of alphabet, but it suggests a shared conceptual world that is implied in the characters. Japanese grammar is another aspect of Japanese culture that is often regarded as unique both by the Japanese as well as the Western students of the language. However, the grammatical similarity of Japanese language to Korean language is only too well known to the Korean students of Japanese language.

The connections between Japan and China, and Japan and Korea, are so deep that there is a tendency among the many students from China and Korea to think that 'everything' in Japan came from their countries. Under these circumstances, the teacher's task is a complex one: it is to balance these two extremes in understanding of Japanese culture as a combined product of an isolated indigenous development and of an imported development; it is to treat Japanese history and culture as a product of a series of interactions of an international system in East Asia, in the same way Britain's history would be understood in the context of the history of Europe. A significant part of exotic Japan is removed by this historical and relational approach to Japan. And the presence of the students from China and Korea in Australian classes provides a stimulating environment for Australian students.

Talking about Japan's involvement in war

Teaching and learning about Japan's colonial and military involvement in Asia conjures up complex reactions in a culturally diverse body of students. In modern Japanese history, Japan's colonial and military involvement in Asia plays a defining role in her historic experience as a modern nation. The memories of colonialism and war also define the character of post-war Japan. This topic is examined as a part of modern Japanese history in the introductory course, and revisited in the advanced course through the topic of post-war nationalism. Most of the students who encounter the topic for the first time in the first year course are intellectually as well as emotionally unprepared. Some students, particularly those from an Asian background, whether they are local or from overseas, know something about the war and colonialism and have negative feelings about Japan at least with regard to this aspect. But rarely was the topic initially important enough to have been one of the main reasons for taking a course on Japan. On the other hand, the majority of Australian students of non-Asian background have little knowledge of the topic and therefore no special feelings about it, though occasionally mature aged students recall their parents and grandparents talking negatively about 'the bloody Japs'. From the beginning, as the teacher, I know that this is a topic that can be controversial to Japan-loving students.

The initial task in teaching about Japan's military expansion in Asia in the late nineteenth century and in the first half of the twentieth century is to provide an understanding about the international context in which Western imperialism dominated the world, including Asia. Thus, Japan's rise as a modern nation and her expansion in Asia is treated in the course as Japan's effort to resist the Western domination and possible subjugation to the West, which many Asian nations fell into. The course sees Japan's rise as a modern nation through the Meiji Restoration and nation-building in a Western-dominated international environment as a remarkable success story that impresses not only the Australian students with European background, but also those with Asian backgrounds, but even more especially the international students from Asia. Japan's willingness to change herself quickly in order to survive and succeed in a new Western-dominated world impresses most students, even the students from China and Korea, where Japan is historically seen more critically due to their negative experience under Japanese military expansion and colonialism.

Japan's colonisation of neighbouring countries and military expansion in Asia can initially be seen as an extension of Japan's determination to resist Western domination, but soon the students realise that Japan became like a Western nation practising imperialism for her own benefit at the expense of other Asian countries. The students who had a middle school or high school education in China or Korea know this story all too well. The Australian students learn for the first time why there were anti-Japanese feelings among the Asian students they came across in the past. The Asian students, on the other hand, learn that the Australian students do not in general share their critical view of Japan, and the members of tutorial classes become more sensitive about the presence of others who may not share their feeling toward Japan in her role in Asia.

The topic that stirs up the uncomfortable feeling most is so-called 'Nanjing Massacre', the killing of a large number of civilians by Japanese soldiers in the fall of Nanjin in 1937. The Chinese government claim of the number of victims is as large as 300,000 whereas the Japanese nationalists view the notion of 'massacre' a pure Chinese government fabrication. This is a controversial topic since there is a strong disagreement not only between China and Japan but even among different groups within Japan about the historical facts and the political use of the history and memory of the event. The most important material I use in teaching of this topic is documentary videos, showing historical footage and interviews with soldiers and victims. There are many versions of the 'Nanjin Massacre' documentary, the number produced growing over the last several years (see list of documentaries at the end of this chapter's bibliography). Some show scenes of extreme, naked brutalities causing considerable upset among students, even with a warning before the documentary. When I showed a version of these videos, some Australian students stated that they felt physically ill during the documentary. Some students from a Chinese background, on the other hand, expressed in tutorial class outrage and anger towards a Japan that continues to deny the fact and responsibility for the massacre. As a result I avoided such videos in following years.

The documentary segments that triggered less emotional feeling but more thought among Australian students were the ones that showed interviews with the Japanese soldiers who fought in China (Choy & Tong 1998). In these segments, the story is not told by a narrator but by ex-Japanese soldiers themselves. They tell, in a matter of fact manner, without emotion, how they regarded the Chinese not as human beings, and how they killed and raped during their military campaigns in China. The Japanese soldiers who told this story were very normal, gentle-looking individuals in their homes in present-day Japan. According to student responses in class, online and in their reflection papers, they seem to be left with strong impression about the logic of the mentality of the soldiers, and the social and political environment that produced them.

On my part as a teacher, I make an effort not to take a side on this controversial issue, and not even to express my personal view. The students, on the other hand, are not prevented from expressing their views, but I place an emphasis, especially in their essays, on showing an understanding and objectively explaining the social and political forces that led to some extreme behaviour among the Japanese soldiers. Some Australian students have become intellectually interested in the topic and pursued it in following years. Some Chinese students have also learned to think less emotionally about the topic. The occasional presence of exchange students from Japan in the two courses have been acutely felt by all when I taught the war topic and discussed it with students in tutorial class. The majority of Japanese students who have been in the class are neither knowledgeable nor interested in history, especially about Japan's involvement in the war in Asia. They remain quiet in tutorial class, and respond minimally when their views are asked, especially because they are not confident in expressing their opinion in English in a foreign university. The Australian students, especially those who want to befriend the students from Japan, are mindful of the discomfort their Japanese friends may be experiencing. Then there are watchful eyes from the students from China. It is not an easy environment to conduct intellectually stimulating discussion. But the tension felt in such a class of students with mixed backgrounds on such topics is difficult for the students to forget. This can serve as an intellectually motivating factor to find out more about the topic.

Occasionally, there have been students from Japan who have a nationalist view, and, at the same time, are competent in English. They are good to have in class because we have a living sample of a Japanese nationalist who expresses his or her opinion vocally, even in English. These individuals are often most active in the discussion board in the course's webpage. A Japanese nationalist is one who tries to propagate his or her pro-Japanese view and challenges any opposing one. Thus, the presence of such a student in class is a challenge for me as a teacher since I am obliged to balance the opinions in class, especially if the Japanese nationalist student acts as an authority on the topic. So, in all these ways, the topic on war and nationalism remains both a controversial and intellectually stimulating topic with students from diverse national backgrounds, one that might profoundly shake the 'I love everything about Japan' belief.

'Korean' teacher

So far, I have talked about some of the most challenging issues in teaching about Japan to the students of diverse national backgrounds. Now I direct the question to the identity of teacher in such a course. Does the cultural or national identity of the teacher matter in teaching on a foreign country? Is it significant? If so, in what way? This aspect adds to the complexity of the cultural composition of the learning environment of teaching about Japan in an Australian university.

One of the first things that I do in introducing myself at the beginning of a Japan course that I teach is to say that I am not a 'Japanese' person, and that I am originally from South Korea. Typically, in the case of a non-'Japanese looking' person, there would be no need to say such a thing, since it is obvious. But for a 'Japanese looking' person like me, I need to say so in a country like Australia where I may be taken for a Japanese. Anyone who is familiar with Asian names should immediately be able to recognise that my surname is Korean. However, for the majority of the Australian students of non-Asian background, this is not the case, especially in the first year of university. However, in a multicultural society like Australia, why would the teacher's ethnic and national identity matter in teaching and learning about a foreign country, Japan in this case?

In this section of this chapter, I would like to point out that the matter of ethnic and national identity is important to Japanese people, and also to Koreans, when it is about teaching about their country, especially when this teaching concerns society and culture. That includes the identity of the teacher, and it is important to convey this point to Australian students. That is, the important significance of the ethnic and national identity of the teacher is firstly, not to us as teacher and students of Japan in Australia, but to the Japanese people; and our job is to appreciate the reason why this is so. However, it turns out that even in Australia, some students raise this matter.

There are many non-ethnic Japanese teaching courses on Japanese society and culture in Western universities, but it is rare to find an ethnic Korean as a teacher. The situation is similar in the case of a course on Korea: it would be difficult to find an ethnic Japanese teaching a full course on Korean society and culture. This situation may be partly due to a low statistical probability of an ethnic Korean teaching on Korea and an ethnic Japanese teaching on Japan. However, beyond the statistical probability of natural linkage of the teacher's ethnic background and the choice of the country, there is an important factor operating in the shaping of this linkage. That is, although no one would think it strange if the courses on Japanese society and culture in a (South) Korean university were taught by a Korean teacher, that may not be the case where the teaching institution is in a Western country, especially in North America or Australia, where there are plenty of teachers of ethnic Japanese background. The situation would be the same in the case of the teacher being an ethnic Japanese where the course is on Korean society and culture. In Japan and Korea, there is a commonplace notion that teaching about their country in a Western country, means an insider teacher teaching the outsider students: the teacher is regarded as their own national representative on a diplomatic mission to spread their culture in a foreign land. The existence of semi-governmental institutions such as the Japan Foundation and its equivalent, the Korea Foundation, and their funding of the academic programs related to their countries in overseas institutions tell the nationalistic side of the cultural diplomacy. There is a natural preference for an insider as a teacher, or at least as a sympathiser to their cause.

Although Japan and (South) Korea share a considerable number of the East Asian cultural traditions as well as democratic values, there is still a great degree of tension between the two nations, due to the historical relations involving Japan's invasion and colonisation of Korea. As a result, there still remains a big dose of distrust between the two countries despite their geographic and cultural proximity. Therefore, there is a common perception that a Korean teacher of Japan, and, conversely, a Japanese teacher of Korea, would have a biased view of the country they teach about. Both anti-Japanese feeling and anti-Korean feelings are strongly aired in established mass media in Korea and in Japan, and even more strongly on the internet. However, the majority of Australian students are not sufficiently aware of this context when they start their first university course on Japan. Under these circumstances, as a teacher of Japan with a Korean ethnic background, I try to make my courses a vehicle through which students are introduced to this matter. It is likely to be better to learn about the tension between Japan and her neighbouring countries through the courses I teach, rather than from the mass media, internet, or through the students from Asia. And my job, naturally, is to try to be above the nationalistic biases of the Japanese as well as those of Korean or Chinese kinds. Consequently, I try to bring this sensitive matter as objectively as I can to uninitiated Australian students, as well as to the students from China and South Korea who are likely to be influenced by their national education in their view on Japan — especially with regard to her role in the war but also with regard to present social attitudes toward war history.

The fact that I am an ethnic Korean teaching Japanese Studies should have no necessary logical pedagogic implication, but in real life people draw their own conclusions. However, the situation is more complex because I am not very Korean in a cultural sense, since I left Korea more than forty years ago, in my mid-teens. I have studied high school in three different languages, and have lived in five different countries, including Japan. Australia is the last country I have lived in, and is now the longest in residency. As can be guessed from my residential history, a person of my background is likely to find the category of nation not only does not fit one's identity, but has lost its original cultural and ideological relevance. The tutorial class in the first week of my courses starts with self-introduction from everyone, which extends far beyond simple name and major. I have been using a student information sheet to collect additional information on students' cultural backgrounds. Additional information is added to the sheet throughout the course. Effort is made to bring out personal history as well as ethnic background. I take part in this in such a way that students get to know my non-linear, mixed cultural background.

Despite all my efforts to communicate my complicated background, many of the students, especially those from Asia, continue to see me as a Korean teacher. The same is true of the exchange students from Japan. Those students from China and Korea do not find having an ethnic Korean teacher in a Japan course an issue. The Japanese students, on the other hand, are curious but also somewhat uncomfortable. The Australian students, especially the Japan-lovers, in general prefer a Japanese teacher for a course in Japanese society and culture. This preference is understandable since there is a strong desire to learn about authentic Japan. This is based on the belief that a Japanese teacher, being an insider, would be better qualified to teach about Japan, or that at least that a Japanese teacher would be less biased when teaching about their own country. My task as a teacher is to show that this belief is unfounded on all grounds.

In one case, a group of exchange students from France told a story that clearly illustrates a case of Japanese teachers acting as cultural ambassadors in France. Unlike the exchange students from the other parts of Europe and the USA, the French students come from a university with a Japanese Studies department. There has been a small flow of one or two students from this university over last three years. The students who have come to The University of Adelaide have been Japanese Studies majors who have already studied a combination of Japanese language and courses on Japan for three years. In Adelaide, they have always taken the first year course on Japanese society. Even though they have not talked about this fact in the beginning of the course, they have usually started the course with the confidence of simply reviewing what they already knew. However, in their final 'Reflection' essays, they commented that they found by the end of the course that they had gained a new perspective on a more 'real Japan' for the first time, even though they may have been studying Japan for three years in their French university. The reason, they have expressed on reflection, is that in the past they had had new teachers from Japan every year who had acted as cultural ambassadors. Several of these students have suggested that most of the students in Japanese studies in the French context had been enthusiastic Japan-lovers, and they had been very happy to have fresh teachers from Japan every year. They had felt privileged to learn directly from 'genuine' Japanese teachers (Student 'Reflection' essay 2007). These students' own earlier perspectives had clearly been problematised when they had a 'Korean' teacher in their exchange program in Australia (Student reflection paper 2007; more about 'reflection' and 'reflection papers' below).

In the case of the French students, most of them were not aware of the tense relationship between Japan and Korea, until they took the introductory course on Japan in Australia. Further, some Australian Japan-lovers who became informed about the Japan-Korea relationship offer a similar story. In the case of one such a student, even though he was majoring in Japanese studies, he had not taken this introductory course on Japan, the only introductory course on Japan in the university. However, he then enrolled in the advanced course because, as he said, he 'had no other course to take' (Student letter 2007). After the course ended and the final mark was out, he wrote me a letter of 'confession' that he took my course even though he had not wanted to. He took the course only because the advanced Japanese language course that he was planning to take was cancelled. Not only had he not intended to take this course, but he had had a negative preconception about a Japan course taught by a 'Korean' teacher, since, he believed, there was a good chance that it may be a Japan bashing session by a Korean person. This view, he wrote, had been confirmed by another student, another Japan lover, who had also anticipated that it was a 'stupid course taught by a Korean', and he too had been unhappy that he was forced to take this course because there had been no other Japan related course left. The letter proceeded, however, to tell me how glad he was to find he was mistaken about having a 'Korean teacher', and how lucky he was having studied with one, since he felt, totally unexpectedly, that he learned more about Japan in depth through this course than in all of the courses he had taken before, including the year he lived in Japan.

The two episodes recounted above may sound self-serving for either my or the students' purposes. Nevertheless, they are authentic citations from student correspondence; my own goals are analytical here, not self-aggrandising, and the student in the second case wrote the letter after completion of the course and we have never met or communicated since then.

What these students missed was a widely known premise in anthropology that we all, as natives, and as native teachers in this case, can often be blind to the 'taken-for-granted' aspects of our daily lives. It can take an outsider to see and point out these aspects. Moreover, in this case, as an outsider I did not have any missionary zeal to impart a 'proper way' of looking at the target country.

In the advanced level course, *Cultures and identities in contemporary Japan*, I examine two topics on minorities in Japan. One of them is the so-called 'Korean residents' in Japan, referred to as *zainichi* (resident) Koreans. These may be fourth generation descendents of the Koreans who came to Japan when Korea was a part of the Japanese Empire, but they are still generally regarded as non-Japanese, that is, even if they have Japanese citizenship. They are invisible minorities since they look Japanese and their mother tongue is Japanese, and they use Japanese names. Having been born and brought up in Japan, their cultural sensitivity is Japanese, but they are still not regarded as Japanese, thus producing a problem of identity to the *zainichi* people. They are 'insider outsiders'. Simply because of their status and position in Japanese society, they see things that the majority of Japanese do not see. In this society, the majority has a general conception that 'we Japanese' are like an extended family, and there is a common presumption that the insiders can understand each other, as expressed by the Japanese expression *ishindenshin* (communication by heart), almost in a sort of telepathic intuition even without talking. In contrast, outsiders, even the 'insider-outsiders', cannot be understood and trusted even if they were born and raised in the same society. Even though there may have been some exaggeration in the portrayal of the insider-outsider distinction in Japan, this illustrates the point that, from the point of view of a Japanese nationalist, even a Japan-born and -raised person cannot be trusted as a teacher of Japanese Studies in Australia. My job as a teacher is then to explain why this kind of phenomenon occurs both inside as well as outside Japan. This is an important understanding about Japan that I try to illuminate for students.

It goes without saying that in reality Japan is a very complex society, and it is only natural to find that the Japanese people are not necessarily all united in their view about many issues. It is important to make students aware that there are many Japans rather than one. But the same would be true of Korea. So, what could a 'Korean teacher' of Japan mean? It could be anyone. Moreover, what meaning could one attribute to the label 'Korean' for a person such as me who has lived in many countries as a global nomad? However, there is a certain kind of very personal Koreanness in me that I would like my students to appreciate. It is Koreanness mixed with Japaneseness. One might conceive of it as a globalised East Asian identity equivalent to an European identity that stands above the national ones. In my personal history, there has been a continuous relationship between me and Japan: my parents were entirely educated in Japanese as were most of the Koreans under the colonial rule of 1917 to 1945. They were Japanese nationals so that, strangely to Australian students, I could say that my parents 'used to be' Japanese. Moreover, both of my parents were among the few 'colonials' who had university education in Japan, when university education was rare even among the local Japanese. Their cultural sensibility was close to the Japanese. Therefore, I grew up in an environment where the traces of Japanese culture were everywhere inside the home, even though the social and cultural atmosphere in (South) Korea after independence was very anti-Japanese. There were always plenty of Japanese books and magazines at home. My parents would speak in Japanese when they wanted to discuss matters that children should not understand.

My parents realised, inside my own family, the love-hate relationship that Korea had with Japan. My mother, having had her university years, the best years of her life according to her, in Japan, had a longing for things Japanese throughout her life. My father, on the other hand, strongly disliked things Japanese even though he not only graduated from the Imperial Tokyo University, the unparalleled top university in pre-war Japan, but had spent altogether eight years of the most formative period of his life, from late teens to early twenties, in Japan. Though he never talked about this matter to children, it appears that the reason he strongly disliked things Japanese was because he had experienced discrimination in employment in a Japanese company that he worked for. Growing up under such parents fostered inside me an ambivalent feeling toward Japan that also created a yearning and fascination about Japan at a period in Korea when Japanese popular culture was not allowed.

In many respects the fact that I ended up being a teacher in Japanese studies is largely an accident, although I kept encountering Japan everywhere I lived, as my family migrated first to Brazil and then to Canada. This was followed eventually by my studying Japanese language and Japanese history and society in North American universities, and finally by four years of living in Japan with my own wife and son. And having become an academic in Asian Studies, it is no accident that as an ethnic Korean teaching about Japan, the Japan-Korea relations, in fact the particular issue of 'peace and reconciliation in East Asia', became a special interest to me. This biographic background inevitably not just influenced but profoundly shaped the way I approached Japan both in my study and my teaching. After all, that was the main driving force behind my interest in Japan.

Self-reflections by students

This self-reflexive process that is at the heart of my own identity is naturally at the core of my teaching. And so, next, we come to the learning experience of the students, especially the reflexive aspect of learning. The study of a foreign country, society, culture and its people, can, and often does, lead students to an Orientalist mode of thinking, in which the subjects they study are 'them', a strange and exotic people, in opposition to 'us', the rational and reasonable people (and this point is also made by Cadman & Song, this volume, Chapter 1). Studying and learning typically involve demystification of previously strange phenomena and behaviours. The process of demystification is not simply about learning new facts that were previously unknown. It involves figuring out how something works. In the case of the study of Japanese society and culture, it is the question of how and why Japanese people might behave in particular ways, and this is an essentially reflective engagement with subject matter. It can also lead to an identification with the actors, that is, leading to a point where the student feels that he or she would act in the same way under the same circumstances. Thus, the process of understanding of Japanese people is the process of the students becoming Japanese.

In the introductory course on Japan, about ten years ago I introduced the writing of a subjective and reflective essay as the final major paper. In this exercise, the students are asked to write about the process they have experienced in learning about Japan rather than about Japan itself. The instruction for the essay is as follows:

> Subjective essay: This essay is about the process through which you acquired a certain understanding of Japan through this course. It is about certain topics on Japan that impressed your views on Japan, but it is less about the facts you learned about these topics and **more about how you reacted to them**. Readers of your essay should be able to learn about 'you' rather than just some facts about 'Japan': what happened to your view of Japan, not simply about 'what I did not know before, but know now'. What is needed is an <u>intellectual as well as introspective</u> **reflection** on your part and <u>your reaction</u> to the exposure to new facts about Japan. Typically students learn new facts about Japan in this course, but do not spend enough time to reflect about them. Even less time is spent reflecting about what happened to their understanding of Japan. In this assignment, you are asked to consciously devote some time to explore what happened to **your understanding and your view** of Japan and share with others. [Bold and underlines as in the original instruction]

Despite the instructions, in the essay, some students talk about what they did not know before and know now, and conclude that they realise now what they knew before was superficial and stereotypical, but now they know better. Many of these students' writings had elements that were self-serving in that they were trying to tell the teacher how much they learned from the course but there was little or no reflection and introspection on their learning process. In contrast, some have succeeded in the task of exploring the learning self as was asked (the French students' reflection papers about which I talked earlier belong to the latter category).

I have picked out below three types of responses that demonstrate effective reflection. The first type is the ones that point out that they found out that 'the Japanese are not so different from us'. For example, some have suggested that the reason why Japanese company men or Japanese students work or study so hard is not because of a work ethic that comes from the exotic and noble value of an ancient culture, but from the structural conditions in which they operate: they have to work hard in order to survive. Many Chinese students immediately identify with the examination hell and pressure exposed by the topic of education in Japan, whereas many Australian students express their amazement and sense of difference of value and culture between their understanding of Japan and Australia. However, good students figure out that anyone, even an Australian, in the same circumstances must work hard. This reflective manner of understanding Japanese behaviour leads to removal of mystery and the sense of uniqueness attributed to the Japanese culture. In these reflections, the presence of the students from China also helps the Australian students to avoid an easy reliance on the uniqueness explanation.

The second type of demystification of Japanese behaviour is to see and show that some Japanese behaviour that is difficult to comprehend by outsiders is a product of education and socialisation of values, or even indoctrination. A prime example is the case of the Japanese soldiers in the Second Sino-Japanese War (1937–1945) who killed the Chinese civilians, not regarding them as human beings. Partly they had no choice because, as soldiers, they had to follow the orders from their superiors and the government. However, it was primarily the system of indoctrination through national educational institutions, and of thought control and censorship, that best explains the Emperor worship (Ienaga 1979, chapter 2). Some students from China came to this understanding of the Japanese soldiers' behaviour during the war campaign in China. They expressed that they had changed their minds about the Japanese people, the negative image of whom they acquired through their own education in China. The responsibility lay less with the common people and more with the education system and the process of socialisation that was led by government authority. They themselves were products of such a system. They felt that they would have been no different if they were in the position of the Japanese people. Studying about Japan together with Australian students also provided them a chance to examine the reasons for the difference in their perception of the Japanese. The Australian students did not share their negative image. This was not simply due to Australian students' lack of knowledge of what happened in China during the war. Some Chinese students are able to reflect this far. By studying Japan in an Australian class, they come to understand something about themselves.

The third type of demystification is of a rather different kind, one based on an understanding of a genuine difference in the patterns of culture between Japan and a Western country such as Australia. In the areas such as religion and philosophy, the Japanese way of thinking is genuinely different from that of the Western pattern. This aspect of Japanese culture and behaviour may also be due to education and socialisation, but it is something closer to a worldview, at the level of civilisation rather than simply a product of government policy during a certain period. The scale of time for the formation and reproduction of cultural tradition of this kind is something close to a millennium in comparison with several decades. The cultural values and worldview associated with Confucianism and Buddhism are in this category. The practice of ancestor reverence (Reader 2002) and the behaviours governed by the concept of '*on*' (indebtedness, obligation) are of this kind (Benedict 1946). These are key concepts in understanding the Japanese view of the world and their behaviour that Australian students find relatively difficult, though, of course, not impossible.

Effective Australian students' reflections focus on this difficulty of comprehension, or, conversely, on the sense of enlightenment when understanding is achieved and growing. Some Australian students have written on this aspect in their reflection papers. The Chinese students' reflection on this matter is naturally most often the opposite, that the Japanese and Chinese share a very similar culture and values, and that they are from similar civilisations. This discovery that they share something so basic and fundamental with Japanese people that it is difficult to explain to the Australians is also an important step toward understanding oneself. Not only the Chinese students but also the Australian students see by looking at and listening to the Chinese reaction that the Japanese culture is not so unique. It is difficult to write a good reflection paper simply to please the teacher so I take these reflective comments as authentic evaluations of the students' learning experience in thee courses.

The material for reflection is unlimited but my understandings are quite clear. The presence of students, and teacher, from diverse backgrounds stimulates the students' minds beyond the learning of facts to comparison, analysis and reflection. In this process, learning about the other is also learning about oneself.

Conclusion

Finally, it is time to reflect on pedagogy and teaching methodology. Was there and is there a methodology in my teaching? A strange thing about teaching at university level is that, unlike the teachers in primary or secondary schools, an aspiring university lecturer is not required to study the theories and practice of teaching or get a formal training for teaching. For sure, most people who become a university lecturer have been exposed to teaching of various styles in various capacities. And we start our first lecturing position by duplicating the styles that we are familiar and comfortable with. Even after this point, there is no mandatory formal training. But, after a while, our teaching style begins to acquire a certain individualistic character. Whatever teaching style that I may have developed was not consciously planned, consistently pursued and followed. It seems simply to have evolved over time.

In retrospect, however, my autobiographic background must have been an important factor in shaping my teaching style. I have consistently tried to show the students *what I have seen and understood*, and *in what way I have done this*. This has meant that the *process* of crossing many cultural boundaries, and *the way I have done so in my past* is the ultimate source of my knowledge and experience in my teaching of a foreign culture and society. It is not something that I studied or learnt from anyone as a pedagogical principle or method. I am sure what I have presented here would be applicable to other teachers of foreign cultures too, whether or not they have developed their teaching methods so consciously.

More specifically, however, in my teaching I have been trying to duplicate among students the *practice of reflection* that I have continued to engage in throughout my experience of crossing many cultural boundaries in several migrations, as well as through my international studies, fieldwork and employment in several countries. When I see Asian international students in Australia, I recall my own experience in a Canadian university, and think about what I felt at the time and how I tried to cope with the situation of language and cultural barriers. This was followed by my experience of studying Japanese language and Asian Studies, including a focus on Japan.

My own learning has taught me to distinguish between two kinds of reflection. The first is students' ability to become aware of the taken for granted knowledge they already have but are not conscious of. Unlike the learning of science, in the study of a foreign society and culture, we make use of *what we already know* about our own society. However, we often 'do not know' that we know. To illustrate this point, an example may be given from the case of a native Korean language speaker learning Japanese language. It is said that the Japanese language is very close to Korean so that Koreans generally find it easier to learn Japanese compared to native English speakers, for example. However, not all Korean speakers find learning of Japanese equally easy. It is only those Korean learners who are able to reflect on their knowledge of Korean language and match the similarities and differences between the two, who can mobilise this knowledge and benefit from the similarities in the two languages. This is about learners 'discovering' what they already know, but did not know that they knew. The natives know about the society and culture they live in far more than non-natives do. But often there are many aspects that they commonly do not think about. Therefore, the first type of reflection is about the practice or cultivation of power of seeing these aspects. This is equivalent to developing anthropologist eyes on their own society and culture.

This can be done without studying a foreign society. However, the study of a foreign culture and society helps a student to be able to revive their unconscious knowledge about their own society. It is said that a foreign country can be a mirror to examine one's own society. The study of a foreign culture provides an opportunity, one that not everyone takes, to develop an understanding of one's own society, culture and identity. Placed in front of a cultural mirror, one is led to reflect introspectively on one's own society. By examining, for example, how the identities of Japanese youth are formed, an Australian or a Chinese student comes to an understanding of how similar and different the processes of formation of his or her identity have been in their own different society. This is the second kind of reflection, which is only present in the study of a society different from the one in which the learner was brought up.

Obviously, in learning to reflect, the process of reflection and the understanding that one gains about another society as well as one's own are gradual and evolving for each student. The teacher's job is to create a structure of incremental steps of reflection in such a way that a momentum is built and maintained. This is also a process in which students and teacher get to know each other, while students' understanding of the target culture, in this case Japan, as well as their ability to reflect, is growing. Although students' factual knowledge of Japan grows as the courses I have described progress, the key objective of these courses is to leave some deep impressions about Japan — not simply from new facts but through the experience of reflections. Some students have stated that they felt a sense of 'revelation' during the exercise of reflection. My goal as a teacher is to achieve such a result with as large a number of students as possible. The result is mixed: sometimes successful and sometimes not. Reflection as a method of teaching and learning is an art.

For the study of a foreign country, the globalised state of the Australian classroom can be an especially favourable environment if its condition is used to educational advantage. A globalised class is a room of many cultural mirrors. If used fruitfully, it can be a stimulating environment for the kinds of reflection and transcultural experience that I have explored in this chapter.

References

Befu, H 1993, 'Nationalism and Nihonjinron', in H Befu (ed.), *Cultural nationalism in East Asia*, University of California Press, Berkeley, pp. 107–135.

Benedict, R 1946, *The Chrysanthemum and the Sword*, Chapter 5: 'Debtor to the ages and the world', Houghton Mifflin, Boston, pp. 98–113.

Chamberlain, BH 1912, *The invention of new religion*, Watts, London.

Choy, C & Tong, N (dir.) 1998, *In the name of the Emperor*, documentary, Filmakers Library, Inc., New York.

Dale, PN 1986, *The myth of Japanese uniqueness*, Croom Helm, London.

Hall, S 1992, 'The West and the rest: discourse and power', in S Hall & B Gieben (eds), *Formation of modernity*, Polity Press in Association with Open University, pp. 275–332.

Hawkins, Mike 1997, *Social Darwinism in European and American Thought 1860–1945*, Cambridge University Press, Cambridge.

Ienaga, S 1979, *Pacific War 1931–1945*, Chapter 2: 'Thought control and indoctrination', Pantheon, New York, pp. 13–32.

Iwabuchi, K 1994, 'Complicit exoticism: Japan and its other', *Continuum: The Australian Journal of Media & Culture*, vol. 8 no. 2, <http://wwwmcc.murdoch.edu.au/ReadingRoom/8.2/Iwabuchi.html>.

Japan Foundation 2000, *Survey report on Japanese-language education abroad 1998*, The Japan Foundation, Tokyo.

Japan Foundation 2004, *Survey report on Japanese-language education abroad 2003*, The Japan Foundation, Tokyo.

McCormack, G 1996, 'Kokusaika: impediments in Japan's deep structure', in D Denoon (ed.), *Multicultural Japan: palaeolithic to postmodern*, Cambridge University Press, Cambridge, pp. 265–286.

Reader, I 2002, 'Contemporary Zen Buddhist tracts for the laity: grassroots Buddhism in Japan', in DS Lopez Jnr (ed.), *Religions of Asia in practice: an anthology*, Princeton University Press, Princeton, pp. 713–724.

Student reflection papers (Every year), Course 1: Introduction to Japanese Society and Culture; Course 2: Cultures and Identities in Contemporary Japan, The University of Adelaide, Adelaide.

Weber, M 1930/1905, *The protestant ethic and the spirit of capitalism*, trans. T Parsons, Unwin Hyman, London & Boston.

List of documentaries

In the Name of the Emperor 1998, documentary film, directed by Christine Choy & Nancy Tong, Filmakers Library, Inc., New York.

Nanking 2007, documentary film, directed by Bill Guttentag and Dan Sturman, USA.

Rape of Nanking — Nanjing Massacre, Part 1 & 2, [year unknown], online documentary film, produced by Rhawn Joseph, Brainmind.com, USA.

The Battle of China 1944, documentary film, directed by Frank Capra.

The Rape of Nanking 1999, documentary film, The History Channel.

10

Critiquing critical thinking: Asia's contribution towards sociological conceptualisation

Shoko Yoneyama

Introduction

Foucault famously begins his book, *The Order of Things*, by saying that the book arose out of the laughter when he came across a 'certain Chinese encyclopaedia' where animals were divided into:

> (a) belonging to the Emperor, (b) embalmed, (c) tame, (d) sucking pigs, (e) sirens, (f) fabulous, (g) stray dogs, (h) included in the present classification, (i) frenzied, (j) innumerable, (k) drawn with a very fine camelhair brush, (l) et cetera, (m) having just broken the water pitcher, (n) that from a long way off look like flies. (1970 & 1994, p. xv)

The laughter was mixed with a sense of disturbance and threat against 'the age-old distinction between the Same and the Other' (1970, 1994, p. xv). Foucault then introduces the notion of a 'tabula', a table or a space where entities (for example, words and things) are sorted out, 'to put them in order, to divide them into classes, to group them according to names that designate their similarities and their differences' (p. xvii).

In the transcultural space of Asian Studies, where I work as a Japan specialist, we regularly face the challenge of sorting out similarities and differences between the 'East' and the 'West'. While this challenge is rarely as preposterous or exotic as in the case of the 'Chinese encyclopaedia', the increasing intermingling of cultures associated with globalisation has added further complexities to the task. One such complexity that has drawn considerable attention in the Western academy is the perceived weakness in critical thinking among international students from Asia (Nichols 2003, p. 141). Studies on this issue proliferated in the 1990s, especially in the area of Teaching English to Speakers of Other Languages (TESOL) in the field of Applied Linguistics, because of the increasing needs of students with English as an Additional Language (EAL) associated with the massive influx of students from Asia, especially East Asia into the Anglophone academy.

Critical thinking no longer appears to be such a fashionable topic in Applied Linguistics. But a question remains as to whether we have adequately sorted out the issue conceptually, that is, whether we have found what constitutes a common ground between the 'East' and the 'West' in relation to critical thinking, a common ground with specific pedagogical implications, applicable not only in the academy of the West but also that of the East. What this chapter proceeds to do is to illuminate the concept of critical thinking itself, by using as leverage the perceived 'problem' faced by international students from Asia. In so doing, my goal here is to explore the possibility that the 'East' can contribute to reach a new understanding of critical thinking that is particularly relevant to the globalising academy.

With this aim, the present chapter attempts to synthesize different strands of discourse on critical thinking, in the fields of philosophy, applied linguistics, education, sociology, and Asian/Japanese studies. In order to do this, I adopt a very broad (and yet generally accepted) working definition of critical thinking: '*critical thinking is reflective and reasonable thinking that is focussed on deciding what to believe or do*' (Ennis 1985, p. 45, emphasis added). By adopting a transdisciplinary approach, I aim in this chapter to provide additional depths to the conventional conceptualisation of critical thinking.

Both 'East' and 'Asia', however, cover such a broad geographical and cultural space. A more specific focus of the chapter is East Asia. This is because, despite some cultural and institutional differences, societies in East Asia seem to share several key characteristics: 1) a sufficiently identifiable cultural tradition that is often referred to as Confucian (Inglehart 1997, p. 335); 2) an extremely competitive modern education system that has also been a main vehicle for modernisation and state formation (Green 1999), and; 3) 'a common challenge in adapting to Western academic expectations' (Durkin 2008, p. 40). I will make particular reference to Japan, from where I can draw non-English (Japanese) sources, with a view to broadening the horizon surrounding the discourse on this topic.

The main thesis this chapter presents is this: Asia, or to be more precise, thinking about the relationship between Asia and critical thinking, can contribute to deepen the prevailing scholarly understanding of critical thinking. First, it accentuates the importance of the sociological (that is, social and relational) milieu in which (critical) thinking takes place. Second, it enables us to identify parameters that constitute key aspects of such a milieu: that is, relationships that are equal (as against hierarchical) and caring (as against atomised). What I intend to do here is to develop a 'tabula' in Foucault's terms that enables us to understand the *sociological milieu* that maximises critical thinking not only for the students from Asia but for all students in the globalising academy.

Let us now begin with an analysis of the discourse of critical thinking that happened relatively early in the field of Applied Linguistics in relation to international students from Asia.

Orientalism and the question of culture

Applied Linguistics is the area where the need to develop pedagogy to enhance critical thinking among students from (East) Asia has been most acutely felt and discussed (e.g. Fox 1994), to the extent that in the 1990s there was seen to be a 'critical thinking bandwagon' (Atkinson 1999, p. 87). It is perhaps not surprising that the topic has attracted so much attention because, apart from practical difficulties in the everyday context of teaching and learning, the issue inevitably touches upon the very core of Western education and academy: the way we think, the way we construct academic argument, or even the way we are. In other words, it challenges the very 'defining concept of the Western university' (Barnett 1997, p. 2) and its education. The remark by Atkinson (1997, p. 89) that 'critical thinking is cultural thinking' is important in that it turned our 'critical gaze upon the cultural context of the critical skills we are emphasising' (Cadman 2000, p. 487).

Atkinson's paper (1997) is based on what McLaren (1994) calls 'second-wave' perspectives of critical thinking, which conceptualise critical thinking not simply as *logical analysis devoid of social context* but as a broader concept that conceives that all thinking occurs 'in concrete situations by concrete individuals ... with meaning, purpose, and nuances' (Walters 1994, p. 16). In other words, the 'second-wave' notion of critical thinking has reflected the 'advances made by feminists, social constructionists, and postmodernists' (McLaren 1994, p. x) in the realm of critical thinking itself.

The second wave of critical thinking is important in that it provides a theoretical basis to put teachers and students on an equal footing, each carrying different yet mutually respected cultural baggage (or 'heritage'). Despite this political implication, Atkinson's claim that critical thinking is culturally specific has been contested on various fronts. First, despite its reflective and self-critical position, the view that critical thinking is 'discoverable ... *only to those* brought up in a cultural milieu in which it operates ... as a socially valued norm' (Atkinson 1997, p. 89, emphasis added) invited the allegation that such a view (re)produces the cultural stereotype that 'Asian students do not think critically and that certain values underlying the notion of critical thinking are incompatible with their cultural beliefs' (Kumaravadivelu 2003, p. 712). Various researchers presented counter-arguments to this 'cultural-specificity model', saying that the critical thinking tradition *does* exist in Asian philosophy (Hongladarom 1998); it is not a cultural issue but a linguistic issue (Lun et al. 2010); it is neither a cultural nor a linguistic issue but a pedagogical issue (Jones 2005; Wang 2010).

An even more fundamental problem underlying the 'cultural-specificity model' of critical thinking lies in its uncritical, monolithic, and static view of the culture of 'the other', that is, in its Orientalism. In other words, the model not only assumes cultural dichotomy between the East and the West, but also (re)produces 'fixed, apolitical, and essentialized cultural representations [of the East/Japan] such as groupism and harmony' (Kubota 1999, p. 10) to explain students' (alleged) weakness in critical analysis and self-expression. Carson and Nelson (1994, p. 20), for instance, cite Triandis et al. (1988) to argue that 'collectivism, a cultural pattern found in Japan and PRC, is characterised as "individuals subordinating their personal goals to the goals of some collectives"'. In the case of Japan, such a reductionist view of Japanese culture is called *nihonjinron* (theory of Japanese) and has been criticised extensively as being primarily an ideological construct (Kubota 1999; Sugimoto & Mouer 1986). Adopting such a view uncritically as 'given' is problematic in two ways. First, it presupposes individuals/students as passive instead of active agents, to be moulded in a given culture. Secondly, it fails to question the social and institutional structures that contribute to produce and reproduce such a culture. In other words, it blinds the viewer to the very mechanism that may function to suppress critical thinking. While the significance of culture cannot be ignored, over-emphasis and over-reliance on cultural explanations lead to determinism, which can provide few suggestions, apart from acculturation ultimately, as to how to enhance critical thinking among learners from such cultures, or among those who teach and learn within those cultures.

This applies not only to Japanese culture but more generally to 'Confucian-Heritage Cultures' or CHCs (Ho & Ho 2008). A recent empirical study found, for instance, that it is not the Confucian culture but a particular mode of learning and teaching that explains students' learning strategies of rote learning and memorisation (Gan 2009, p. 49). Thus, in order to identify parameters of critical thinking, it is necessary to shift the focus from culture (of the other) to more specific aspects of learning and teaching, as well as to the broader social structure of which they are part.

A perspective from Japan

The discourse on thinking (if not critical thinking) in the context of Japanese education may enable us to examine the question from a different angle. Although critical thinking *per se* has not been a key concept in Japanese education, how to develop 'creative, individual, and independent thinking' has been advocated as one of the key objectives in school education since the mid-1990s (MEXT 2008), to be further developed at the tertiary level into the ability 'to respond autonomously to changing situations, to identify issues relevant to the future, and to make decisions about them, comprehensively and flexibly, based on a wide perspective' (Daigaku shingikai 1998: 31, my translation). Underlying this is the recognition that in order for the nation to survive in an increasingly competitive, post-industrial 'knowledge society', it is necessary to develop what might be called 'post-modern competencies', including such qualities as being highly independent, innovative, creative, motivated, active and skilled in communication and negotiation (Williams & Yoneyama 2011; Honda 2005: 22).

Behind this is even a greater pressure from the international community to enhance these competencies. The field of education has reaffirmed the significance of analytical thinking in the globalising, high-tech world. Critical thinking in the West is considered a prerequisite for reflectivity, which in turn has been pointed out as 'a mental prerequisite for key competencies' in the OECD's international collaborative research 'Definition & Selection of Competencies' (DeSeCo) (Rychen 2003, p. 82). DeSeCo's notion of key competencies constitutes a conceptual foundation of the 2003 Programme for International Student Assessment (PISA), widely known as the international test for 15-year-olds for OECD countries around the world. The impact of PISA upon school education in the world is immeasurable, as it is often seen by politicians, educators and others as a tool with which countries 'compete' with each other. Thus, the recent development means that critical thinking is likely to be considered increasingly significant worldwide, including by countries in Asia. Thus, issues arising from the 'encounter' of critical thinking with the 'East' is likely to expand from the Western academy to the Eastern academy. The pedagogy to enhance critical thinking will be the concern of a much broader community in the world.

For societies like Japan the challenge posed by critical thinking creates a major dilemma across its social structure (Rear 2008). This ranges from: 1) generally hierarchical, competitive and conformist *institutional* structures 2) the nature of the modern education system that, implicitly or explicitly, has functioned in many ways to silence *students and teachers* (Yoneyama 1999), and 3) the rise of neo-liberalism and neo-conservatism since the mid-1990s, which has pushed competition and the pressure to conform to a new height, creating a hotbed of bullying in Japanese society (Yoneyama 2008). Instead of revisiting these social structures, however, I would like to examine this issue by looking at how Japanese society has tackled the challenge of improving thinking skills among students. My aim here is to identify parameters to think about critical thinking.

Critical pedagogy

One of the key policies adopted to improve thinking skills among school students in Japan is the introduction in 2002 of a course called *Integrated Study* in primary and lower secondary schools. In this course:

> [c]ontent for all children to study in common is carefully selected, and each school is allowed to devise plans to give children enough time to think, to provide supplemental teaching individually, or to involve them in developing learning. It also substantiates the experiential and problem-solving approach to learning so that children can understand what they are learning with a feeling of reality. The aim is to enable children to learn basics and fundamentals, and to develop 'Academic Ability', including natural gifts and faculties to find assignments, learn, and think by themselves, make decisions independently, take actions, and solve problems better. (MEXT 2002)

The course, which allows maximum liberty for teachers to be innovative and creative and encourages students to think outside the textbook, is a major step forward from learning and teaching based on a highly-prescribed, centrally-controlled national curriculum, used primarily as the preparation for entrance examinations at all levels (Yoneyama 1999). Although *Integrated Study* has to date constituted only a small part of curricula, it has potentially provided a space to allow both teachers and students to develop their (critical) thinking. Varieties of themes actually selected for the course, including the environment, international understanding, caring and health, seem in line with the topics Noddings (2006) has selected for 'critical lessons' to promote critical thinking at school. Referring to school education in the US, Noddings writes:

> Although free debate is rarely so directly forbidden, the suppression of discussion and critical thinking in our educational system is widespread. *Usually it is accomplished by defining the curriculum so narrowly and specifically that genuinely controversial issues simply do not arise. Without controversial issues, critical thinking is nonexistent or, at best, weak.* Students are encouraged now and then to exercise a bit of critical thinking in science or mathematics as they try to solve word problems or think of alternative hypotheses, but such exercises are usually constrained tightly by the topic at hand and the limited

knowledge of young students. Further, this sort of critical thinking does not challenge deeply held beliefs or ways of life. (Noddings 2006, p. 1, emphases added)

Given the carefully depoliticised nature of education in Japan (Yoneyama 1999), it may not have been easy to introduce controversial issues to the *Integrated Study* class to promote the deep critical thinking that Noddings advocates. Teachers in Japan, for instance, have been under increasing control until recently by the conservative LDP (Liberal Democratic Party) government. Between 1998 and 2005, over one thousand teachers were officially disciplined and/or verbally reprimanded for not complying with the order to stand up and sing *kimigayo*, the emperor-praising national anthem (Yoneyama 2008). And it is not just teachers in Japan who work in an environment that undermines their own critical thinking. Nodding writes that 'when the United States invaded Iraq in 2003, many public school teachers were forbidden to discuss the war in their classrooms' (Noddings 2006, p. 1). Obviously, in order to cultivate critical thinking in the classroom, there must be the social environment that allows it to happen, and this is not just the problem of the 'East'.

The significance of controversial topics to stimulate critical thinking has been supported by a 2006 empirical study in Japan. This study found that the more students were exposed to 'provocative' class content, the more they tended to develop the ability to think critically (Hirooka et al. 2006). Although the specificity of the 'provocative' content was not made clear, given the fact that the tendency was observed only with students in humanities (and not science), it is probable that it included controversial topics.

It appears that controversial topics help stimulate critical thinking; however, they are not sufficient for it. I once observed a Japanese Grade 6 class on 'human rights' where the extremely controversial issue of the *burakumin*, one of the most discriminated minorities in contemporary Japan, was taken up as the topic. In that particular class, after watching a film on the *burakumin*, the teacher literally ordered each student to stand up one by one and say at the top of their voice, 'I would not discriminate against people!' This was then followed by the whole class repeating it in unison. A few dozen parents, teachers and visitors observed the class complacently.

Setting aside the question of how common such pedagogy is in Japan, it is hard to imagine that this class would have cultivated critical thinking among students. The example reaffirms the two points made by Gonczi (2003) that were subsequently adopted in the OECD's DeSeCo report mentioned above (Rychen & Salganik 2003). First, in order to promote critical thinking, the 'traditional notion of learning in terms of filling up the mind of the learner with facts, knowledge, beliefs, and ideas as if the mind were a container' (Rychen & Salganik 2003, p. 57), or what Freire (1970) has called the 'banking concept of education' or the 'jug and mug approach' to education, needs 'to be replaced by a new one which links learners to the environment in which learning is taking place. Such a conception of learning takes account of the affective, *moral*, physical, as well as cognitive aspects of individuals' (Goncsi 2003, quoted in Rychen & Salganik 2003, p. 58, emphasis added). Second, in order to meet complex demands in the coming age, it is necessary to develop critical thinking and a reflective approach, which in turn calls for not only altering or expanding school curricula or programs (Rychen & Salganik 2003, p. 59), but *'a fairly significant shift in the teacher-student relationship'* (Gonsci 2003 quoted in Rychen & Salganik 2003, p. 59, emphasis added).

Based on the discussion above, a set of summative points to be made with reference to the Japanese example are:

1. *controversial issues* help stimulate critical thinking
2. critical thinking requires a *politically free social environment*
3. critical thinking involves deep *moral engagement* with the issue
4. critical thinking necessitates a *non-authoritarian teacher-student relationship*.

To put it differently, what is needed to promote critical thinking is in fact *critical pedagogy*. This is actually the contention of 'second-wave' advocates of critical thinking (McLaren 1994). While critical thinking and critical pedagogy are often used interchangeably, critical pedagogy is a more powerful concept for the humanities and social sciences because its ultimate aim is to emancipate and empower individuals to bring about social transformation to achieve greater social justice (McLaren 1994, p. xii). It should be noted that, although it may not be stated as explicitly as this, critical (or reflective) thinking is presented as the foundation for a new education paradigm envisaged in the OECD's DeSeCo project, in its conceptualisation of key competencies in the globalising world. Here, this new paradigm is called 'holistic' (Rychen & Salganik 2003).

Relationship, connectedness and caring

At the shoreline of the encroaching wave of globalisation of critical thinking, researchers in Japan have been asking the question of whether this kind of analytical approach is something for Japanese education to 'adjust to' or to accept being imposed upon it as a form of 'cultural invasion'. Kakai (2004) explores the possibility of 'collaborative critical thinking' and addresses the significance of the relationship between individuals engaged in critical dialogue. Michida (2002) also asserts the importance of a 'soft heart', by which he means the sense of care (*omoiyari*), empathy and respect for the person with whom one holds a critical dialogue. What he means here by empathy is more than just not being aggressive and being sensitive to the feelings of another. It means also trying to understand the other person's point of view and, by doing so, to reflect upon one's own point of view critically, so that the dialogue becomes a collaborative endeavour by those who examine the same issue.

What Michida proposes as a 'soft heart' approach to critical thinking resonates with what, in an early discussion, Clinchy (1994) calls 'connected knowing'. Clinchy, one of the advocates of 'second-wave' critical thinking, writes: 'There is nothing wrong with trying to teach critical thinking, but something goes wrong when we teach *only* critical thinking' (p. 33, emphasis in original). What Clinchy considers missing is feeling, and a sense of connectedness with oneself and another, thus she proposes 'connected knowing' by a 'connected knower' as follows:

> Connected knowers are not dispassionate, unbiased observers. They deliberately bias themselves in favour of what they are examining. They try to get inside it and form an intimate attachment to it. The heart of connected knowing is imaginative attachment: trying to get behind the other person's eyes and 'look at it from that person's point of view'. (Clinchy 1994, p. 39)

Clinchy suggests that connected knowing, whether it occurs in a social context or in relation to text, represents what Martin Buber (1970) calls the 'I-Thou' relationship, rather than the 'I-It' relationship, in the sense that the text is seen as a 'thou', a subject and something to relate and hold a dialogue with, rather than 'it', an object of analysis (Clinchy 1994, p. 39).

This remark potentially links the discourse on critical thinking with that on holistic education in a deep sense. Buber sees the 'I-Thou' relationship as the key to having the sense of connectedness with one's inner self, another person, and the external environment, and he sees that this sense of connectedness can lead to spirituality (which is not necessarily religious) (Yoshida 2007). Seen in this way, it can be interpreted that this dialogical (and relational) critical thinking is at the core of holistic education, which includes the realms of soul and spirit, and which goes much deeper than (w)holistic education as a buzz word (Yoshida 1999, p. 17).

While Michida (2005) does not use the word 'spiritual', he discusses the case of a student who demonstrated an exceptional advancement in critical thinking in the four years of undergraduate study. An in-depth interview with the student found that his reflective thinking had been cultivated through a continued relationship with a senior student whose words, though difficult to take at times, helped him to continue the dialogue within himself (with his 'second I'), which not only made him a better (that is, deeper) critical thinker, but led him to transform himself to reach a new stage of self-awareness. This case perhaps describes critical thinking in its deepest sense — critical thinking that involves the transformation of the inner-self. The point is that it was achieved through the encounter with another with whom the student could develop an 'I-Thou' relationship, which allowed the sense of connectedness through which he developed the high level critical thinking ability that caught the eye of Michida.

This story illustrates how human relationships are a key to considering critical thinking. In the field of education, the significance of the relational mode of thinking has been recognised (for example, by Vygotsky 1962), and it has been pointed out that interpersonal relationships, nurtured in the safe space of a classroom free of surveillance by authority, can foster a 'pedagogy of connection', where empowerment of learners is made possible by connecting 'people, understandings, knowledge and feelings' (Cadman 2005: 355). Concerning students from East Asia in the Western academy, it has been found that they adopted 'the middle way' between Western-style academic critical argumentation (a 'wrestling debate') and much gentler 'conciliatory dialogue' where harmony is stressed (Durkin 2008). That is, the students showed a high sensitivity to the social and relational aspects of learning, and considered it important to have empathy for another who holds a different view, while at the same time trying to engage in meaningful discussion (Durkin 2008). Gallo (1994), another advocate of 'second-wave' critical thinking, maintains that empathy fosters analytical skills as it is essential for 'multiple perspective-taking and genuine open-mindedness' (p. 59). If so, it may be possible that in these ways (East) Asia contributes positively to the conceptualisation of insightful critique in that it can provide a stronger case for including empathy and positive human relations as important factors in fostering critical thinking.

One would have to be cautious, however, not to revert again here to the cultural stereotype of a group-oriented society. Empirically, such things as group-orientedness, harmony, empathy, and sensitivity to the feelings of others may come as a package of 'high-context' East Asian or Confucian culture. In relation to critical thinking, however, the implications of 'empathy' and harmony, for instance, can be vastly different. An emphasis on harmony can very well suppress empathy toward a non-conforming individual and thus extinguish critical thinking, as in the case of the pressure in Japan to conform to the atmosphere of particular time and space by 'reading-the-vibes' (or *kukiyomi*) (Rear 2008; Yoneyama 2008).

A further concept that does not allow this confusion is 'caring', which Thayer-Bacon (1993) argues to be an essential ingredient in critical thinking. Thayer-Bacon writes:

> Most critical thinking theories address the problems of how to develop reasoning abilities and encourage students to be more rational. I would like to argue that there is another necessary quality for being a critical thinker that is as important as the propensity to be rational: the ability to be receptive

and caring, open to others' ideas and willing to attend to them, to listen and consider their possibilities. ... My position is that without caring, one cannot hope to be a good critical/constructive thinker. (p. 323)

While the difference between empathy and caring may seem trivial, caring is more relational than empathy and is free of the cultural implications of collectivism and conformity. In that sense, it constitutes a superior parameter for conceptualising critical thinking.

Equality, hierarchy and competition

The final point this chapter explores concerning the relationship between critical thinking and Asia is the question of hierarchy. Amid all the pressure to cultivate abilities to think critically and creatively among university students, university faculties often feel contradictory pressure. In a revealing, published discussion among three Japanese professors, anonymous Professor 'P' from a leading university candidly comments:

> As long as the employment criteria in large corporations remain the same, universities can't produce students with originality and creativity, because such students are never employed. In reality, large corporations employ only students with lots of potentialities and no character, i.e. colourless and transparent kind. ... Company executives often talk about individuality and creativity, but that's just glib. Once such a personality enters the company and makes a suggestion, he will be oppressed by being told that 'it's ten years too early for you to say so'. (Professors P, Q, R 2000)

Clearly, corporations recognise that they are in need of a competitive workforce, but do not want to be challenged by it. There are contradictory needs among firms to recruit the most competent workforce while keeping the labour cost to a minimum. As far as Japan is concerned, there is a possibility that the contradiction is met by the polarisation of education: to provide education designed to facilitate such abilities as autonomy and creativity while dumbing down the quality of a conformist education for the 'masses' (Yoneyama 2002). The result of PISA indicates that this polarisation of academic ability may have already been happening (Williams & Yoneyama 2011).

A recent study (Ogihara & Mochizuki 2007) on the pedagogy of critical thinking in four leading universities in Asia (Singapore, Thailand and Malaysia) found that this mode of learning is taught with English as a working language, by importing the business model of critical thinking, with the objective of students' acquiring problem-solving skills in a given situation in the shortest time. It was also found that critical thinking courses in leading universities tended to be positioned as part of an élite education. In the case of Singapore, for instance, in 2006 'Writing and Critical Thinking' was part of the core curriculum for 180 scholarship students who constituted the top three per cent of the student population (p. 45).

What this limited information on critical thinking education in Asia suggests is the possibility that such education may become a vehicle to accelerate two trends that are very much underway worldwide. One is the increasing economic and social gap ubiquitous in the world, and especially in Asia. The other is what Bauman (2000), a sociologist, describes by using a caravan park as a powerful metaphor to expose the paradoxical lack of (deep) critical thinking in the world where (shallow) critical thinking is a norm. Bauman argues that, in late-modern or post-modern society, 'order-obsessed', 'heavy/solid/condensed/systemic modernity' is gradually being replaced with a light, fluid, diffuse and network-like society of 'fluid modernity' (p. 25), and one of the biggest challenges of this process is the decline of critical thinking, in the deep sense. He writes:

> We are perhaps more 'critically predisposed', much bolder and intransigent in our criticism than our ancestors managed to be in their daily lives, but our critique, so to speak, is 'toothless'. ... The kind of 'hospitality to critique' characteristic of modern society in its present form may be likened to the pattern of a caravan site. The place is open to everyone with his or her own caravan and enough money to pay the rent. Guests come and go; none of them takes much interest in how the site is run, providing that [all facilities work well] ... When they leave, following their own itineraries, the site remains much as it was before the arrival, unaffected by past campers and waiting for others to come. (Bauman 2000, pp. 23–4)

If, under the pressure of globalisation, only the shallow version of critical thinking is adopted in the Eastern academy, it could nullify the advancement (that is, the 'second wave') made in the conceptualisation of critical thinking itself, by regressing back to, primarily, a form of logical analysis devoid of insight into any broader socio-political or moral implications, and disconnected biographically, emotionally and socially from the thinker and others around her/him. In other words, it would regress to the kind of critical thinking that does not lead either to emancipation or empowerment of the learner, nor to the transformation of society towards greater social justice. If the élite are 'empowered' with this kind of (shallow) 'critical thinking' in what is an increasingly polarising Asia, it is possible that the power structures in Asia will become increasingly more rigid and immobile, while the real issues will become less and less visible, and the voices of the oppressed less and less audible, in the continuously fluid, soft-controlled, 'harmonious', Confucian Asia.

Towards a 'tabula': A sociological model of critical thinking

The discussion above suggests that there might be two sociological (social and relational) parameters that influence the deepest and most highly valued forms of critical thinking. One is the quality of human relations centred on the notion of *caring*, and the other is the level of *equality* in human relations. Each parameter constitutes the horizontal and vertical axis respectively, as shown in Figure 1.

Although Figure 1 indicates simply a conceptual model and no single society would fit perfectly in any of the four divided spaces, if anything quadrant 'A' can be seen to resemble those East Asian societies with a fairly robust hierarchical social structure and high sensitivity to human relations, including 'caring' and a 'soft-heart' approach to interpersonal interchange. When the sensitivity to human relations surfaces as conformism, however, this becomes the least hospitable environment for critical thinking. 'B' can be visualised as representing highly industrial, neo-liberal 'Western' societies, the kind of 'caravan park' society described by Bauman above, although strictly speaking, Bauman's 'fluid society' should have much broader applicability. Here, individuals are very much atomised; caring relationships are not predominant; people are little aware of the covert conformism; and there is a fluid and yet unmistakable social hierarchy based on competition and social class. Critical

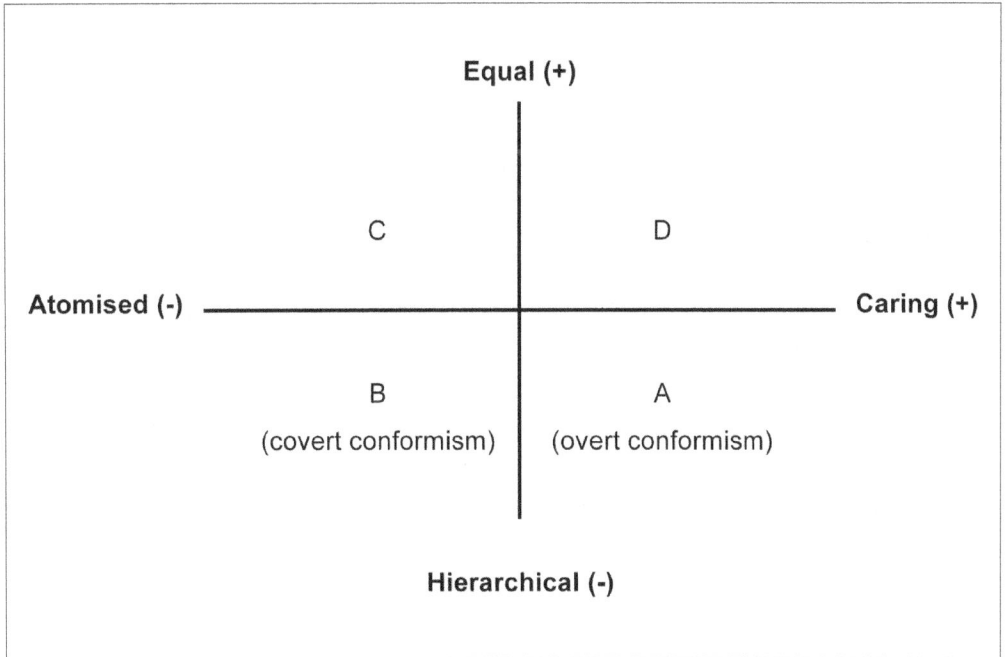

Figure 1: Sociological milieus of critical thinking

thinking is a norm, but it rarely questions the deepest assumptions that underpin the system, leaving little chance for major social change or for a paradigm shift. 'C' can be envisaged as the mainstream Western academy. Although it is the system that supports 'B', it still allows human relations to be relatively equal, as in the case of non-authoritarian teacher-student relationships, and critical pedagogy can be pursued relatively well in this social space. When the human relations are more atomised than caring, however, this can greatly reduce the epistemic possibilities of reciprocal teacher-student exchange, as well as alienate those students whose need for a caring relationship are greater.

Space 'D' represents the social space where critical pedagogy flourishes most productively and critical thinking is developed most effectively. Learners benefit from equal and caring human relations that enable them to practise critical thinking in a safe and secure social atmosphere. The caring relationships and critical pedagogy enable them to develop connected knowing with one another, reflectively involving one's inner self as well as society through the examination of social issues. The space enables learners to be emancipated and empowered, as well as generating the energy to bring about social transformation to create a fairer, sustainable society. This space thus provides the optimum social environment for holistic education as well. In this way, then, Figure 1 indicates that the sociological milieu that can generate critical thinking most positively emerges from the synthesis of the best of the Western academy and the positive aspects of Eastern social relations.

Conclusion

In this chapter I have explored the concept of critical thinking by using as leverage the often-claimed weakness in critical thinking among higher education students in and from Asia, who are often seen as 'the other' in the discourse on critical thinking. This exploration, conducted on the basis of a widespread, broad understanding of critical thinking as reflective and evaluative of 'what to believe or do' (Ennis 1985, p. 45), has revealed that the term 'critical thinking' actually covers a vast range of activities with very different pedagogical and practical implications. Through the 'transdisciplinary' perspective taken in this discussion, I have traced the development and transformation of the conception of critical thinking. Namely, I observed what began as a mere *exercise in logic* devoid of social context to have developed into *critical pedagogy* where, ideally, controversial issues are discussed in a politically-free, social environment, in such a way that calls forth deep moral engagement among the thinkers, to emancipate and empower them, ultimately to bring about a better society. We have also seen that critical thinking in its deepest sense means *connected knowing* where the thinker experiences a sense of connectedness with the material/text, with their own inner self, with an 'other', and ultimately with the spiritual as envisaged in holistic education.

'Asia' as 'the other' has enabled us to sharpen our understanding of critical thinking at almost every step of the analysis. It has helped us to reflect on our own position working in the Western academy as 'teachers' (as against students), and as those who take a 'Western' (as against 'Eastern') view on thinking and analysis. It has thus helped us direct our own critical gaze upon ourselves. To put 'Asia' into the 'critical thinking equation' has also stimulated us to integrate the knowledge accumulated in our field of study (here Japanese Studies) into the discourse on critical thinking. Thus, this chapter flagged the danger of slipping into Orientalism by adopting an uncritical and monolithic view of the culture of 'the other'. This in turn directed our attention more critically towards the pedagogical, sociological and political aspects of learning and teaching which are 'within our reach', unlike those 'cultural' aspects which are largely beyond our reach. Reviewing literature on critical thinking in Asia/Japan, has further sharpened awareness of the significance of socio-political aspects, and shown that equal and caring relationships supported with political freedom are the prerequisite for critical thinking in its deeper sense.

As seen with the discussion of the OECD's DeSeCo project and recent developments in Eastern academic thought, it is likely that the significance of critical thinking will be increasingly recognised in the globalising academy. In this context, we need to stop and think once again about the meaning of our promoting critical thinking in tertiary education: to empower each learner as an individual so that each will be able to contribute one way or another to create a more just, equitable and sustainable society. The world we live in today faces unprecedented challenges such as climate change, global financial crises, nuclear disasters, and increasing social and economic polarisation. All demand complex and profound moral and political engagement, and only critical thinking that goes beyond what Bauman calls the 'critical thinking at the caravan park' will help us to face these challenges and find a way towards a sustainable future. Asia, as *the centre* of the world's growth in population and economy, holds the key to our survival. It is precisely at this very juncture of Eastern and Western academies that the significance of the *deep* critical thinking needs to be recognised, and to be reflected in our pedagogy, with the view to bring about a positive change to the world.

References

Atkinson, D 1997, 'A critical approach to critical thinking in TESOL', *TESOL Quarterly*, vol. 31 no. 1, pp. 71–94.

Bauman, Z 2000, *Liquid modernity*, Polity, Cambridge, UK.

Burnett, R 1997, *Higher education: a critical business*, Milton Keynes, Bucks, Society for Research into Higher Education & Open University Press.

Buber, M 1970, *I and Thou*, Charles Scribner & Sons, New York.

Cadman, K 2000, '"Voices in the air": evaluations of the learning experiences of international postgraduates and their supervisors', *Teaching in Higher Education*, vol. 5 no. 4, pp. 475–491.

Cadman, K 2005, 'Towards a "pedagogy of connection" in critical research education: a REAL story', *Journal of English Academic Purposes*, vol. 4 no. 4, pp. 353–367.

Carson, J & Nelson, G 1994, 'Writing groups: cross-cultural issues', *Journal of Second Language Writing*, vol. 3 no. 1, pp. 17–30.

Clinchy, BM 1994, 'On critical thinking and connected knowing', in K Walters (ed.), *Re-thinking reason: new perspective in critical thinking*, State University of New York Press, New York, pp. 33–42.

Daigaku shingikai (Higher Education Council of Japan) 1998, 21 *seiki no daigaku zo to kongo no henkaku housaku ni tsuite* [The vision of universities in the 21st century and the reform measures in future: University where individuality shines in a competitive environment], viewed 11 September 2010, <http://www.mext.go.jp/b_menu/shingi/12/daigaku/toushin/981002.htm>.

Durkin, K 2008, 'The middle way: East Asian Masters students' perceptions of critical argumentation in U.K. universities', *Journal of Studies in International Education*, vol. 12 no. 1, pp. 38–55.

Ennis, R 1985 October, 'A logical basis for measuring critical thinking skills', *Educational Leadership*, vol.4 3 no. 2, pp. 44–48.

Foucault, M 1970/1994, *The order of things*, trans., Vintage Books, New York.

Freire, P 1970, *Pedagogy of the oppressed*, Continuum, New York.

Fox, H 1994, *Listening to the world: cultural issues in academic writing*, National Council of Teachers of English, Urbana, IL.

Gallo, D 1994, 'Education for empathy, reason, and imagination', in K Walters (ed.), *Re-thinking reason: new perspective in critical thinking*, State University of New York Press, New York, pp. 43–60.

Gan, Z 2009, '"Asian learners" re-examined: an empirical study of language learning attitudes, strategies and motivation among Chinese and Hong Kong students', *Journal of Multilingual and Multicultural Development*, vol. 30 no. 1, pp. 41–58.

Gonczi, A 2003, 'Teaching and learning of the key competencies', in DS Rychen, LH Salganik & ME McLaughlin (eds), *Selected contributions to the 2nd DeSeCo symposium*, Swiss Federal Statistical Office, Neuchatel, Switzerland.

Green, A 1997, *Education, globalization and the nation state*. St. Martin's Press, New York.

Hirooka, S, Yokoya, T & Nakanishi, Y 2006, 'Relationship between "the orientation towards critical thinking" and "daily experiences" among university students' (published in Japanese), *Mie daigaku kyoiku gakubu kenkyu kiyo* [Research bulletin of Department of Education, Mie University], vol. 57, pp. 121–131.

Ho DYF & Ho RTH 2008, 'Knowledge is a dangerous thing: authority relations, ideological conservatism, and creativity in Confucian-Heritage Cultures', *Journal for the Theory of Social Behaviour*, vol. 38 no. 1, pp. 67–86.

Honda, Y 2005, *Tagenka suru 'noroyoku' to nihon shakai* [Japanese society and diversification of 'competence'], NTT, Tokyo.

Hongladarom, S 1998, May 6–8, 'Asian philosophy and critical thinking: divergence or convergence?', paper presented at the Second APPEND Conference, Chulalongkorn University, viewed 11 September 2010, <http://homepage.mac.com/soraj/web/APPEND.html>.

Inglehart, R 1997, *Modernization and postmodernization*, Princeton University Press, Princeton, NJ.

Jones, A 2005, 'Culture and context: critical thinking and student learning in introductory macroeconomics', *Studies in Higher Education*, vol. 30 no. 3, pp. 339–354.

Kakai, H 2004, 'A prospect of critical thinking education in Japanese higher education of the 21st century: exploring a possibility of collaborative critical thinking' (published in Japanese), *Aoyama Journal of International Politics, Economics and Business*, vol. 63, pp. 129–156.

Kubota, R 1999, 'Japanese culture constructed by discourses: implications for Applied Linguistics research and ELT', *TESOL Quarterly*, vol. 33 no. 1, pp. 9–35.

Kumaravadivelu, B 2003, 'Problematizing cultural stereotypes in TESOL', *TESOL Quarterly*, vol. 37 no. 4, pp. 709–719.

Lun, VMC, Fisher, R & Ward, C 2009, 'Teaching critical thinking across cultures: a study of the university course syllabi in New Zealand and Hong Kong', in R Ismail, MEJ Macapagal, NM Noor, J Takai & T Hur (eds), *Global issues and challenges in a changing world: psychological, cultural and group relationships*, Centre for Research and Innovation, Universiti Malaysia Sabah, Kota Kinabalu, Sabah, pp. 131–147.

Lun, VMC, Fisher, R & Ward, C 2010, 'Exploring cultural differences in critical thinking: is it about my thinking style or the language I speak?', *Learning and Individual Differences*, vol. 26 no. 6, pp. 604–616.

McLaren, P 1994, 'Critical thinking as a political project', in K Walters (ed.), *Re-thinking reason: new perspective in critical thinking*, State University of New York Press, New York, pp. ix–xv.

MEXT (Japan Ministry of Education, Culture, Sports, Science and Technology) 2002, 'Japanese government policies in Education, Culture, Sports, Science and Technology 2002, Chapter 2, Section 3', viewed 11 September 2010, <http://www.mext.go.jp/b_menu/hakusho/html/hpac200201/hpac200201_2_013.html>.

MEXT (Japan Ministry of Education, Culture, Sports, Science and Technology) 2008, '*Chuo kyoiku shingikai toshin 2008*' [Deliberations of the Central Council for Education] p. 9, viewed 11 September 2010, <http://www.mext.go.jp/a_menu/shotou/new-cs/news/20080117.pdf>.

Michida, Y 2002, 'Importance of a soft heart in critical thinking' (published in Japanese), *Ryukyu daigaku kyoikugakubu kiyo* [Research Bulletin of the Department of Education, Ryukyu University], vol. 60, pp. 161–170.

Michida, Y 2005, 'Some notes on critical thinking in a strong sense' (published in Japanese), *Ryukyu daigaku kyoikugakubu kiyo* [Research Bulletin of the Department of Education, Ryukyu University], vol. 66, pp. 75–91.

Nichols, S 2003 '"They just won't critique anything": the "problem" of international students in the Western academy', in J Satterthwaite, E Atkinson and K Gale (eds), *Discourse, power, resistance: challenging the rhetoric of contemporary education*, Stoke on Trent, Trentham Books, pp. 135–149.

Noddings, N 1992, *The challenge to care in schools*, Teachers College, Columbia University, New York and London.

Noddings, N 2006, *Critical lessons: what our schools should teach*, Cambridge University Press, New York.

Ogihara, S & Mochizuki, T 2007, 'In search of an Asian model of teaching critical thinking: educational practices in the universities in Southeast Asian Countries: NUS, KMUTT, CU, and USM', *Osaka daigaku kyoiku jissen senta kiyo* [Bulletin of Osaka University Education Research Center], vol. 4, pp. 43–52.

Professors, P, Q, R 2000, May, 'Sankyojyu gakuryoku mondo' [Three professors talk about 'academic abilities'], *Sekai*, pp. 94–97.

Rear, D 2008, 4 March, 'Critical thinking and modern Japan: conflict in the discourse of government and business', *Electronic Journal of Contemporary Japanese Studies*, Article 2 in 2008.

Rychen, D 2003, 'Key competencies: meeting important challenges in life', in D

Rychen & L Slaganik (eds), *Key competencies: for a successful life and a well-functioning society*, Hogrefe & Huber, Göttingen, pp. 63–107.

Rychen, D & Salganik, L 2003, 'A holistic model of competence', in D Rychen & L Slaganik (eds), *Key competencies: for a successful life and a well-functioning society*, Hogrefe & Huber, Göttingen, pp. 41–62.

Sugimoto, Y & Mouer, R 1986, *Images of Japanese society*, Kegan Paul, London.

Thyayer-Bacon, B 1993, 'Caring and its relationship to critical thinking', *Educational Theory*, vol. 43 no. 3, pp. 323–340.

Triandis, HC 1988, 'Collectivism vs. individualism: a reconceptualization of a basic concept in cross-cultural social psychology', in GK Verma and C Bagley (eds), *Personality, cognition, and values*, Macmillan, London, pp. 60–95.

Vygotsky, LS 1962, *Thought and language*, MIT Press, Cambridge, MA.

Walters, K 1994, 'Beyond logicism in critical thinking', in K Walters (ed.), *Re-thinking reason: New perspective in critical thinking*, State University of New York Press, New York, pp. 1–22.

Wang, L 2010, 'Chinese postgraduate students in a British university: their learning experiences and learning beliefs', Unpublished PhD thesis, Durham University, Durham UK.

Williams, B and Yoneyama, S 2011, 'Japan's education system: problems and prospects in the post-industrial age', in P Jain and B Williams (eds), *Japan in decline: fact or fiction?*, Global Oriental, Kent.

Yoneyama, S 1999, *The Japanese high school: silence and resistance*, Routledge, London and New York.

Yoneyama, S 2002, 'Japanese "educational reform": the plan for the twenty-first century', in J Maswood, J Graham & H Miyajima (eds), *Japan: change and continuity*, Routledge Curzon, London, pp. 192–213.

Yoneyama, S 2008 December 31, 'The era of bullying: Japan under neoliberalism', *The Asia-Pacific Journal*, vol. 1–3–09.

Yoshida, A 1999, *Holistic kyoikuron* [A theory of holistic education], Nihon hyoronsha, Tokyo.Yoshida, A 2007, *Buber taiwa ron to holistic kyoiku* [Buber's theory of dialogue and holistic education], Keiso shobo, Tokyo.

Yoshida, A 2007, *Buber taiwa ron to holistic kyoiku* [Buber's theory of dialogue and holistic education], Keiso shobo, Tokyo.

Part V

Bridging learning gaps

11

Chinese culture and plagiarism: A convenient cause for an inconvenient issue in the academy

Ming Hwa Ting

> There is a most absurd and audacious Method of reasoning avowed by some Bigots and Enthusiasts, and through Fear assented to by some wiser and better Men; it is this. They argue against a fair Discussion of popular Prejudices, because they say, tho' they would be found without any reasonable support, yet the Discovery might be productive of the most dangerous Consequences. Absurd and blasphemous Notion! As if all Happiness was not connected with the Practice of Virtue, which necessarily depends on the Knowledge of Truth. (Edmund Burke, *A vindication of natural society*, 1757).

The internationalisation of the Australian higher education sector is not a recent phenomenon. As early as 1904, Asian international students were pursing tertiary studies in Australia (Radford, Ongkili & Toyoizumi, 1984, cited in Burke 2006, p. 333). However, the numbers were low and only increased significantly with the introduction of the Colombo Plan in 1950 as the Australian government provided scholarships for students from developing countries to study in Australia. These scholarships were highly competitive and recipients were selected primarily on the basis of their academic performances. Then, the introduction of full-fee paying places for international students in 1985 changed the make-up of foreign students coming to Australia, as academic results no longer constituted the primary consideration for gaining admission. Due to the income generated from enrolling international students, they became an attractive recruitment target. As a result, Australia's tertiary education experienced a qualitative change. Australian universities, in a departure from the vision of the Colombo Plan when it was implemented in 1950, have increasingly regarded higher education as a tradeable commodity (Skilbeck & Connell 2006). As a result, they are no longer enrolling students on the primary basis of their academic performance. Now, it seems that it is more important for international students to be able to pay for courses than for them to excel academically in these courses (Kayrooz et al. 2001, p. 38).

With this change in student demographics, it comes as no surprise if their academic performances are not as stellar as those of their predecessors, an observation common among academics in relation to deteriorating standards and increasing magnitude of problems such as plagiarism. These students are different, and academics need to openly acknowledge that differences exist. As reflected in Burke's quote, it is necessary to air such issues. The objective in doing this is not to stereotype Chinese international students. Instead, the present objective is to actively explore reasons for the presence of academic problems such as plagiarism and to implement possible strategies to counter them, not to sweep them under the carpet or to place them in the 'too-hard' category, favouring procrastination over solution.

The issue of plagiarism in the academy is currently highly divisive, and academics fall into two broad camps. Generally, one camp holds that Chinese culture is somehow conducive to plagiarism because referencing and acknowledging sources are unfamiliar concepts and practices (Deckert 1993; McCormick 1998; Sowden 2005). For instance, Ouyang Huhua, professor of English at Guandong University of Foreign Studies, provides a typical account of this supposed nexus. He believes that:

> The notion of plagiarism is alien to Chinese culture, where there is no individual claim, no ownership over intellectual property, and it is hard for Chinese students to conceptualise the idea. In China, knowledge-making is not open to everybody as it is in the West. It is a privilege belonging to a handful. (cited in Gill 2008)

Consequently, it is understandable that Chinese students are very prone to committing plagiarism in their written work. It is held by adherents in this camp that Confucian culture somehow promotes plagiarism, or at the very least, does not discourage this serious academic transgression (Friedman 2010). The perceived link especially between Chinese culture and plagiarism persists because it provides a convenient cause to account for a serious problem within the academy today. Attributing plagiarism essentially to Chinese culture implies this is the way Chinese international students are, meaning that serious actions would be fruitless, so nothing needs to be done. Instead, time and effort are all too often devoted to the easier and more passive approach — which is patently less effective — of warning students of the dire consequences if they were found to commit plagiarism, and requiring them to sign often meaningless plagiarism declarations certifying that submitted work is not plagiarised. These strategies are much easier than adopting an active approach that teaches students how to write, paraphrase, and reference appropriately in their work (Carroll 2002, p. 58; Chandrasoma et al. 2004).

In the other camp, there are also sympathetic academics who believe that Chinese students commit [unintentional] plagiarism because it is part of their learning process. To these sympathetic academics, Chinese students face a double bind. Not only do they have to express themselves in English, which is not their mother tongue and so they are not highly proficient in this language, but these students also have to express themselves in a discipline-appropriate manner that they are unfamiliar with. Imitating the works of other scholars is therefore regarded as an inevitable developmental stage they have to go through (McGowan 2009). Some scholars, such as Rebecca Moore Howard, believe that this unintentional plagiarism, which she names 'patchwriting', is an integral part of students' learning process, especially if English is an additional language for them. In her opinion:

> Students' patchwriting is often a move toward membership in a discourse community, a means of learning unfamiliar language and ideas. Far from indicating a lack of respect for a source text, their patchwriting is a gesture of reverence.
>
> The patchwriter recognizes the profundity of the source and strives to join the conversation in which the source participates. To join this conversation, the patchwriter employs the language of the target community. (Howard 1999, p. xviii cited in Blum 2009, p. 165)

Similarly, Ivanič believes that the practice of re-using texts among EAL students is to be expected because the 'only way an apprentice member can learn to become a full member is by copying, adapting and synthesizing from the works of other members' (Ivanič 1998, p. 3). As Alastair Pennycook (1996) points out, students learning English — or, for that matter, other languages — face significant problems with understanding new ideas presented in the new language as well as articulating them in English. For instance, Pennycook recalls an incident in which he set an assignment in which students had to write a biography of a famous individual. One of the students then reproduced a passage he had previously memorised from a high school textbook (pp. 201–2). Rather than labelling such behaviour instantly as plagiarism, Pennycook was instead intrigued by this episode because it raised issues concerning 'questions about ownership of texts, practices of memory, and writing' (p. 202). For scholars in this camp, it is therefore important for Western tertiary institutions to cater to increasing cultural diversity within the academy and to have a more tolerant approach towards international students who commit academic transgression.

As a Singaporean academic with an English and Chinese background in Australia, I situate myself squarely in the middle ground. I do so not because I am indecisive. I do so because I find both camps to be rather inadequate in dealing with the issue of plagiarism in today's globalising academy. Subscribing to the notion that there is a link between Chinese culture and plagiarism fosters the view that nothing needs to be done because this is just the way Chinese international students behave. On the other hand, condoning and defending international students' plagiarism rewards inappropriate behaviour and is unfair to those local students who do not receive positive discrimination in this area. Not only is there no link between Chinese culture and plagiarism, I also believe that it is possible to teach Chinese international students strategies to avoid plagiarism, as for me, committing this academic transgression is not necessarily an integral part of the learning process. In addition, I, like Blum (2009), subscribe to the belief that plagiarism or other forms of inappropriate academic practice among students is a 'correctable stage of learning how to write' (p. 27).

Yet, cultural dissonance still seems to be present in Western academies (Phan 2006). Many Western academics, who are neither proficient in Asian languages nor have direct experience of Asian forms of education, seem to have enduring misperceptions that Chinese culture, in the belief that its perceived deference and respect for authority and seniority, somehow encourages plagiarism (Brennan and Durovic 2005). Although Chinese culture in general does place more emphasis on authority and tradition, and rote learning is more common in Chinese education systems (Holmes 2004, p. 294), this does not mean that Chinese students are therefore unable to adapt and orientate themselves to a Western education system that places different emphasis on different aspects of learning. Unsurprisingly, there are also scholars who hold the opposing view, that Chinese culture does not in fact facilitate plagiarism. For instance, Liu Dilin points out that acknowledging and crediting the source for one's information is not unique to Western culture and therefore foreign to Chinese culture. When quoting the words of Confucius, it is common to preface the statement with *zi yue*, which is translated to mean 'Confucius says' (Liu 2005, p. 235). As Liu elaborates:

> Based on my educational experience as a native of China and the research I have conducted … the claim that copying others' writing as one's own is allowed, taught/or encouraged in China is not accurate. I received all my education, with the exception of my graduate study in China, and I never recall any of my teachers telling us it was acceptable to copy others' writing and turn it in as one's own, be it in a paragraph or a couple of sentences. On the contrary, all my teachers often warned us not to copy others' work. In fact, the concept of 'plagiarism' as an immoral practice has existed in China for a very long time. (2005, p. 235)

From the above discussion, it is clear that, as yet, there is no consensus on the link between Chinese culture and plagiarism. Furthermore, if some aspects of

Chinese culture really do encourage plagiarism, there ought to be as many cases of plagiarism among other ethnic Chinese students from countries such as Singapore and Taiwan who are exposed to, and belong to the same Confucian culture, a correlation that I have yet to detect in my experience so far.

As to why I do not situate myself with sympathetic academics, I believe that it is important to remember that just as we know that a rose, by any other name, would smell as sweet,[1] labelling plagiarism by any other name is an exercise in semantics and does not change the nature of the act. Conversely, the very notion that academics ought to be more sympathetic towards Chinese students because such behaviours are somehow part of *the* Chinese culture, or that Chinese international students are less capable than other students of adapting to the existing academic culture they are exposed to, is in itself 'a form of intellectual imperialism' (Liddicoat & Crichton 2008, p. 379). This view assumes Chinese culture is somehow inferior to Western culture in terms of failing to encourage original scholarship, or that Chinese students are unable to acknowledge their sources. Apart from anecdotal accounts that plagiarism is a problem among Chinese students, it is quite difficult for academic staff to validate or falsify this hypothesis, which discriminates against the Chinese students who, perhaps on account of the large numbers currently enrolled, are almost invariably singled out as the main culprits responsible for committing plagiarism at the University. Adrian Slater, legal adviser at the University of Leeds in the UK, believes that it is wrong to perceive any one group of students as more 'high-risk' than another group because any increase in the rates of detection could be due to increased checking, and not necessarily due to the fact that more students from that particular group are plagiarising (Gill 2008). This sentiment is congruent with my experience teaching *Research Project for Chinese Speakers* in the Centre for Asian Studies at a research-intensive Australian university in the second semester of 2009.

This chapter draws on my personal experience teaching this upper-level course targeted at native Chinese speakers who were not very familiar with Western academic culture and norms. There were 64 students in this class. Forty-nine out of the 64 students were pursuing Commerce/Economics degrees, and almost all of them came from the Greater China region, comprising the People's Republic of China, Republic of China, and the Special Administrative Region of Hong Kong. Unsurprisingly, the vast majority of the students in this course came from the People's Republic of China. Even though all these Chinese students had studied in Australia for at least a year, I found that they were not skilled in meeting the requirements of Western academic culture and norms. This issue came to the fore when I marked their first significant written assignment for this course, which was an annotated bibliography. When I marked the assignments, I discovered many cases of plagiarism even though these students were writing in Chinese. In fact, I found that 25 out of the 64 students had plagiarised. In all the 25 cases I detected, I identified the original source texts from the Internet.

Despite the serious implications of these numbers, I argue that Chinese culture is not the dominant factor in why cases of plagiarism are so common among Chinese international students. I hypothesise here that instances of plagiarism are high because Chinese international students in Australia, or in other Western countries today, are possibly less academically proficient than their forbears and may initially lack the social or cultural capital to immediately excel in the Western, English language academy. Furthermore, anecdotal accounts suggest that the vast majority of Chinese international students now seek tertiary education as a pathway to securing permanent residency in Australia, and so they may lack the intrinsic motivation to excel academically. As reported by *The Australian* in its *Higher Education Supplement* on 30 April 2010, the number of Chinese students applying to study in Australia was expected to plunge very dramatically because of proposed changes to the Skilled Occupations List [SOL] issued by the Department of Immigration and Citizenship [DIAC] (Sainsbury & Healy 2010). The dire forecast proved to be accurate as the number of Chinese students applying for visas to study in Australia decreased significantly. From July 1 to December 31 2010, there were 13,969 applications; in the corresponding period for 2011, there were only 12,425 applications, representing a decrease of 11 per cent in a year (Sainsbury 2012). The Australian government is clearly aware of the problem in which many Chinese international students pursue studies in Australia with the primary purpose of securing permanent residency rather than for educational purposes. It has even gone to the extent of reminding students that:

> [You] are encouraged to undertake study in a field they intend to work in once they graduate. It is strongly advised that you do not undertake studies with the sole purpose of obtaining a migration outcome. (Department of Immigration and Citizenship 2010)

Hence, at one level I am pointing to what seems obvious, and suggesting that since many individuals' main objective is to secure permanent residency, they are maybe then less likely to perform as well as their academically-motivated predecessors. This is a point that has been similarly observed in the United States in the context of general immigration:

> Think back to the immigrant at the turn of the century. America was the Land of Opportunity — but that was all. There were no guarantees, no safety nets. One way or another, an immigrant had to make it on his own. Add to that the wrench of tearing himself and family away from a place where his people might have lived for centuries, the terrors of having to learn a new language and culture, often the prospect of working at jobs he had never tried

before, a dozen other reasons for apprehension, and the United States had going for it a crackerjack self-selection mechanism for attracting immigrants who were brave, hard-working, imaginative, self-starting — and probably smart. Immigration can still select for those qualities, but it does not have to. Someone who comes here because his cousin offers him a job, a free airplane ticket, and a place to stay is not necessarily self-selected for those qualities. On the contrary, immigrating to America can be for that person a much easier option than staying where he is, (Herrnstein & Murray 1994, p. 361)

Just as current emigrants to the US may lack some of the stellar qualities of earlier emigrants, the current generation of Chinese international students may also lack some of the impressive academic qualities of their predecessors. In the past, the costs associated with an overseas education were prohibitive. Generally, only those who secured highly competitive scholarships could enjoy this privilege. In the current context, rising incomes in China mean that overseas education becomes more affordable to more families, and students heading overseas are now not necessarily selected based primarily on their academic achievements. Hence, it would not be surprising if these current Chinese students encountered more academic problems than previous cohorts.

As a result of my teaching experience, I wanted to gain a better understanding of these students who plagiarised in their mother tongue. In so doing, I sought to evaluate literature arguing that students commit this error as they attempt to mimic the writing of other more experienced practitioners within the field. To this end, I calculated the Grade Point Average [GPA] for these 25 students, which was approximately 3.5. Since a GPA of 4 indicates a pass, it is therefore clear that these students, on average, only managed to achieve an average grade of conceded pass in the various subjects they took for their degrees. The grades individuals obtain arguably provide the most objective gauge of their academic proficiency in their primary role as a student. This is because, as Clegg and Flint (2006) observe:

> The only thing that should matter in a university is the quality of your academic work, not your race, class, gender, sex, sexuality, physical disabilities or your social background or anything like this. In other words people shouldn't be unduly advantaged by any factor other than academic merit. (p. 381)

As already discussed, since these students are not generally admitted on the basis of their academic performance, they may encounter more problems in their studies (Clegg & Flint 2006 p. 381), making it more likely that they would consider adopting pragmatic strategies and shortcuts when completing their assignments, in order to meet deadlines. Furthermore, it is also counter-intuitive, in my view, for Chinese students to incur high financial costs to study an elective subject in Australia that is taught in Chinese about Chinese society and culture. This supports my belief that such students may be more interested in gaining 'easy' credit points for their studies, rather than challenging themselves academically.

Most significantly, within the context of the *Advanced Chinese* course I was teaching, these Chinese students were writing in their mother tongue on subjects of their own choosing, which meant that they were not beginners coming to grips with an additional language. Firstly, these students would have little difficulty with reading and understanding the source texts that are frequently, though not exclusively, in their own language. Secondly, they would also have no difficulty in expressing ideas and content in the original source text in their own words. Hence, the copying and re-using of source text cannot be reasonably interpreted as 'a coping strategy to meet the demands of producing fluent-sounding academic discourse' (Percorari 2008, p. 20). This is because these students do not have any special problem expressing themselves. Thus, there is no need to rely on, or remember, formulaic phrases in an additional language, which Weinert (1995) defines as:

> generally expressed in terms of processes, and refer to multi-word or multi-form strings which are produced or recalled as a whole chunk, much like an individual lexical item, rather than being generated from individual lexical items/forms with linguistic rules. (p. 182)

Hence, the typical difficulties EAL students face when expressing themselves in an academically appropriate manner are not applicable in this instance. However, whatever the reasons, intents or factors responsible for plagiarism, my experience convinced me that such problems are not insurmountable. Such a problem exists because undergraduate students are rarely expressly taught strategies for effective academic writing, academic skills that can be acquired through explicit and consistent instruction, opportunities for practice, and targeted checking.

After I had identified clear instances of plagiarism, I spoke with some of the offending students. They informed me that their assignments for other subjects had not been subjected to such meticulous checking. Hence, they assumed that this assignment would not be any different. Although in other courses they had been warned about the gravity of the offence of plagiarism, no systematic checking had ever been carried out. In these students' experience, checking for plagiarism by the tutors is therefore a custom more honoured in its *breach* rather than in its *observance*.[2] As a result, these Chinese students had been lulled into a false sense of security, assuming that the markers and tutors are only making empty threats, which are nearly always full only of sound and fury, but essentially signifying nothing.[3] It was apparent that these students have committed plagiarism before, and in their own estimation had 'got away with it', which had emboldened and misled them.

The first significant written assignment in the course was an annotated bibliography, and many of these Chinese students had not done an annotated bibliography before. Consequently, they did not have a clear idea of the requirements of this assignment. This is because Commerce subjects tend to be more 'coursework' in nature whereas Social Sciences subjects tend to be more 'research' in nature. In my informal interactions with these students, I got the impression that undergraduate Commerce subjects tend to focus on the teaching of new contextual knowledge such as economic theories, with less emphasis on teaching academic skills. It could be possible that teaching staff, including myself, assumed that advanced level students would be familiar with writing in this genre, even though it was probably their first exposure. Due to the lack of clarity on our part, it was possible that some students mistook an annotated bibliography to be a mere book summary, and so they assumed that they could easily copy the relevant information from a book's blurb. It has to be acknowledged that teaching staff such as I, must therefore bear some responsibility for this problem. Furthermore, since these students might not be clear about what is expected of them, they might become anxious as the deadline approaches, and resort to copying from relevant sources in order to present accurate information and finish the assignment, thereby committing plagiarism.

As part of my own research into the plagiarism issue, I sought to gain insights into its occurrence at the University. To this end, I requested access to the University's central plagiarism register. However, the University denied my request for access, informing me that such information is confidential and cannot be released, even for legitimate research purposes related to a project conducted at the University. From my perspective, this lack of transparency perpetuates the problem of plagiarism within the University. In order for tutors and markers to take the issue of plagiarism seriously, and be more meticulous when assessing assignments, they need to first know the severity of the problem. In relation to this, it must be acknowledged that part-time and casual staff now carry the bulk of the teaching and marking load. Even though tenured academic staff have privileged access to such information, they are not the ones assessing assignments. In order to deter students from committing plagiarism, it is important to provide tutors and markers with access to such information. With the internationalisation of the academy, class sizes have increased. In large classes, it is not always possible to check every single piece of submitted work. With such information, it would make it possible for tutors and markers to focus their attention on students whose work has been problematic in the past, which is surely the rationale behind the register.

With the internationalisation of the higher education sector, there has been much pressure on academics to take into account the myriad of social and cultural values that are now present on campus. This has led to much debate on the significance of plagiarism and how to handle the issue when, and not if, it arises. In an early analysis, Michael Eraut (1984, in Clegg 2006, p. 384) identified the three main ways in which academics impart values to their students, namely: through implicit transmission by 'assuming them or taking them for granted'; explicit transmission by 'advocating them or refuting them and taking up a definite value proposition', and; explicit discussion by 'making them the subject of his or her teaching with the intention of promoting pupil's value awareness while still preserving their autonomy'.

This last method of education is arguably the most effective way to address the issue of plagiarism with students, but seems to be rarely done. Informal discussions with my colleagues have revealed a general belief that there is not enough time to teach students academic skills *as well as* contextual knowledge. The lack of emphasis on teaching students academic skills might also arise from the misplaced belief that students already have these skills, or that they are able to acquire them quickly through observation. This is not necessarily the case in the present context. Instructors might have forgotten that they have been socialised into their various discipline areas through undergoing years of specialised training during their graduate studies. It is therefore quite unreasonable for them to assume that overseas trained undergraduate students are able to fully master such challenging skills in a short period, especially given the complex diversity of today's student population.

In my own teaching, when I first brought up the issue that I had detected widespread plagiarism in the first written assignment, many students were very surprised. I learned this was because they did not expect me to check their work thoroughly since their previous instructors seemed to have had a more *laissez faire* approach to this issue. The detection of a high incidence of plagiarism in this class seems to indicate that there is a link between Chinese students and plagiarism since within Confucian culture 'memorization and imitation are [deemed to be] the mark of an educated person' (Moder & Halleck 1995, p. 16). Although there is a culture of rote learning in China, it is important to note that it does not represent the entire Chinese education culture (Angélil-Carter 2000, p. 39). Rote learning may be more common, but this issue can be easily resolved if explicit and sustained training in source use and citation are present, as in this Chinese-language cultural studies course. In this particular course, students did not face any language barriers. Therefore, it was possible to focus more attention on teaching them on how to reference and paraphrase appropriately — important academic skills that are transferable and applicable to studies in English in other disciplines and contexts.

Clearly, in order to address the issue of plagiarism, my experience would suggest that having more assignments, rather than just one major essay at the end of a semester, is an effective method to solve this problem. Although such an approach adds to the instructor's workload, it is positive from a pedagogical perspective. This is because such an incremental approach provides a student with consistent practice and feedback, which then allows for early remedial action to be taken if needed. In this Chinese cultural studies course, my belief was validated by the complete turnaround I noted when I marked the students' final essay and did not detect any instances of plagiarism. One of the most common perceived shortcomings of Asian education systems is believed to be the undue emphasis on rote learning and memorisation, which has a detrimental effect on students' creativity and critical thinking skills (Ballard & Clanchy 1991). Yet, through explicit and sustained instruction, it is possible to teach academic skills as well as contextual knowledge. Students may lack these skills at the beginning of the course, but this does not mean they cannot learn them when given the opportunity through structured and targeted attention to the required skills.

More importantly, if there are more assignments, the assessed weight for each would be lower. Consequently, at each stage, the stakes would be lower for students and so they would be more receptive to what instructors have to say, and to experimenting with what, to them, are new techniques. Conversely, if there were problems with the major assignment, and the result of the major assignment determines whether a student passes or fails a course, it is likely that students would try harder to justify their inappropriate actions and be less likely to see things from the instructor's educational perspective. In this latter high-stakes context, it is more likely that students would feel compelled to contemplate appealing the decision to the academic board, a lengthy and time-consuming process. It is quite possible that a student's decision to 'escalate' the issue would be sufficient to cause an instructor to re-think the earlier assessment and not report the problem to higher authorities (Murray 1996 cited in Brennan and Durovix 2005). After all, it would be much easier to award the student a grade of conceded pass than to go through the time-consuming appeal process. In such a scenario, academic transgressions are indirectly rewarded, which then perpetuates the problem as students may then feel that they can 'get away with' plagiarism.

With the internationalisation of Australia's higher education sector, foreign students, and especially those from the People's Republic of China, have become a visible and integral part of campus life in almost all Australian universities. It is now possible that the current generation of Chinese international students is different from their academic predecessors of the 1980s and 1990s who came to study in Australia after securing highly competitive scholarships. The current Chinese students are more likely to be self-funded, and may lack the social and cultural capital to perform academically in comparison with earlier generations of Chinese students who were previously selected based on their academic achievements, and not based on their financial status. This later generation is thus more likely to encounter problems in their studies. The perceived higher incidence of plagiarism among Chinese students, which is anecdotal since the University does not release such figures, is perhaps the clearest representation of their lack of success in acclimatising to the Western learning environment that they are now exposed to.

In the current context of equity and non-discrimination, it may be politically incorrect to make such a generalisation on the academic performance of Chinese international students. However, this issue is the proverbial elephant in the room; it needs to be seen and addressed for what it is, in order to put in place measures to address the problems. It is important for all academics to adopt an active approach that teaches Chinese international students the requisite academic skills to write, paraphrase, and reference in a manner appropriate to their various disciplines, and not just to emphasise the dire consequences they will experience *after* they are caught committing plagiarism. At the same time, there also needs to be a coherent and consistent pedagogic approach towards this issue so that the students are not confused by mixed signals. There is a need for all teaching staff to rigorously check assignments, or to finance such checking for plagiarism so that students do not develop the attitude that they can take a chance since there is a high probability that they will not be penalised for plagiarism. Given the income levels generated by enrolling international students, such costs are not likely to prove prohibitive, and investing to maintain academic integrity is, I believe, not an unreasonable outlay.

The situation, though, is perhaps not entirely bleak. Instead, the prognosis is rather optimistic. As Bourdieu & Passeron (1994, p. 8) point out, 'Academic language is a dead language for the great majority of … people, and is no one's mother tongue'. The democratisation of the academy has led to improved access to higher education, which has allowed international students without the prerequisite social and cultural capital to attend universities in the present context. Problems exist and educators should not ignore this challenge. This new generation of students may initially lack the academic and social capital to excel in a Western education context, but it does not mean that they cannot improve. It is up to the educators to train and assist them in their academic development. After all, universities admit these students after they satisfy the admission criteria, and it is not unreasonable for them to believe that they are able to cope with academic demands.

In the course discussed here, many students plagiarised in the first written assignment. However, the teaching staff adopted a pro-active approach, teaching these Chinese students academic writing skills and assessing their learning rigorously. It was complex and time-consuming, but there were no instances of plagiarism detected in subsequent essays. This turnaround, within the space of a semester, shows that there is no fixed link between aspects of Chinese culture and its perceived propensity to condone or even encourage plagiarism. If Chinese culture were connected to plagiarism, it would take much longer than one semester to rectify these 'congenital' or socially indoctrinated traits. As educators, it is important for us to note that even though these current students may well lack the cultural and intellectual capital to immediately excel in their Anglo-Celtic academic studies, this does not mean that such capital cannot be gained. All motivated students can be taught and can learn the requisite skills to do well in their studies. However, to achieve this goal, active and consistent intervention needs to be present, which is considerably more productive than complaining that these students' performance is not as good as their predecessors or their current local counterparts. In order to equitably address the issue of plagiarism among Chinese international students, it is important to be upfront and transparent about the possible factors, and not persist with a deterministic approach that invariably leads back to the role of the Chinese culture, nor to accept that plagiarism is inevitably a part of students' learning process and so should be tolerated.

Notes

1. *Romeo and Juliet.*
2. *Hamlet.* (Even though I am paraphrasing it here, this is considered to be common knowledge and so does not require referencing. Hence, I am not committing plagiarism.)
3. *Macbeth.* (The same disclaimer applies.)

References

Angélil-Carter, S 2000, *Stolen language?: plagiarism in writing*, Pearson Education Limited, Essex.

Ballard, B & Clanchy, J 1991, *Teaching students from overseas: a brief guide for lecturers and supervisors*, Longman Cheshire Melbourne.

Blum, SD 2009, *My word! Plagiarism and college culture*, Cornell University Press, Ithaca and London.

Bourdieu, P & Passeron, J-C 1994, 'Language and relationship to language in the teaching situation', in PBJ-C Passeron & MDS Martin (eds.), *Academic discourse: linguistic misunderstanding and professorial power*, Polity Press, Cambridge.

Brennan, L & Durovic, J Year, "Plagiarism' and the Confucian heritage culture

(CHC) student', in 2nd Asia-Pacific Educational Integrity: Values for Teaching, Learning and Research, 2–3 December 2005, University of Newcastle.

Burke, R 2006, 'Constructions of Asian international students: the 'casualty' model and Australia as 'educator'', *Asian Studies Review*, vol. 30 no. 4, pp. 333–354.

Carroll, J 2002, *A handbook for deterring plagiarism in higher education*, Oxford Centre for Staff and Learning Development, Oxford.

Chandrasoma, R, Thompson, C & Pennycook, A 2004, 'Beyond plagiarism: trangressive and nontragressive intertextuality', *Journal of Language, Identity, and Education*, vol. 3 no. 3, pp. 171–193.

Clegg, S & Flint, A 2006, 'More heat than light: plagiarism in its appearing', *British Journal of Sociology of Education*, vol. 27 no. 3, pp. 373–387.

Deckert, GD 1993, 'Perspectives on plagiarism from ESL students in Hong Kong', *Journal of Second Language Learning*, vol. 2 no. 2, pp. 131–148.

Department of Immigration and Citizenship 2010, *Onshore International Students*, viewed 3 June 2010, <http://www.immi.gov.au/skilled/general-skilled-migration/pdf/faq-onshore-student.pdf>.

Friedman, P 2010, *Plagiarism and China's future economic development*, East Asia Forum, viewed 3 June 2010, <http://www.eastasiaforum.org/2010/05/26/plagiarism-and-chinas-future-economic-development/>.

Gill, J 2008, 'Cultural insight can help tackle plagiarism', *Times Higher Education*, 24 April.

Herrnstein, RJ & Murray, C 1994, *The bell curve: intelligence and class structure in American life*, The Free Press, New York.

Holmes, P 2004, 'Negotiating differences in learning and intercultural communication: ethnic Chinese students in a New Zealand university', *Business Communication Quarterly*, vol. 67 no. 3, pp. 294–307.

Ivanič, R 1998, *Writing and identity: the discoursal construction of identity in academic writing*, John Benjamins, Amsterdam.

Kayrooz, C, Kinnear, P & Preston, P 2001, *Academic freedom and commercialisation of Australian universities: perceptions and experiences of social scientists*, The Australian Institute, Canberra.

Liddicoat, AJ & Crichton, J 2008, 'The monolingual framing of international education in Australia', *Sociolinguistic Studies*, vol. 2 no. 3, pp. 367–384.

Liu, D 2005, 'Plagiarism in ESOL Students: is cultural conditioning truly the major culprit?', *ELT Journal*, vol. 59, pp. 234–241.

McCormick, F 1988, 'The plagiario and the professor in our peculiar institution', *Journal of Teaching Writing*, vol. 8, no. 2, pp. 133–145.

McGowan, U 2009, 'Research apprenticeship: is this the answer to inadvertent plaigiarism in undergraduate students' writings', *4th Asia-Pacific Conference on*

Educational Integrity, Wollongong.

Moder, CL & Halleck, GB 1995, 'Solving the plagiary puzzle with role plays', *TESOL Journal*, vol. 4 no. 3, pp. 16–19.

Murray, B 1996, 'Are professors turning a blind eye to cheating? Schools facing a plague of cheating. Beware the 'A' student. Overachievers can be cheaters', *The APA Monitor*, vol. 27, pp. 1–42.

Pennycook, A 1996, 'Borrowing others' words: text, ownership, and plagiarism', *TESOL Quarterly*, vol. 30 no. 2, pp. 201–230.

Percorari, D 2008, *Academic writing and plagiarism: a linguistic analysis*, Continuum, London and New York.

Phan, LH 2006, 'Plagiarism and overseas students: stereotypes again?', *ELT Journal*, vol. 59 no. 3, pp. 76–78.

Sainsbury M. 2012, 'China crisis as numbers tumble', *The Australian*, 8 February, viewed 21 March 2012, <http://www.theaustralian.com.au/higher-education/china-crisis-as-numbers-tumble/story-e6frgcjx-1226265112359>.

Sainsbury M & Healy, G 2010, 'Plunge in Chinese University Students Coming to Australia', *The Australian*, 30 April, viewed 30 April 2010, <http://www.theaustralian.com.au/higher-education/plunge-in-chinese-university-students-coming-to-australia/story-e6frgcjx-1225860383768>.

Skilbeck, M & Connell, H 2006, *Meeting the world halfway: towards an Australian school sector strategy*, Department of Education, Science and Training, Canberra.

Sowden, C 2005, 'Plagiarism and the culture of multilingual students in higher education abroad', *ELT Journal*, vol. 59 no. 3, pp. 226–233.

Weinert, R 1995, 'The role of formulaic language in second language acquisition: a review', *Applied Linguistics*, vol. 16 no. 2, pp. 180–205.

12

Education with(out) distinction: Beyond graduate attributes for Chinese international students[1]

Xianlin Song and Kate Cadman

> 有教无类
>
> Everyone, without distinction, is educable;
>
> Education should be provided for all without distinction
>
> — Confucius, *Analects* 15.39

Introduction

Recently a scholar from the Chinese National Academy of Educational Administration, Jianfu Yu (2009), has argued strongly for the continued relevance of Confucian educational principles in a pluralistic cultural world, especially for contemporary European-based civilizations. One of the principles unequivocally embraced by Yu and others (Yang 1999/1993; Cheng, 2009) lies at the heart of Confucian educational philosophy (*Analects* 15; see epigraph). In our research-intensive Australian university, we found ourselves challenged by this principle as we investigated curriculum for a new initiative, a research-based Asian Studies course for the final-year of the Bachelor of Arts and Bachelor of International Studies degrees. This course is one of a suite of courses offered under the banner of *Advanced Chinese* by the University's Centre for Asian Studies (CAS). Entitled *Research Project for Chinese Speakers* (*RPFCS*), it is designed to address the rapidly increasing numbers of Chinese international students in the University, and is thus only offered to students who are Chinese speakers.

Interestingly, through our investigations it became clear that this famous Confucian edict offers two possibilities for translation into English. The first of these (see epigraph) suggests that everyone, equally, has the *capacity* to be educated, placing the focus of the Analect's meaning on the learner. The second translation moves the burden of responsibility to the education provider, implying that everyone, equally, has the *right* to be educated. First, all students, without distinction, are capable of learning the skills that we respect in accomplished students, and are not automatically remedial by definition of their cultural and linguistic backgrounds. Second, they have the right to an education which is appropriate for the skills and knowledges that they bring to their learning contexts, and it is the role of educators to devise the most appropriate content and environment for their access to such an education.

Grounded in both these beliefs, we set about to explore how they shift, intersect and become realised in our own context. Scholars in a special issue of *Higher Education* (2001) have clearly advocated the need for new conceptual approaches to social science education in response to globalisation. Tierney (2001), for example, argues strongly for the importance of recognising the multiple and hybrid identities of today's university education stakeholders. In this light, our primary objective was to investigate how we might provide Chinese-speaking students with fair and rigorous educational opportunities that are directly relevant to their specialised positions and life experiences — in other words, to bridge some of the gaps they may have experienced between their previous and present education contexts. Our goal was to put into practice a pedagogy that would privilege 'connecting' with these students (see Cadman 2005) rather than emphasising disciplinary content or language. Through such a pedagogy we sought to capitalise on students' multilingual competency and thus prepare them for transnational futures while remaining firmly grounded within the University's mandated 'Graduate Attributes'. In this way we hoped to secure equity for these students, beyond and including commercial success for the Australian institution.

In this article we begin by locating our work in the present climate of internationalised higher education in Australia in order to foreground the situations of the large numbers of Chinese students presently being educated here. Our aim is then to review the educational imperatives, both institutional and philosophical, that underpinned the curriculum design of this exclusively Chinese-speakers' course, before presenting the structure, objectives and course content that resulted along with the unique, bilingual pedagogic processes we implemented. Finally, we offer a qualitative analysis of the students' learning outcomes in response to course objectives and to the pedagogic approach we implemented. In this analysis we follow Guba and Lincoln's (1989) conditions for rigorous constructivist inquiry that, in summary, are as follows:

- a natural setting … in the same time/context frame that the inquirer seeks to understand
- enquirers who enter the frame as learners, not claiming to know preordinately what is salient … not knowing what it is they don't know
- employing qualitative methods … talking to people, observing their activities, reading their documents, responding to their non-verbal cues and so on
- drawing on *tacit knowledge*, that is, all that we know minus all that we can say, judgement developed out of experience (pp. 174–7).

Our goal in this discussion is not to present quantitative findings but to open up widening lines of inquiry into possibilities for transcultural learning, and to contribute to current debates around a genuinely international higher education for Northern, metropolitan universities.

Chinese students in the university

Chinese students are an exponentially growing, aggressively recruited minority group in Australian universities. According to Australian Education International (AEI) statistics (2010), in 2009 there were almost 95,000 Chinese international students between the ages of 20 and 29 in Australian institutions, over 40 per cent of the total number of international students in the Higher Education sector. Clearly, such global commercialisation of degree programs in English impacts not only on the knowledge capital of developing nations but also on educational outcomes in our own developed market contexts, as the work of researchers such as Marginson (2009; Marginson & Eijkman 2007) and Birrell (2006) convincingly demonstrates. Marginson (2009), in particular, demonstrates in some detail how the natural corollary of this commercialising trend is the failure of programs to develop innovative and inventive curricula to meet the pressing challenges of student diversity.

In our own context in the Centre for Asian Studies, 67 students enrolled in the inaugural semester of the *RPFCS* course. In our pre-course diagnostic survey, these students confirmed the expectations we anticipated in that they were largely enrolled in social science and humanities disciplines, majoring in Commerce, Economics, Media, Politics, with a minority in the applied sciences. All but a very few had previously had to do major assignments in discursive English and they had all shown interest in various cultural studies subjects offered by the Centre, especially those focussing on historical and contemporary issues in China.

These students were bilingual in that they speak both Chinese (their native language) and English (having met the University's entry requirements of overall IELTS score of 6.0). In conversations held in their own language, this cohort emotionally described their ongoing negative study experiences and outcomes to date; a closer check later revealed that their average Grade Point Average (GPA) was 3.5, on a scale from 1 to 7. Like many of their fellow international students, having met the university's admissions criteria and having had good learning outcomes in the past, these students were at a loss as to why they could not succeed in the Australian institution (see Coley 1999). Most of them were extremely disillusioned by their experiences of unsatisfactory academic performance and brought to light the agony of constantly feeling inadequate in relation to the expectations they encountered.

Educational imperatives
Institutional requirements

In our curriculum design we were first required to address a set of generic 'Graduate Attributes' defined and mandated by the University. Such an approach to education clearly reflects recent Australian Government trends for national testing in schools, and rests on an unshakeable belief in the value of dealing with student diversity by creating homogenised measures of assessment. As such, it seriously reinforces the discourse of remediation that attends international students' education.

The homogenous 'attributes' that are required to be addressed in this faculty context include such examples as:

- An appreciation of students' potential contribution to knowledge through engagement with the traditions and innovations in their field of enquiry
- Analytic and critical skills
- The ability to argue from evidence
- An awareness of their potential leadership roles in the community of scholars and in the wider community (University of Adelaide, 2005/6; underlining added).

The underlined phrases here show universalised criteria, invisibly embedded within key assumptions underpinning this 'international' education. Their power as gatekeepers remains fixed paradoxically *because* they are unarticulated and undefined. They clearly exemplify the 'monolingual framing' recently identified in higher education (Liddicoat & Crichton 2008); indeed, it is only possible to interpret these educational goals from within the dominant Anglo-Celtic worldview that generates them (see MacKinnon & Manathunga 2003). The sense that our learners might make of these attributes, and the relevance they might have for their 'life-long learning' — given that these are exclusively Chinese-speaking students engaged in extending their knowledge and ability to communicate about issues in their own culture and language — are extremely problematic. Nevertheless we seek to engage these educational goals, and integrate them into the learning experiences of our students.

Philosophy of teaching

As curriculum designers, our professional goals run counter to this trend toward 'generic' educational outcomes and are, by contrast, inspired primarily by two philosophical considerations that emerge directly from previous research and practice.

The first of these involves the principle of 'transculturalism' that we have developed from Salvadori's (1997) application of an early concept by Cuban historian Fernando Ortiz (1975/1995; see Chapter 1, pp. 12, this volume). *Trans*culturalism is the process of reaching beyond interculturalism in education, to create a shared culture that is different from the original cultures of both teachers and students (see Cadman 2000). Thus, we reject the model of higher education described as a 'one-way process of knowledge exchange' (Liddicoat & Crichton 2008, p. 379; also Pennycook 1989). Today, in our present contexts of continually accelerating internationalisation, we follow Salvadori in arguing that, for 'real' education to occur, 'the challenge to change is on both sides' (Cadman 2000, p. 487) and we need to find ever more creative ways of promoting multicultural and multilingual flows of reciprocal knowledges.

Striving then to develop an effectively transcultural curriculum for each specific cohort of students, we draw on some of the key aspects of the 'pedagogy of connection' (see Cadman 2005). Such a pedagogy is inspired by a teaching context of 'team collaboration (of creativity, fact and affect), lots of discussion, and mutual respect and support' (Cadman 2005, p. 354). Most importantly, it informs the creation of the classroom learning space as a 'safe house in the contact zone' (Cadman 2005, p. 356; see also Canagarajah 1997) in which we can structure opportunities for students' agency and engagement through the generation of self-reflexive, exploratory intellectual dialogues. Here the primary goal is to integrate 'what students know, speak, experience, and feel, as starting points from which an empowering curriculum can be built' (Shor 1992, cited in Cadman 2005, p. 359).

The *RPFCS* course

In these ways the core philosophy underpinning the *RPFCS* course was designed to provide a critical lens through which Australian 'Graduate Attributes' are viewed and put into practice. The personal higher education stories of these Chinese-speaking students in social and cultural studies indicated that there are specific areas of skill development that they actively recognise and seek in order to succeed — skills that are most often 'hidden' and unarticulated, though everywhere assessed. Fundamentally these involve conducting research to develop independent perspectives on targeted topic questions, and the writing of convincingly logical, 'Western' arguments in support of those perspectives, paying contextually appropriate attention to conventions of plagiarism. Our own strong view is that, in multilingual and multiracial university contexts, such requisite skills should not be assumed and left 'invisible', but must be explicitly taught in ways that make them equally accessible to all students. It thus became our goal to foreground the teaching and learning of these skills, and to treat them as *education* not *remediation*, in other words to embed them integrally into the taught and assessed components of the course.

Issues in Chinese culture – a strategic co-requisite

A common problem for explicitly skills-based courses in tertiary settings is how to allocate teaching and study time to the intellectual content that the developing academic skills are required to communicate. Basic Vygotskian educational theory leads us to understand that the research skills we are targeting cannot be learned in a vacuum but must be built upon what students already know, that learning can only occur in a '*Zone of Proximal Development*' (ZPD) for the student (see Vygotsky 1978). Consequently we devised the *RPFCS* course to be structured with a relevant co-requisite, *Issues in Chinese Culture for Chinese Speakers*, which strategically presents course content in Asian studies of interest to the students, and directly capitalises on their previous knowledge and cultural and language backgrounds.

The primary role of the *Issues in Chinese Culture* course for *RPFCS* is thus to provide the content material and to define the scope of research topics possible for students to select from, in order to pursue independent research. Topics of the *Issues* co-requisite included Chinese culture, globalisation, orientalism and occidentalism, Confucianism, and gender in Chinese contexts. In this way, the lectures, tutorials and *Course Reader* of *Issues in Chinese Culture* contextually ground the students for the learning of skills required in *RPFCS*.

RPFCS *course objectives*

In *RPFCS* there are two intersecting sets of goals under the broad rationale of the *Advanced Chinese* program. First, using theoretical frameworks developed in the *Issues* course, students are required to engage critically and analytically with some of the central concerns of Chinese culture and to demonstrate the key research and logical communication skills that are rewarded in Western humanities and social science research environments.

To achieve these goals the *RPFCS* uses a student-centred, scaffolded course structure that explicitly sets up the following learning objectives for students:

- to frame a research problem or question, and devise appropriate and effective ways of investigating it
- to develop a clear and well argued answer to the question, based on an Annotated Bibliography on the topic, and give a formal oral presentation
- to be able to analyse and evaluate the strengths of a successful student assignment presenting an argument on a social or cultural studies topic
- to write a research paper which provides an informed answer to the original question as a logically organised, formal, deductive argument, and appropriately integrates published literature in its support.

Most significantly, all the assessment components are presented in Chinese. Students are first required to negotiate and produce a research question on a topic covered in the co-requisite *Issues* course. They present orally on their question and their plans for the research journey they intend to undertake to answer it. Finally, they produce a research report which, while it should adhere to the Aristotelian deductive argument structures that have been taught, may be written in English or Chinese (5000 Chinese characters).

RPFCS *course content*

To meet the skills development objectives of the *RPFCS*, the content of the course focuses directly on how successful research and its expression are evaluated in the present global research contexts of social and cultural studies. How to perform 'researcher', how to write effective and acceptable arguments in the global, Anglicised academy, become the substantive material of the teaching.

Becoming 'international' researchers

Initially we engage students' experience of key research concepts by demystifying the often 'secret' terms associated with the Western academy: research, question, objective, qualitative, quantitative, primary and secondary data, methodology, methods, results, discussion, logic, argument, conclusion. Activities require students to share their often diverse understandings with each other, to interrogate how these concepts might be interpreted differently in different research contexts, and to educate the lecturers from their own experience. Thus they are launched with us on an authentically *trans*cultural learning journey. Strategically, teaching attention is given to the conventional criteria associated with a research question in this context: students' draft and redraft their questions, share and critique each other's, and consider the implications of question words and content phrases for the focus and scope of the argument that will eventually provide the question's answer.

Western/Northern logic for academic writing and speaking

Gradually, as the students become more immersed in their own research process, teaching emphasis moves to research writing in order to problematise the analytic argument that will express the research outcome. Steeped in a cultural heritage that prides itself on the use of imagery both in thinking and texts, Chinese-speaking students are here introduced to the principles of Eurocentric logic, which have continued to be debated along rhetorical lines since the ground-breaking 'contrastive rhetoric' arguments of Kaplan in 1966 (see Connor 2002; Kubota & Lehner 2004; Panetta 2001). Interestingly, recent studies by Chinese-background researchers have returned to endorse the view that '[t]here are differences in the structuring of Chinese and English scholarly arguments' (Singh & Fu 2008, p. 135; also Ji 2001); that 'different cultural values and assumptions may influence how people express themselves both orally and in written texts' (Chien 2007, p. 135), and; that 'the L2 [English] writing process is strategically, rhetorically, and linguistically different from the L1 [Chinese] writing process' (Mu & Carrington 2007, p. 14). One scholar, Li Ming (2004), presents a diagrammatic representation of Chinese thought as a *yin-yang* circular symbol located at the centre of a five-pointed star representing the 'five elements' of Chinese logic, and thus demonstrates its difference from Western rhetorical structure (Li 2004, p. 50).

Frequently in class the *RPFCS* students articulately explained their belief that it was their inability to reproduce the expected rhetorical arguments, rather than grammatical problems, that had routinely produced a lack of respect for the intellectual content of their writing (an assessment soundly demonstrated by Mackinnon & Manathunga's 2003 study in *HERD*). Consequently, in the *RPFCS* course we make both the purpose and logical structure of academic argument an explicit focus of students' own contrastive analysis. They are encouraged to interrogate their understanding of their own Chinese writing style, and to conceptualise the Aristotelian conventions of logical organisation as they make sense of the ideas they develop (Ren, 2009).

An extremely significant difference in this *Advanced Chinese* context, however, from all other linguistic and pedagogic studies, is that here there is no assumption that any form of logical reasoning is attached to a particular language. Models and examples in written English provide evidence for deconstructing and reconstructing arguments in both English and Chinese, and the students' final research reports demand Aristotelian logic written in either language. The assumptions that underpin this teaching are explicit: that all logical structures are culturally embedded in educational traditions; that they express different rather than superior or inferior modes of organising ideas; they are not esoteric or mysterious, and; above all, they are learnable.

Avoiding plagiarism

In relation to successful academic writing, a final focus for our teaching goals must of course address the escalating concern expressed by students and staff about plagiarism. It is not appropriate here to review the plethora of published research addressing the issue of plagiarism in English language higher education (see *International Journal for Educational Integrity*; also Abasi & Graves 2008). What remains uncontested in this scholarship is that there are 'countless cases of plagiarism' in Australian universities every year (Devlin 2006, p. 45), and that policy and course documents continue to represent plagiarism in a discourse of intellectual dishonesty, as a breach of appropriate moral or ethical conduct (as in a heading such as 'Plagiarism, Collusion and Related Forms of Cheating' [2010] and in the rise of entrapment software packages entitled *Turnitin* and *Ferret*, and so on). A very convincing body of literature has linked international students' educationally-developed writing practices to their likelihood of 'unintentionally' plagiarising (for examples, see Sutherland-Smith 2005; Devlin 2003, 2006; McGowan 2005, 2008; Gu 2009), but still unresolved complexities continue to be unearthed for both students and staff (Stappenbelt, Rowles & May 2009). Inevitably for our Asian students, to develop both a concrete understanding of what actually counts as 'plagiarism', as well as a confidence in the practice of writing that does not contravene accepted global academic practices, in any language, is an unavoidable priority.

Curriculum implementation through a connecting, inter-lingual pedagogy

In all these ways the central learning concerns of this particular student cohort presented us with some very specific, in addition to homogeneous and generic, challenges for curriculum implementation. We engaged with these by effecting the 'pedagogy of connection' we were aiming for through two distinct frameworks.

The first of these rigorously applies a well-established 'genre pedagogy', to work through scaffolded writing activities (see Hammond et al. 1992). This text-based approach involves guiding students through a series of articulated learning stages: the role of a scholarly argument text in its context; deconstruction and evaluation of authentic, relevant examples; facilitated group construction of the target 'genre', and; independent text construction. Throughout this process, students are given explicit guidance and materials so they can learn and practise the key elements of Aristotelian, deductive academic argument, framed within the 'Western' education tradition that they came to Australia to receive. Simultaneously, course content engages their previous knowledge, their intellectual aptitude, and their first language competence, so how to 'connect' with them as holistic learners remains at the heart of the teaching project.

The second aspect of this approach — and perhaps the most significant and far-reaching innovation to the 'pedagogy of connection' here — is that in the *RPFCS* course, teaching and learning are effected bilingually. The course is structured so that dialogues are generated in both elective and assessable components, and communications can take place in English, in Chinese, in both languages simultaneously, and in any newly-minted hybrid combinations. Some lectures/workshops are delivered in Chinese, some in English; questions are asked in either language; students control the interactive group work, which is carried out in the most appropriate language for the content of the discussion, very often in Chinese with key issues (such as 'epistemology', 'positivist', 'post-structural', and so on) being interrogated in English. Since one of us is not bilingual English-Chinese — the only class member in fact — we noticed that students and staff freely request, volunteer, conduct, and share translations. Interruptions for clarification are common, modelled by us as staff and gradually taken up by students. Switching between languages clearly does not inhibit communication but rather enhances learning, and above all, facilitates connecting with new understandings and with other people.

In our view, the effectiveness of this pedagogic approach cannot be underestimated. Instead of furthering the notion that monolingualism is the natural state of learning, *RPFCS* creates a living bilingual classroom environment that engages with students' linguistic competence, thus granting legitimacy to the bilingual experience that is these students' lived realities in Australia (Ellis 2006, cited in Liddicoat & Crichton 2008, p. 368). In a linguistic setting such as this, where lecturers, tutors and students are free to use both English and Chinese, communication is observed by all to be a two-way reciprocal dialogue where the emphasis focuses on intelligibility and exchange of meaning (see Jenkins 2006). Students' capabilities are developed through their hybridised use of both languages, engaging their 'capacity to draw on, combine and move between' their linguistic and cultural identities in the communication process (Liddicoat 2011, p. 839). Negotiation of meaning, critique of ideas and deductive reasoning are performed through bilingual exchange so students are able to capitalise actively on what they know, and what they think.

Evaluation outcomes – developing 'attributes' and bridging gaps

As a new course in the Faculty, *RPFCS* was required to conduct the University's 'Students Experience of Learning and Teaching' (SELT) evaluation, which took place in week 12 of teaching. The items in this survey were generic for the Centre and not designed specifically for the *RPFCS* course. We were pleased to see the mean response to the key trigger, 'Overall, I am satisfied with the quality of this course', was 6.1 (range 1–7, n = 47), which is above the Faculty average, and there were no negative indications about the course.

Then, in line with our own constructivist goals for course development, we distributed an informal questionnaire employing open-ended questions in which students were asked to give discursive responses to the course objectives both in writing and in oral discussion, again in the language of their choice, Chinese or English. In these responses, many students valued the pragmatic skills focus of the course, and spoke of their deeper understanding of gaps between their Chinese and Australian educations, particularly in terms of logical writing and critical argumentation. Several students noted with regret that they had not been able to take the course in their first year and suggested that *RPFCS* should be a first year foundation course in the Faculty. There was considered advice for course development, but no student indicated a negative experience; among the vast majority of strong positive comments, one quite vehemently thanked us for 'Let[ting] me know what I wouldn't know for a life time in China'.

Becoming researchers

An immediate observation with respect to how the students engaged with the prevailing expectation of 'researcher' was how slow they were to enter dialogues with each other and with us about the learning issues they felt confident or under-confident about. We found we had to provide specific scaffolding on how to reflect on your own experience and skill levels, how to engage in group discussion, and how to draft collaborative documents. The gradual transition to independent learning evidenced through critical, scholarly questioning was demonstrably achieved by a majority of the students, and expressed clearly:

> I think research is the most important skill I learned at University. (S27)
> Before I start my research, I need to think and read my research question

deeply and carefully. (S6)

Significantly, in the oral discussion this student group responded extremely warmly to the bilingual teaching and learning environment, attributing newly gained skills to the relaxed and constructive dialogues. In the written responses in our informal questionnaire, 34 chose to comment positively on this classroom culture. We also noted that the bicultural and bilingual environment was associated with agency by many students, with valued aspects such as:

> Study Chinese culture in Australia. Stand at different position. Negative or positive. (S19)
>
> Bi-language teaching system through research[ing] two-language writing about the same issue can provide a opportunity to learn a lot about transcultural experience. (S2)
>
> The research [is] directly relevant to our future life. (S41)
>
> The course require[s] us to use both Chinese and English resources. (S29)

Interestingly, during the course students' agency became increasingly evident in relation to practical skills, as they requested us to revisit issues they were unsure of, challenged definitions, clarified their research questions and negotiated their 'thesis' construction. It remained problematic, however, in their perceived 'loss of face'; they remained uncomfortable to admit any lack of required knowledge, even where the topic was new and unfamiliar, and to talk openly about their own initial 'plagiarisms'.

Deductive reasoning and logical argument

The final research essays were assessed by Chinese-speaking bilingual tutors who were required to evaluate them on the following grounds: evidence of scholarly research appropriate for the focus and scope of the developed research question; a precise thesis statement; a series of relevant propositions supporting the thesis; well selected scholarly evidence to support each argument; a clear principle of organisation, with logical links provided; confident paraphrasing of published material with appropriate attribution, and; a consistent bibliographical style. In this cohort, only two chose to submit their essays in English and they were clearly amongst the most confident students, with one achieving a Credit and the other a Distinction.

Interestingly, the assessed outcomes were very similar to what we would have expected from any typical range of cultural studies essays, with three failing, 28 receiving Passes, 31 receiving Credits, and five receiving Distinctions and High Distinctions (n = 67). The failures were as expected by the markers[2] in that they showed no evidence of scholarly research, they provided no clear thesis, with weak, largely irrelevant, evidence drawn only from personal, often biased, experience, there were no citations or reference to scholarly publication, and only incoherent and incomplete reference lists. At the other end of the spectrum, those that scored most highly provided succinct thesis statements, followed up by relevant and well formed topic sentences which 'sustained coherence' and provided 'a very clear roadmap' to the logic. Scholarly research was evident in that validated measures were provided as evidence for argument assertions, and scholarly arguments were summarised and paraphrased effectively so that argument 'came across as original rather than a collage of academic resources'.

These results were of particular interest to us, in that they strongly supported our initial hypotheses that Western research skills are learnable, that Aristotelian logical argument can be developed through practice and that it does not demand expression in tailored English sentences. Student enthusiasm was forcefully expressed: 'No questions, this course teach[es] us how to write a research essay!' (S36)

Plagiarism

For diagnostic purposes at the beginning of the course we conducted a short survey aimed at getting an understanding of students' motivation for taking the *RPFCS*, and their expectations of it. The results indicated that 67 out of the 69 respondents associated 'plagiarism' with cheating or academic dishonesty. Judging from this, we assessed that these students had a reasonably good understanding of what 'plagiarism' entails. That is, they recognised that plagiarism is associated with concepts of honesty, integrity and cheating, which may be deemed universal in a globalising environment. In reality, however, our experience with the first major assignment, an Annotated Bibliography on their chosen topic, told us a different story (see Table 1).

Overall, 38 per cent of the 64 submissions contained what, in Australian higher institutions, we would consider to be 'improper referencing' to the published works of others, and three were almost entirely comprised of passages of 'copied', unattributed text. It is noteworthy here that these assignments were written *after* explicit workshopping on the practice of appropriate referencing and plagiarism, and that they were written in Chinese.

Our response strategy was to be uncompromising but sympathetic. We advised all students that *some* had not followed the instructions on plagiarism, and offered individual consultations to those who sought them. All the students who had extensively 'copied' took up this offer and each agreed that they had plagiarised. One student suggested he did so out of respect for published material, and the other two provided weak excuses about time constraints. None of the other students elected to discuss the issue, though as a group they were observed repeatedly discussing the situation with some agitation. When the time came to return the assignments, the 21

	Completed assignments	Referenced inappropriately	Comprised entirely of copied extracts
Annotated bibliography	64	21	3
Final essay assignment	64	0	0

Table 1: Instances of plagiarism in major assignments

that had demonstrated 'improper' referencing techniques were not returned. Instead, all the students were advised that those whose marks had been withheld would be given the opportunity to resubmit on a pass or fail basis. Subsequent rigorous checking of the 21 re-submissions revealed no further instances of plagiarism, nor, very significantly, did that of the final Research Report assignments (see Table 1).

We concluded that this very welcome outcome resulted from two pedagogic strategies: the uncompromising stand we took to implement the University's plagiarism policy (The University of Adelaide 2009; see Stappenbelt et al. 2009), together with an informed, non-judgemental and empathetic educational line. The culturally sensitive and unconfrontational strategy we adopted seemed to provoke a genuine learning response from this cohort of students and, not unexpectedly, this was expressed in emotional terms in the informal evaluations: 'The Chinese tutor never told us how to avoid plagiarism in writing' (S20, respondent's emphasis); 'in China the plagiarism is different from here, I learned here plagiarism' (S33).

Conclusion

Through the design, implementation and analysis of the *Research Project for Chinese Speakers* course, we have been able to identify key considerations for the education of Chinese international students, of which there are escalating numbers in Australian universities. First and foremost we conclude that it is possible to reconcile the invisible monolingual framing of the institutional policy and assumptions that we are required to engage with, with our educational imperative to offer Chinese-speaking international students meaningful, relevant and, above all, equitable possibilities for learning. A large majority of the first *RPFCS* student cohort patently met the demands of the Faculty's 'Graduate Attributes', and extended their learning outcomes beyond the restricted Anglo-Celtic assumptions these attributes represent. The pragmatic skills such students have developed are rigorously assessed, but crucially here, students' academic performance is graded on their demonstration of the explicit criteria that are taught and exemplified in detail; there are no taken-for-granted, assumed or hidden criteria so these students are offered the same chances of success as the local students they are being educated alongside.

For ourselves, by integrating theoretical understandings of transculturalism and critical pedagogy in higher education, through this course we increased our understanding of the significance of student agency in learning. We assessed that, as educators, we were successful in actively creating a bilingual learning environment which constitutes a 'safe house' for these students, thus recognising, engaging, and connecting 'with students' previous knowledge, experiences and academic practices and languages' (Liddicoat & Crichton 2008, p. 380). Nevertheless, we aim in future to build decision-making more specifically into assessed tasks, and to encourage more students to experiment with English by offering a percentage loading for those who write or present orally in English. Overall, we estimate that we fulfilled our own overarching objective to bridge some of the gaps these students experience between Chinese and Australian education systems. As a result we may offer them access to an education *with* distinction, in terms of Aristotelian content, and *without* distinction as translated in the epigraph at the opening, with both the connotative inferences that can be taken from the Confucian philosophy which originally inspired our project.

Notes

[1] An earlier version of this chapter appeared in the journal *Higher Education Research & Development*. The authors thank Taylor & Francis (www.tandfonline.com) for permission to republish.
[2] A bilingual tutor/assessor was asked to present detailed notes in English to indicate the ways in which a range of essays were assessed in relation to the mandated criteria.

References

Abasi, AR & Graves, B 2008, 'Academic literacy and plagiarism: conversations with international graduate students and disciplinary professors', *Journal of English for Academic Purposes*, vol. 7 no. 2, pp. 221–233.

Australian Education International AEI 2010, March, 'Research snapshot: international student enrolments in higher education in 2009', viewed 21 May 2010, <www.aei.gov.au/AEI/PublicationsAndResearch/Snapshots/Default.htm>.

Birrell, B 2006, 'Implications of low English standards amongst overseas students at Australian universities', *People and Place*, vol. 14 no. 4, pp. 53–64.

Cadman, K 2000, '"Voices in the air": evaluations of the learning experiences of international postgraduates and their supervisors', *Teaching in Higher Education*, vol. 5 no. 4, pp. 475–491.

Cadman, K 2005, 'Towards a 'pedagogy of connection' in research education: a 'REAL' Story', *Journal of English for Academic Purposes*, vol. 4 no. 4, *Special Edition on Advanced Academic Literacy*, pp. 353–367.

Canagarajah, S 1997, 'Safe houses in the contact zone: coping strategies of African-American students in the academy', *College Composition and Communication*, vol. 48 no. 2, pp. 173–196.

Cheng, CY 2009 12–14 November, 'Confucian global leadership: classical and contemporary, from both historical and philosophical points of view', keynote presentation at the *10th International Leadership Academic Conference*, Los Angeles, viewed 13 October 2009, <www.ph.url.tw/document/leadership_1.pdf>.

Chien, S 2007, 'The role of Chinese EFL learners' rhetorical strategy use in relation to their achievement in English writing', *English Teaching: Practice and Critique*, vol. 6 no. 1, pp. 132–150.

Coley, M 1999, 'The English language entry requirements of Australian universities for students of non-English-speaking background', *Higher Education Research and Development*, vol. 18 no. 1, pp. 7–17.

Connor, U 2002, 'New directions in contrastive rhetoric', *TESOL Quarterly*, vol. 36 no. 4, pp. 493–510.

Devlin, M 2003, 'The problem with plagiarism', *Campus Review*, vol.12, pp. 4–5.

Devlin, M 2006, 'Policy, preparation, and prevention: proactive minimization of student plagiarism', *Journal of Higher Education Policy and Management*, vol. 28 no. 1, pp. 45–58.

Gu, Q 2009, 'Maturity and interculturality: Chinese students' experiences in UK higher education', *European Journal of Education*, vol. 44 no. 1, pp. 37–52.

Guba, E & Lincoln, Y 1989, *Fourth generation evaluation*, Sage, Newburg Park, CA.

Hammond, J, Burns, A, Joyce, H, Brosnan, D & Gerot, L 1992, *English for social purposes: a handbook for teachers of adult literacy*, National Centre for English Language Teaching and Research, Macquarie University, Sydney.

Jenkins, J 2006, 'Points of view and blind spots: ELF and SLA', *International Journal of Applied Linguistics*, vol. 16 no. 2, pp. 137–291.

Kaplan, RB 1966, 'Cultural thought patterns in intercultural communication', *Language Learning*, vol. 16, pp. 1–20.

Ji, S 2001, 'Reading vs. writing', *ELT Newsletter 80*, viewed 30 April 2010, <www.

eltnewsletter.com/back/November2001/art802001.htm>.

Kubota, R & Lehner, A 2004, 'Toward critical contrastive rhetoric', *Journal of Second Language Writing*, vol. 13, pp. 7–27.

Li, M 2004, 'Weishenme yaozai 21 shiji tichang renxue de chuangzao [Why advocate for human studies in the 21 century]', in *Tanjiu xinling* [Exploring the Soul], (ed.) S Zhang, Zhengzhou daxue chubanshe, Henan, pp. 39–60.

Liddicoat, AJ 2011, 'Language teaching and learning from an intercultural perspective', in E Hinkle (ed.), *Handbook of research in second language teaching and learning, Volume 2*, Routledge, New York, pp. 837-855.

Liddicoat, AJ, & Crichton J 2008, 'The monolingual framing of international education in Australia', *Sociolinguistic Studies*, vol. 2 no. 3, pp. 367–384.

MacKinnon, D & Manathunga, C 2003, 'Going global with assessment: what to do when the dominant culture's literacy drives assessment', *Higher Education Research & Development*, vol. 22 no. 2, pp. 131–144.

Marginson, S 2009, 'University rankings and the knowledge economy', in MA Peters, S Marginson & P Murphy (eds), *Creativity and the global knowledge economy*, Peter Lang, New York, pp. 185–216.

Marginson S & Eijkman, H 2007, *International education: financial and organisational impacts in Australian universities*, Monash University Centre for Economics of Education and Training, Clayton, Vic.

McGowan, U 2005, 'Does educational integrity mean teaching students NOT to "use their own words"?', *International Journal for Educational Integrity*, vol. 1 no. 1, viewed 04 April 2010, <www.ojs.unisa.edu.au/index.php/IJEI/article/view/16/6>.

McGowan, U 2008, 'International students: a conceptual framework for dealing with unintentional plagiarism', in TS Roberts (ed.), *Student plagiarism in an online world: problems and solutions*, Hershey, New York, pp. 92–107.

Mu, C & Carrington, S 2007, 'An investigation of three Chinese students' English writing strategies', *Teaching English as a Second or Foreign Language*, vol. 11 no. 1, pp. 1–23.

Ortiz, F 1975/1995, *Cuban counterpoint: tobacco and sugar*, H de Onís, trans., Duke University Press, Durham, NC.

Panetta, CG (ed.) 2001, *Contrastive rhetoric revisited and redefined*, Lawrence Erlbaum, Mahwah, NJ.

Pennycook, A 1989, 'The concept of method, interested knowledge, and the politics of language teaching', *TESOL Quarterly*, vol. 23, pp. 589–618.

Ren, K 2009, 'On the difference between Chinese-English logic: a reasoning and thinking model of the aspects of the structure of composition', *Journal of Liaoning Normal University*, vol. 32 no. 4, pp. 91–94.

Salvadori, RG 1997, 'The difficulties of interculturalism', *European Journal of Intercultural Studies*, vol. 8 no. 2, pp. 185–191.

Singh M, & Fu, D 2008, 'Flowery inductive rhetoric meets creative deductive arguments: becoming transnational researcher-writers', *International Journal of Asia Pacific Studies*, vol. 4 no. 1, pp. 121–137.

Stappenbelt B, Rowles C & May, E 2009, Jan 29–30, 'Cultural influence on attitudes to plagiarism', Refereed proceedings of the 18th Annual Teaching Learning Forum *Teaching and learning for global graduates*, Curtin University of Technology, Perth, WA, viewed 28 March 2010, <http://otl.curtin.edu.au/tlf/tlf2009/refereed/stappenbelt.html>.

Sutherland-Smith, W 2005, 'Pandora's box: academic perceptions of student plagiarism in writing', *Journal of English for Academic Purposes*, vol. 4 no. 1, pp. 83–95.

Tierney, WG 2001, 'The autonomy of knowledge and the decline of the subject: postmodernism and the reformulation of the university', *Higher Education*, vol. 41 no. 4, pp. 353–372.

The University of Adelaide 2005/6, *University of Adelaide Graduate Attributes*, viewed 28 March 2010, <www.adelaide.edu.au/dvca/gradattributes>.

The University of Adelaide 2009, *Policy statement on plagiarism, collusion and related forms of cheating*, viewed 01 June 2010, <http://www.adelaide.edu.au/policies/230>.

Vygotsky, LS 1978, *Mind in society*, Harvard University Press, Cambridge, MA.

Yang, H 1993/1999, *Confucius K'ung Tzu 551–479 BC*, UNESCO International Bureau of Education, Paris.

Yu, J 2009, 'The influence and enlightenment of Confucian cultural education on modern European civilisation', *Frontiers of Education in China*, vol. 4 no. 1, pp. 10–26.

This book is available as a fully-searchable pdf from
www.adelaide.edu.au/press

www.ingramcontent.com/pod-product-compliance
Lightning Source LLC
Chambersburg PA
CBHW080023110526
44587CB00021BA/3829